10/05

$45.00

D0215719

THE CRUSADES

Titles in the Series
Greenwood Guides to Historic Events of the Medieval World

The Black Death

The Crusades

Eleanor of Aquitaine, Courtly Love, and the Troubadours

Genghis Khan and Mongol Rule

Joan of Arc and the Hundred Years War

Magna Carta

Medieval Castles

Medieval Cathedrals

The Medieval City

Medieval Science and Technology

The Puebloan Society of Chaco Canyon

The Rise of Islam

THE CRUSADES

Helen Nicholson

Greenwood Guides to Historic Events of the Medieval World
Jane Chance, Series Editor

GREENWOOD PRESS
Westport, Connecticut • London

Library of Congress Cataloging-in-Publication Data

Nicholson, Helen J., 1960–
    The Crusades / Helen Nicholson.
      p. cm.—(Greenwood guides to historic events of the medieval world)
    Includes bibliographical references and index.
    ISBN 0–313–32685–1 (alk. paper)
    1. Crusades. I. Title. II. Series.
  D157.N48 2004
  909.07—dc22   2004043642

British Library Cataloguing in Publication Data is available.

Library of Congress Catalog Card Number: 2004043642
ISBN: 0–313–32685–1

First published in 2004

Greenwood Press, 88 Post Road West, Westport, CT 06881
An imprint of Greenwood Publishing Group, Inc.
www.greenwood.com

Printed in the United States of America

The paper used in this book complies with the
Permanent Paper Standard issued by the National
Information Standards Organization (Z39.48–1984).

10 9 8 7 6 5 4 3 2 1

Copyright Acknowledgment

CONTENTS

Illustrations   ix

Series Foreword   xi

Advisory Board   xxiii

Preface   xxv

Acknowledgments   xxix

Chronology   xxxi

Introduction: Definitions and Motivations   xxxix

Chapter 1. Crusading Expeditions to the Holy Land,
              1095–1291   1

Chapter 2. Expeditions in the Iberian Peninsula   21

Chapter 3. The "Crusade" in Northeastern Europe   37

Chapter 4. Crusades against Heretics: The Albigensian
              Crusades and the Hussite Crusades   53

Chapter 5. Crusades against the Ottoman Turks in the
              Balkans   77

Chapter 6. Conclusion: The Impact of Crusading on
              History   91

Biographies   **101**

    Baibars al-Bunduqdāri   101

    Boabdil (Abū ʿAbd Allāh Muḥammad XI)   102

    Bohemond "of Taranto"   103

    Frederick II of Hohenstaufen   105

    Gediminas of Lithuania   106

    Giraude of Lavaur   108

    Hermann von Salza   109

    Innocent III   110

    Jadwiga, queen of Poland   112

    James I, king of Aragon   113

    John Hunyadi   115

    John Žižka   117

    Margaret of Beverley   119

    Mehmed II   120

    Saladin   122

    Shajar al-Durr   123

    Süleyman I "the Magnificent"   126

Primary Documents   **129**

   1.   Letter of Count Stephen of Blois to His
       Wife, Adela of Normandy, March 29, 1098   129

   2.   The Battle of Antioch, June 28, 1098   134

   3.   Brother Thierry of the Order of the Temple
       Writes to All the Templars about the Capture
       of the Kingdom of Jerusalem by Saladin,
       July 1187   136

4. Saladin's Secretary 'Imād al Dīn Describes
the Assault on Jerusalem, September 20, 1187–
October 2, 1187   138

5. *Audita tremendi*: Pope Gregory VIII Calls the
Third Crusade   140

6. The Albigensian Crusades: The Massacre at
Béziers, July 22, 1209, according to Caesarius of
Heisterbach   145

7. The Crusade of Emperor Frederick II of
Hohenstaufen, 1228–29   148

8. King James I of Aragon Plans an Attack on the
Muslim Kingdom of Valencia: 1233   153

9. The Prussian Crusade, 1260–61   155

10. The Douglas Goes on Crusade, 1329   158

11. The Second Crusade against the Hussites,
September 1421   160

12. John Kaye's 1482 Translation of Guillaume
Caoursin's Eyewitness Account of the 1480 Siege
of Rhodes by the Ottoman Turks   163

Glossary   169

Annotated Bibliography   175

Index   185

ILLUSTRATIONS

Maps

1. The Holy Land, 1099–1291   11
2. The Iberian Peninsula during the "Reconquest," showing
   the approximate frontier lines between the Christian and
   Muslim regions   24
3. Northeastern Europe during the Baltic Crusades   38
4. Southern France during the Albigensian Crusades   61
5. The Kingdom of Bohemia and the Hussite Crusades   66
6. The Balkans and the Middle East during the Ottoman
   invasions   79

A key for the symbols on these maps is shown on map 1.

Figures

1. Marqab (Margat) castle, Syria   16
2. Almourol castle, Portugal   27
3. Bayezid I routs the crusaders at the battle of Nicopolis,
   1396   83
4. Crusade leaders and Muslims meet outside Acre, 1250–54   94
5. The assault on Belgrade in 1456 by the forces of Sultan
   Mehmed II   116
6. King Louis IX attacks Damietta in 1249   124
7. The crusaders' siege of Antioch in 1097–98   132

SERIES FOREWORD

The Middle Ages are no longer considered the "Dark Ages" (as Petrarch termed them), sandwiched between the two enlightened periods of classical antiquity and the Renaissance. Often defined as a historical period lasting, roughly, from 500 to 1500 C.E., the Middle Ages span an enormous amount of time (if we consider the way other time periods have been constructed by historians) as well as an astonishing range of countries and regions very different from one another. That is, we call the "Middle" Ages the period beginning with the fall of the Roman Empire as a result of raids by northern European tribes of "barbarians" in the late antiquity of the fifth and sixth centuries and continuing until the advent of the so-called Italian and English renaissances, or rebirths of classical learning, in the fifteenth and sixteenth centuries. How this age could be termed either "Middle" or "Dark" is a mystery to those who study it. Certainly it is no longer understood as embracing merely the classical inheritance in the west or excluding eastern Europe, the Middle East, Asia, or even, as I would argue, North and Central America.

Whatever the arbitrary, archaic, and hegemonic limitations of these temporal parameters—the old-fashioned approach to them was that they were mainly not classical antiquity, and therefore not important—the Middle Ages represent a time when certain events occurred that have continued to affect modern cultures and that also, inevitably, catalyzed other medieval events. Among other important events, the Middle Ages saw the birth of Muhammad (c. 570–632) and his foundation of Islam in the seventh century as a rejection of Christianity which led to the imperial conflict between East and West in the eleventh and twelfth centuries. In western Europe in the Middle Ages the foundations for modern nationalism and modern law were laid and the concept of romantic love arose in the Middle Ages, this latter event partly one of the indirect consequences of the Crusades. With the shaping of national identity came the need to defend boundaries against invasion; so the castle emerged as a military outpost—whether in northern Africa, during the Crusades, or in Wales, in the eleventh century, to defend William of Normandy's newly acquired provinces—to satisfy that need. From Asia the invasions of Genghis Khan changed the literal and cultural shape of eastern and southern Europe.

In addition to triggering the development of the concept of chivalry and the knight, the Crusades influenced the European concepts of the lyric, music, and musical instruments; introduced to Europe an appetite for spices like cinnamon, coriander, and saffron and for dried fruits like prunes and figs as well as a desire for fabrics such as silk; and brought Aristotle to the European university through Arabic and then Latin translations. As a result of study of the "new" Aristotle, science and philosophy dramatically changed direction—and their emphasis on this material world helped to undermine the power of the Catholic Church as a monolithic institution in the thirteenth century.

By the twelfth century, with the centralization of the one (Catholic) Church, came a new architecture for the cathedral—the Gothic—to replace the older Romanesque architecture and thereby to manifest the Church's role in the community in a material way as well as in spiritual and political ways. Also from the cathedral as an institution and its need to dramatize the symbolic events of the liturgy came medieval drama— the mystery and the morality play, from which modern drama derives in large part. Out of the cathedral and its schools to train new priests (formerly handled by monasteries) emerged the medieval institution of the university. Around the same time, the community known as a town rose up in eastern and western Europe as a consequence of trade and the necessity for a new economic center to accompany the development of a bourgeoisie, or middle class. Because of the town's existence, the need for an itinerant mendicancy that could preach the teachings of the Church and beg for alms in urban centers sprang up.

Elsewhere in the world, in North America the eleventh-century settlement of Chaco Canyon by the Pueblo peoples created a social model like no other, one centered on ritual and ceremony in which the "priests" were key, but one that lasted barely two hundred years before it collapsed and its central structures were abandoned.

In addition to their influence on the development of central features of modern culture, the Middle Ages have long fascinated the modern age because of parallels that exist between the two periods. In both, terrible wars devastated whole nations and peoples; in both, incurable diseases plagued cities and killed large percentages of the world's population. In both periods, dramatic social and cultural changes took place as a result of these events: marginalized and overtaxed groups in societies rebelled against imperious governments; trade and a burgeoning middle class came to the fore; outside the privacy of the family, women began to have a greater role in Western societies and their cultures.

How different cultures of that age grappled with such historical change is the subject of the Greenwood Guides to Historic Events of the Medieval World. This series features individual volumes that illuminate key events in medieval world history. In some cases, an "event" occurred during a relatively limited time period. The troubadour lyric as a phenomenon, for example, flowered and died in the courts of Aquitaine in the twelfth century, as did the courtly romance in northern Europe a few decades later. The Hundred Years War between France and England generally took place during a precise time period, from the fourteenth to mid-fifteenth centuries.

In other cases, the event may have lasted for centuries before it played itself out: the medieval Gothic cathedral, for example, may have been first built in the twelfth century at Saint-Denis in Paris (c. 1140), but cathedrals, often of a slightly different style of Gothic architecture, were still being built in the fifteenth century all over Europe and, again, as the symbolic representation of a bishop's seat, or chair, are still being built today. And the medieval city, whatever its incarnation in the early Middle Ages, basically blossomed between the eleventh and thirteenth centuries as a result of social, economic, and cultural changes. Events—beyond a single dramatic historically limited happening—took longer to affect societies in the Middle Ages because of the lack of political and social centralization, the primarily agricultural and rural nature of most countries, difficulties in communication, and the distances between important cultural centers.

Each volume includes necessary tools for understanding such key events in the Middle Ages. Because of the postmodern critique of authority that modern societies underwent at the end of the twentieth century, students and scholars as well as general readers have come to mistrust the commentary and expertise of any one individual scholar or commentator and to identify the text as an arbiter of "history." For this reason, each book in the series can be described as a "library in a book." The intent of the series is to provide a quick, in-depth examination and current perspectives on the event to stimulate critical thinking as well as ready-reference materials, including primary documents and biographies of key individuals, for additional research.

Specifically, in addition to a narrative historical overview that places the specific event within the larger context of a contemporary perspective, five to seven developmental chapters explore related focused aspects of the event. In addition, each volume begins with a brief chronology and ends with a conclusion that discusses the consequences and impact of the event. There are also brief biographies of twelve to twenty key individuals (or places or buildings, in the book on the cathedral); primary documents from the period (for example, letters, chronicles, memoirs, diaries, and other writings) that illustrate states of mind or the turn of events at the time, whether historical, literary, scientific, or philosophical; illustrations (maps, diagrams, manuscript illuminations, portraits); a glossary of terms; and an annotated bibliography of important books, articles, films, and CD-ROMs available for additional research. An index concludes each volume.

No particular theoretical approach or historical perspective characterizes the series; authors developed their topics as they chose, generally taking into account the latest thinking on any particular event. The editors selected final topics from a list provided by an advisory board of high school teachers and public and school librarians. On the basis of nominations of scholars made by distinguished writers, the series editor also tapped internationally known scholars, both those with lifelong expertise and others with fresh new perspectives on a topic, to author the twelve books in the series. Finally, the series editor selected distinguished medievalists, art historians, and archaeologists to complete an advisory board: Gwinn Vivian, retired professor of archaeology at the University of Arizona Museum; Sharon Kinoshita, associate professor of French literature, world literature, and cultural studies at the University of California–Santa Cruz; Nancy Wu, associate museum educator at the Metropolitan Museum of Art, The Cloisters, New York City; and Christopher A. Snyder, chair of the Department of History and Politics at Marymount University.

In addition to examining the event and its effects on the specific cultures involved through an array of documents and an overview, each volume provides a new approach to understanding these twelve events. Treated in the series are: the Black Death; the Crusades; Eleanor of Aquitaine, courtly love, and the troubadours; Genghis Khan and Mongol rule; Joan of Arc and the Hundred Years War; Magna Carta; the medieval castle, from the eleventh to the sixteenth centuries; the medieval cathedral; the medieval city, especially in the thirteenth century; medieval science and technology; Muhammad and the rise of Islam; and the Puebloan society of Chaco Canyon.

The Black Death, by Joseph Byrne, isolates the event of the epidemic of bubonic plague in 1347–52 as having had a signal impact on medieval Europe. It was, however, only the first of many related such episodes involving variations of pneumonic and septicemic plague that recurred over 350 years. Taking a twofold approach to the Black Death, Byrne investigates both the modern research on bubonic plague, its origins and spread, and also medieval documentation and illustration in diaries, artistic works, and scientific and religious accounts. The demographic, economic, and political effects of the Black Death are traced in one chapter, the social and psychological patterns of life in another, and cultural expressions in art and ritual in a third. Finally, Byrne investigates why bubonic plague disappeared and why we continue to be fascinated by it. Documents included provide a variety of medieval accounts—Byzantine, Arabic, French, German, English, and Italian—several of which are translated for the first time.

The Crusades, by Helen Nicholson, presents a balanced account of various crusades, or military campaigns, invented by Catholic or "Latin" Christians during the Middle Ages against those they perceived as threats to their faith. Such expeditions included the Crusades to the Holy Land between 1095 and 1291, expeditions to the Iberian Peninsula, the "crusade" to northeastern Europe, the Albigensian Crusades and the Hussite crusades—both against the heretics—and the crusades against the Ottoman Turks (in the Balkans). Although Muslim rulers included the concept of jihâd (a conflict fought for God against evil or his enemies) in their wars in the early centuries of Islam, it had become less important in the late tenth century. It was not until the middle decades of the twelfth century that jihâd was revived in the wars with the Latin Christian Crusaders. Most of the Crusades did not result in victory for the Latin Christians, although Nicholson concedes they slowed the advance of Islam. After Jerusalem was destroyed in 1291, Muslim rulers did permit Christian pilgrims to travel to holy sites. In the Iberian Peninsula, Christian rulers replaced Muslim rulers, but Muslims, Jews, and dissident Christians were compelled to convert to Catholicism. In northeastern Europe, the Teutonic Order's campaigns allowed German colonization that later encouraged twentieth-century German claims to land and led to two world wars. The Albigensian Crusade wiped out thirteenth-century aristocratic families in southern France who held to the Cathar heresy, but the Hussite crusades in the 1420s failed to eliminate the Hussite heresy. As a result of the wars, however, many positive changes occurred: Arab learning founded on Greek scholarship entered western Europe through the acquisition of an extensive library in Toledo, Spain, in 1085; works of western European literature were inspired by the holy wars; trade was encouraged and with it the demand for certain products; and a more favorable image of Muslim men and women was fostered by the crusaders' contact with the Middle East. Nicholson also notes that America may have been discovered because Christopher Columbus avoided a route that had been closed by Muslim conquests and that the Reformation may have been advanced because Martin Luther protested against the crusader indulgence in his Ninety-five Theses (1517).

Eleanor of Aquitaine, Courtly Love, and the Troubadours, by ffiona Swabey, singles out the twelfth century as the age of the individual, in which a queen like Eleanor of Aquitaine could influence the development of a new social and artistic culture. The wife of King Louis VII of France and later the wife of his enemy Henry of Anjou, who became king of England, she patronized some of the troubadours, whose vernacular lyrics celebrated the personal expression of emotion and a passionate declaration of service to women. Love, marriage, and the pursuit of women were also the subject of the new romance literature, which flourished in northern Europe and was the inspiration behind concepts of courtly love. However, as Swabey points out, historians in the past have misjudged Eleanor, whose independent spirit fueled their misogynist attitudes. Similarly, Eleanor's divorce and subsequent stormy marriage have colored ideas about medieval "love courts" and courtly love, interpretations of which have now been challenged by scholars. The twelfth century is set in context, with commentaries on feudalism, the tenets of Christianity, and the position of women, as well as summaries of the cultural and philosophical background, the cathedral schools and universities, the influence of Islam, the revival of classical learning, vernacular literature, and Gothic architecture. Swabey provides two biographical chapters on Eleanor and two on the emergence of the troubadours and the origin of courtly love through verse romances. Within this latter subject Swabey also details the story of Abelard and Heloise, the treatise of Andreas Capellanus (André the Chaplain) on courtly love, and Arthurian legend as a subject of courtly love.

Genghis Khan and Mongol Rule, by George Lane, identifies the rise to power of Genghis Khan and his unification of the Mongol tribes in the thirteenth century as a kind of globalization with political, cultural, economic, mercantile, and spiritual effects akin to those of modern globalization. Normally viewed as synonymous with barbarian destruction, the rise to power of Genghis Khan and the Mongol hordes is here understood as a more positive event that initiated two centuries of regeneration and creativity. Lane discusses the nature of the society of the Eurasian steppes in the twelfth and thirteenth centuries into which Genghis Khan was born; his success at reshaping the relationship between the northern pastoral and nomadic society with the southern urban, agriculturalist society; and his unification of all the Turco-Mongol tribes in 1206 before his move to conquer Tanquit Xixia, the Chin of northern China, and the lands of Islam. Conquered thereafter were the Caucasus, the Ukraine, the Crimea, Russia, Siberia, Central Asia, Afghanistan, Pakistan, and Kashmir. After his death his sons and grandsons continued, conquering Korea, Persia, Armenia, Mesopotamia, Azerbaijan, and eastern Europe—chiefly Kiev, Poland, Moravia, Silesia, and Hungary—until 1259, the end of the Mongol Empire as a unified whole. Mongol rule created a golden age in the succeeding split of the Empire into two, the Yuan dynasty of greater China and the Il-Khanate dynasty of greater Iran. Lane adds biographies of important political figures, famous names such as Marco Polo, and artists and scientists. Documents derive from universal histories, chronicles, local histories and travel accounts, official government documents, and poetry, in French, Armenian, Georgian, Chinese, Persian, Arabic, Chaghatai Turkish, Russian, and Latin.

Joan of Arc and the Hundred Years War, by Deborah Fraioli, presents the Hundred Years War between France and England in the fourteenth and fifteenth centuries within contexts whose importance has sometimes been blurred or ignored in past studies. An episode of apparently only moderate significance, a feudal lord's seizure of his vassal's land for harboring his mortal enemy, sparked the Hundred Years War, yet on the face of it the event should not have led inevitably to war. But the lord was the king of France and the vassal the king of England, who resented losing his claim to the French throne to his Valois cousin. The land in dispute, extending roughly from Bordeaux to the Pyrenees mountains, was crucial coastline for the economic interests of both kingdoms. The series of skirmishes, pitched battles, truces, stalemates, and diplomatic wrangling that resulted from the confiscation of English Aquitaine by the French form the narrative of this Anglo-French conflict, which was in fact not given the name Hundred Years War until the nineteenth century.

Fraioli emphasizes how dismissing women's inheritance and succession rights came at the high price of unleashing discontent in their male heirs, including Edward III, Robert of Artois, and Charles of Navarre. Fraioli also demonstrates the centrality of side issues, such as Flemish involvement in the war, the peasants' revolts that resulted from the costs of the war, and Joan of Arc's unusually clear understanding of French "sacred kingship." Among the primary sources provided are letters from key players such as Edward III, Etienne Marcel, and Joan of Arc; a supply list for towns about to be besieged; and a contemporary poem by the celebrated scholar and court poet Christine de Pizan in praise of Joan of Arc.

Magna Carta, by Katherine Drew, is a detailed study of the importance of the Magna Carta in comprehending England's legal and constitutional history. Providing a model for the rights of citizens found in the United States Declaration of Independence and Constitution's first ten amendments, the Magna Carta has had a role in the legal and parliamentary history of all modern states bearing some colonial or government connection with the British Empire. Constructed at a time when modern nations began to appear, in the early thirteenth century, the Magna Carta (signed in 1215) presented a formula for balancing the liberties of the people with the power of modern governmental institutions. This unique English document influenced the growth of a form of law (the English common law) and provided a vehicle for the evolution of representative (parliamentary) government. Drew demonstrates how the Magna Carta came to be—the roles of the Church, the English towns, barons, common law, and the parliament in its making—as well as how myths concerning its provisions were established. Also provided are biographies of Thomas Becket, Charlemagne, Frederick II, Henry II and his sons, Innocent III, and many other key figures, and primary documents—among them, the Magna Cartas of 1215 and 1225, and the Coronation Oath of Henry I.

Medieval Castles, by Marilyn Stokstad, traces the historical, political, and social function of the castle from the late eleventh century to the sixteenth by means of a typology of castles. This typology ranges from the early "motte and bailey"—military fortification, and government and economic center—to the palace as an expression of the castle owners' needs and purposes. An introduction defines the various contexts—military, political, economic, and social—in which the castle appeared in the Middle Ages. A concluding interpretive essay suggests the impact of the castle and its symbolic role as an idealized construct lasting until the modern day.

Medieval Cathedrals, by William Clark, examines one of the chief contributions of the Middle Ages, at least from an elitist perspective—that is, the religious architecture found in the cathedral ("chair" of the bishop) or great church, studied in terms of its architecture, sculpture, and stained glass. Clark begins with a brief contextual history of the concept of the bishop and his role within the church hierarchy, the growth of the church in the early Christian era and its affiliation with the bishop (deriving from that of the bishop of Rome), and the social history of cathedrals. Because of economic and political conflicts among the three authorities who held power in medieval towns—the king, the bishop, and the cathedral clergy—cathedral construction and maintenance always remained a vexed issue, even though the owners—the cathedral clergy— usually held the civic responsibility for the cathedral. In an interpretive essay, Clark then focuses on Reims Cathedral in France, because both it and the bishop's palace survive, as well as on contemporary information about surrounding buildings. Clark also supplies a historical overview on the social, political, and religious history of the cathedral in the Middle Ages: an essay on patrons, builders, and artists; aspects of cathedral construction (which was not always successful); and then a chapter on Romanesque and Gothic cathedrals and a "gazetteer" of twenty-five important examples.

The Medieval City, by Norman J. G. Pounds, documents the origin of the medieval city in the flight from the dangers or difficulties found in the country, whether economic, physically threatening, or cultural. Identifying the attraction of the city in its *urbanitas*, its "urbanity," or the way of living in a city, Pounds discusses first its origins in prehistoric and classical Greek urban revolutions. During the Middle Ages, the city grew primarily between the eleventh and thirteenth centuries, remaining essentially the same until the Industrial Revolution. Pounds provides chapters on the medieval city's planning, in terms of streets and structures; life in the medieval city; the roles of the Church and the city government in its operation; the development of crafts and trade in the city; and the issues of urban health, wealth, and welfare. Concluding with the role of the city in history, Pounds suggests that the value of the city depended upon its balance of social classes, its need for trade and profit to satisfy personal desires through the accumulation of wealth and its consequent economic power, its political power as a representative body within the kingdom, and its social role in the rise of literacy and education and in nationalism. Indeed, the concept of a middle class, a bourgeoisie, derives from the city—from the *bourg*, or "borough." According to Pounds, the rise of modern civilization would not have taken place without the growth of the city in the Middle Ages and its concomitant artistic and cultural contribution.

Medieval Science and Technology, by Elspeth Whitney, examines science and technology from the early Middle Ages to 1500 within the context of the classical learning that so influenced it. She looks at institutional history, both early and late, and what was taught in the medieval schools and, later, the universities (both of which were overseen by the Catholic Church). Her discussion of Aristotelian natural philosophy illustrates its impact on the medieval scientific worldview. She presents chapters on the exact sciences, meaning mathematics, astronomy, cosmology, astrology, statics, kinematics, dynamics, and optics; the biological and earth sciences, meaning chemistry and alchemy, medicine, zoology, botany, geology and meteorology, and geography; and technology. In an interpretive conclusion, Whitney demonstrates the impact of medieval science on the preconditions and structure that permitted the emergence of the modern world. Most especially, technology transformed an agricultural society into a more commercial and engine-driven society: waterpower and inventions like the blast furnace and horizontal loom turned iron working and cloth making into manufacturing operations. The invention of the mechanical clock helped to organize human activities through timetables rather than through experiential perception and thus facilitated the advent of modern life. Also influential in the establishment of a middle class were the inventions of the musket and pistol and the printing press. Technology, according to Whitney, helped advance the habits of mechanization and precise methodology. Her biographies introduce major medieval Latin and Arabic and classical natural philosophers and scientists. Extracts from various kinds of scientific treatises allow a window into the medieval concept of knowledge.

The Puebloan Society of Chaco Canyon, by Paul Reed, is unlike other volumes in this series, whose historic events boast a long-established historical record. Reed's study offers instead an original reconstruction of the Puebloan Indian society of Chaco, in what is now New Mexico, but originally extending into Colorado, Utah, and Arizona. He is primarily interested in its leaders, ritual and craft specialists, and commoners during the time of its chief flourishing, in the eleventh and twelfth centuries, as understood from archaeological data alone. To this new material he adds biographies of key Euro-American archaeologists and other individuals from the nineteenth and twentieth centuries who have made important discoveries about Chaco Canyon. Also provided are documents of archaeological description and narrative from early explorers' journals and archaeological reports, narratives, and monographs. In his overview chapters, Reed discusses the cultural and environmental setting of Chaco Canyon; its history (in terms of exploration and research); the Puebloan society and how it emerged chronologically; the Chaco society and how it appeared in 1100 c.e.; the "Outliers," or outlying communities of Chaco; Chaco as a ritual center of the eleventh-century Pueblo world; and, finally, what is and is not known about Chaco society. Reed concludes that ritual and ceremony played an important role in Chacoan society and that ritual specialists, or priests, conducted ceremonies, maintained ritual artifacts, and charted the ritual calendar. Its social organization matches no known social pattern or type: it was complicated, multiethnic, centered around ritual and ceremony, and without any overtly hierarchical political system. The Chacoans were ancestors to the later Pueblo people, part of a society that rose, fell, and evolved within a very short time period.

The Rise of Islam, by Matthew Gordon, introduces the early history of the Islamic world, beginning in the late sixth century with the career of the Prophet Muhammad (c. 570–c. 632) on the Arabian Peninsula. From Muhammad's birth in an environment of religious plurality—Christianity, Judaism, and Zoroastrianism, along with paganism, were joined by Islam—to the collapse of the Islamic empire in the early tenth century, Gordon traces the history of the Islamic community. The book covers topics that include the life of the Prophet and divine revelation (the Qur'an) to the formation of the Islamic state, urbanization in the Islamic Near East, and the extraordinary culture of Islamic letters and scholarship. In addition to a historical overview, Gordon examines the Caliphate and early Islamic Empire, urban society and economy, and the emergence, under the Abbasid Caliphs, of a "world religious tradition" up to the year 925 C.E.

As editor of this series I am grateful to have had the help of Benjamin Burford, an undergraduate Century Scholar at Rice University assigned to me in 2002–2004 for this project; Gina Weaver, a third-year graduate student in English; and Cynthia Duffy, a second-year graduate student in English, who assisted me in target-reading select chapters from some of these books in an attempt to define an audience. For this purpose I would also like to thank Gale Stokes, former dean of humanities at Rice University, for the 2003 summer research grant and portions of the 2003–2004 annual research grant from Rice University that served that end.

This series, in its mixture of traditional and new approaches to medieval history and cultures, will ensure opportunities for dialogue in the classroom in its offerings of twelve different "libraries in books." It should also propel discussion among graduate students and scholars by means of the gentle insistence throughout on the text as primal. Most especially, it invites response and further study. Given its mixture of East and West, North and South, the series symbolizes the necessity for global understanding, both of the Middle Ages and in the postmodern age.

Jane Chance, Series Editor
Houston, Texas
February 19, 2004

Advisory Board

Sharon Kinoshita
Associate Professor of Literature
(French Literature, World Literature, and Cultural Studies)
University of California–Santa Cruz

Christopher A. Snyder
Chair, History and Politics
Marymount University

Gwinn Vivian
Archaeologist
University of Arizona Museum

Nancy Wu
Associate Museum Educator
Metropolitan Museum of Art, The Cloisters

PREFACE

This book is about wars. Specifically, it is about a series of military campaigns fought by Catholic, or Latin, Christians in the Middle Ages against peoples who, they believed, were threatening the existence of their Christian faith. Some of those campaigns were against Muslims, some were against other Christians, and some were against pagans. There was nothing new about the concept of fighting in defense of religion; ever since humans first had state religions they have claimed that their wars are fought in the name of their god(s). Yet the crusades were distinctive because they were an invention of Latin Christians, they had their own symbols and traditions, and they were not one war but many, fought over a long period of time.

Other religions also have their holy wars; Islam, for example, has the concept of *jihād*. The *jihād* is a struggle in God's name against the spiritual forces of evil or the physical enemies of Islam. The individual's struggle against the forces of evil within that individual is more important than military battles against Islam's enemies. The first battles that the Muslims fought against the crusaders in the Middle East during the First Crusade were not fought as *jihād*. Although some preachers did declare that war against the crusaders should be *jihād*, it was not until the reign of the ruler Zengi of Mosul (d. 1146) that Muslim writers systematically began to present the war as *jihād*, rather than as a simple conflict over land. Zengi's son Nūr al-Dīn (d. 1174) depicted his own war against the crusaders in the Middle East as a *jihād*. Arguably he used the concept of *jihād* as propaganda to unite his subjects behind him and make him appear to be a legitimate ruler and overlord.

Yet throughout the Middle Ages, the Muslim rulers who fought the crusaders in the Middle East had more dangerous and significant enemies on their other frontiers. At the period when this book begins, Christian western Europe was not a major world power but a relatively barbarous backwater, largely cut off from world trade and culture. The greatest power on Earth in 1050, on the eve of the crusades, was the Chinese Empire in the far east of Asia. The Christian Byzantine Empire in eastern Europe and Asia Minor, and the Islamic Fatimid Empire in northeastern Africa were in decline but were still powerful military forces. In the Middle East, the up-and-coming power was the Seljuk Turks, who conquered the Islamic Abbasid Caliphate in Baghdad in 1055 and who were expanding westward into Asia Minor. Islamic culture had absorbed the culture and learning of those civilizations it encountered or conquered, including the philosophy and science of ancient Greece, Persia, and India. Islamic scholars had developed the study of medicine, astronomy, and mathematics. In contrast, Christian western Europe was a relatively underdeveloped, backward region.

For the Muslim rulers who fought the crusaders, their wars against the crusaders often took second place to conflicts against other, more formidable powers. For example, Saladin spent the years 1174–86 fighting to establish his authority over Muslim territory in northern Syria and in what is now eastern Turkey and northern Iraq. He did make brief incursions into the "crusader kingdom," but for most of this period his attention was elsewhere. Even during the Third Crusade, a part of Saladin's forces was fighting Muslims in the north, where his nephew Taqī al-Dīn 'Umar was killed. In the thirteenth century, the greatest threat to Islam was not the crusaders but the Mongols—nomadic warriors whose great armies swept across central Asia and into eastern Europe, capturing the city of Baghdad in 1258 and executing the Sunni caliph, the religious leader of the Sunni Muslims. Later in the Middle Ages, the Ottoman Turks, at the same time as invading eastern Europe, were attacking and conquering their Muslim neighbors in the east and south. So it is not surprising that Muslim writers of the Middle Ages often did not regard the crusades as being as important as other wars in which the rulers of Islam were involved.

For the Latin Christians of western Europe, however, the crusades were of great importance. Crusading was the most honorable form of warfare for Latin Christian warriors. All sections of Latin Christian society were involved in it; it could take many different forms, against different enemies; and, through taxation and the sale of the "crusade indulgence," it affected the whole of society. So western European writers regarded the crusades as far more important than did Muslim writers of the same period. The crusades were very much a Latin Christian movement, and arguably their biggest impact was on the society that created them rather than the societies they fought. For this reason, this book concentrates mostly on the Latin Christian view of the crusades rather than the viewpoints of their opponents.

Throughout the crusades, the warriors fighting on both sides believed that they were in the right—that they were, to use the modern phrase, "the good guys." Warriors on both sides believed that they were good, moral, upright people; that they were fighting with the best intentions to make the world a better place; and that God was supporting them. We, looking back on these wars with the benefit of hindsight, might be tempted to judge them according to our own values and in the light of our views on modern events. However, the historian's task is to gather evidence, to assess it objectively, and to try to understand why people of the past acted as they did, not to impose judgments. If we impose our own views on the past, we will never be able to understand it. The concluding chapter in this book considers the legacy of the crusades, and how some modern commentators have interpreted the crusades to suit their own political agendas.

ACKNOWLEDGMENTS

I would like to thank Jane Chance, Kevin Ohe, and the readers and editorial staff at Greenwood Press for their help in bringing this book to completion. In writing it, I am indebted to colleagues and friends working within the field of crusading history whose research and interpretations have shaped my own approach to the subject. Many of their works are listed both in the notes to the essays in this book and in the bibliography.

I am very grateful to Professors Denys Pringle and Joan Fuguet Sans, who allowed me to reproduce their photographs of the castles of Marqab and Almourol respectively, and to John Morgan of the School of History and Archaeology, Cardiff University, for producing the actual photographs. Other pictures are by courtesy of Bridgeman Art Library. The maps were drawn by Nigel Nicholson and myself. I am particularly grateful to Thomas Fudge and to Ashgate Publishing for allowing me to reproduce the translated text "Crusade armies thwarted again at Žatec," from Thomas Fudge, *The Crusade against Heretics in Bohemia, 1418–1437* (Aldershot: Ashgate, 2002), pp. 130–32. All other translations, except where otherwise stated, are my own. L'Académie des Inscriptions et Belles-Lettres kindly allowed me to translate a section from Henri Massé's translation of 'Imâd al-Dîn al-Iṣfahânî, *Conquête de la Syrie et de la Palestine par Saladin* (Paris: Librarie orientaliste Paul Geuthner, 1972), in their series "Documents relatifs à l'histoire des croisades," vol. 10. I am also grateful to Wissenschaftliche Buchgesellschaft of Darmstadt, Germany, for permission to include a translated extract from Peter von Dusburg, *Chronik des Preussenlandes*, ed. and trans. Klaus Scholz and Dieter Wojtecki (Darmstadt: Wissenschaftliche Buchgesellschaft, 1984).

A NOTE ON NAMES

Many of the places and individuals mentioned in this book have more than one name, or a name with several possible spellings. I have tried to use the form of the name that is generally used by historians or, if there is none, the form most familiar to English-speaking readers. Where appropriate, I have given alternative versions of the name where it is first mentioned.

In this book I often refer to "Europe." Europe did not exist as a political region in the Middle Ages. I use the word here as a convenient term for the geographical area now called Europe.

CHRONOLOGY

1064	Barbastro (Iberian Peninsula) is captured by a combined Christian force.
1085	Toledo (Iberian Peninsula) is captured by King Alfonso VI of Castile.
1086	Alfonso VI of Castile is defeated by the Almoravids at Sagrajas.
1087	A Christian naval force attacks and plunders al-Mahdiyyah (North Africa).
1095	The First Crusade is preached by Pope Urban II at the Council of Clermont.
1099	The First Crusade captures Jerusalem. The Latin kingdom of Jerusalem is founded.
1100–1101	A follow-up expedition to the East is defeated by the Turks.
1107–10	King Sigurd of Norway brings an army to the Holy Land.
1119	Battle of the "Field of Blood." Prince Roger of Antioch is defeated by Il-ghazi ibn Artuk of Mardin.
1120	The military religious Order of the Temple is founded in Jerusalem.

1122–24	A Venetian naval expedition goes to the Holy Land; Tyre is captured.
1129	A crusader expedition sets out to attack Damascus but is unsuccessful.
1136	King Fulk of Jerusalem entrusts Beit Jibrin castle to the Hospital of St. John of Jerusalem—the first clear indication of this religious order's military involvement.
1144	Zengi, ruler of Mosul and Aleppo, captures Edessa.
1146	Death of Zengi.
1147	Lisbon is captured by Afonso I of Portugal and crusading forces.
1147–49	The Second Crusade. The crusaders besiege Damascus, but fail to capture it.
1153	The forces of King Baldwin III of Jerusalem capture Ascalon.
1154	Nūr al-Dīn (Zengi's son) captures Damascus. The Almohads win control of Granada.
1158	Count Thierry of Flanders goes on pilgrimage to Jerusalem.
1163–69	King Amaury (Amalric) of Jerusalem campaigns against Egypt.
1169	Saladin becomes vizier of Egypt.
1172	Duke Henry the Lion of Saxony goes on pilgrimage to Jerusalem. The Almohad caliph takes control of Seville.
1174	Death of Nūr al-Dīn. Saladin seizes Damascus.
1177	Count Philip of Flanders goes on pilgrimage to Je-

	rusalem. The forces of Saladin and King Baldwin IV of Jerusalem fight a battle at Montgisard. Baldwin is victorious.
1187	Saladin captures Jerusalem.
1189–92	The Third Crusade. Aim: to recover Jerusalem. It fails, but recovers some territory.
1197–98	The German crusade recovers some territory and converts the Teutonic Hospital at Acre into a military religious order, known as the Hospital of St. Mary of the Teutons ("the Teutonic Order").
1202–4	The Fourth Crusade. Aim: to assist Christians in Holy Land. It captures Constantinople.
1209–26	The Albigensian Crusades.
1212	The "Children's Crusade." It breaks up before it leaves Europe.
1212	Battle of Las Navas de Tolosa. The Almohads are defeated by a combined Christian force.
1213	Battle of Muret. The crusaders under Simon de Montfort defeat King Peter II of Aragon.
1218–21	The Fifth Crusade. Aim: to conquer Egypt. It is initially successful, but the crusaders are cut off when the Muslims open the sluice gates of the Nile.
1228–29	Crusade of the Emperor Frederick II. He recovers Jerusalem for the kingdom of Jerusalem by a treaty with al-Kāmil, the Ayyūbid sultan of Egypt.
1229	King James I of Aragon captures the Balearic Islands.
1230s	The Teutonic Order begins military operations in Prussia.

1233	King James I of Aragon invades the kingdom of Valencia.
1237	The Teutonic Order takes over the Swordbrothers in Livonia.
1238	King James I of Aragon captures the city of Valencia.
1239–40	Crusade of Theobald, count of Champagne and king of Navarre, to Acre. Theobald negotiates a peace treaty with al-Ṣāliḥ Ismāʿīl, Ayyūbid ruler of Damascus.
1240–41	Crusade of Earl Richard of Cornwall, to Acre. Richard recovers territory for the kingdom of Jerusalem by negotiation with al-Ṣāliḥ Ayyūb, sultan of Cairo.
1242	The Livonian branch of the Teutonic Order is defeated at Lake Chud (Peipus) by a Russian force led by Prince Alexander Nevsky.
1244	The crusaders finally lose Jerusalem.
1248–54	First crusade of King Louis IX of France, to Egypt. The crusade captures the port of Damietta, but is defeated at Manṣūra in February 1250. Louis then goes to Acre.
1250	A Mamluk coup in Egypt overthrows the Ayyūbids.
1251	First "Shepherds' Crusade": a popular religious movement that sets out to help King Louis. The crusaders begin to attack clergy and Jews, and their movement is crushed.
1258	The Mongols capture Baghdad.
1260	Battle of ʿAin Jālūt (Ayn Jalut). The Mamluks of Egypt defeat the Mongols. In the same year, Baibars becomes sultan of Egypt.

1261	Michael Palaeologos recaptures Constantinople.
1263–71	Sultan Baibars campaigns in Syria and Palestine.
1269	The princes of Aragon go to Acre on crusade.
1269–70	A Frisian crusade arrives in Acre.
1270	The second crusade of King Louis IX of France besieges Tunis, but achieves nothing.
1271–72	The crusade of the Lord Edward of England (later King Edward I of England) to Acre: ends with a truce.
1274	The Second Church Council of Lyons discusses plans for recovering the Holy Land. No decision is reached.
1277	Death of Baibars.
1282	The Sicilian Vespers: the Sicilians revolt against Charles of Anjou, king of Naples.
1285	The French launch a crusade against Aragon, in revenge for the Aragonese assisting the Sicilian revolt.
1291	Acre is captured by al-Ashraf Khalīl, sultan of Egypt. The remaining "Latin" territories in the Holy Land fall to the Muslims soon afterward.
1306	The Hospital of St. John of Jerusalem begins the conquest of the Greek Orthodox Christian island of Rhodes.
1309	The Teutonic Order moves its headquarters to Marienburg in Prussia. The Hospital of St. John moves its headquarters to Rhodes.
1312	Pope Clement V dissolves the Order of the Temple.
1320	The second "Shepherds' Crusade": a popular movement that aims to reach the Holy Land. The cru-

saders kill Jews and attack the clergy, and the movement is crushed.

1332–34	The first naval crusading league is set up to fight Muslims at sea.
1344	A naval crusading league captures Smyrna (now Izmir).
1365	Peter I of Cyprus' crusade captures Alexandria, but withdraws soon afterward.
1374	Pope Gregory XI entrusts the defense of Smyrna to the Hospitallers of St. John.
1375	Cilician Armenia is conquered by the Mamluks.
1386	Queen Jadwiga of Poland marries Duke Jagiełło of Lithuania. Lithuania accepts Christianity.
1389	Battle of Kosovo Polje: the Ottoman Turks claim victory.
1390	A French expedition sets out to capture al-Mahdiyyah (North Africa). The siege ends with a peace treaty and the French withdraw peacefully.
1396	Battle of Nicopolis: the western European crusaders are defeated by the Ottoman Turks under Bayezid I.
1399–1404	Boucicaut, marshal of France, raids Turkish settlements in the eastern Mediterranean.
1402	"Tamerlane" (Timur the Lame) captures Smyrna.
1410	The Teutonic Order is defeated by a combined Catholic Christian Polish-Lithuanian force at Tannenberg/Grunwald.
1420–31	Hussite Crusades.
1434	Battle of Lipany: the Hussite moderates defeat the radicals.

1444	The crusade of Varna: fails to defeat the Ottoman Turks.
1453	Constantinople is conquered by the Ottoman Turks under Mehmed II.
1456	Belgrade is successfully defended against the Ottoman Turks by crusaders led by John Hunyadi.
1480	The Hospitallers successfully defend Rhodes against the Ottoman Turks. The Ottomans capture Otranto in Italy, but lose it the following year.
1492	The Muslim city of Granada falls to the forces of Isabella and Ferdinand of Castile-Aragon.
1497	The Spanish capture Melilla in North Africa.
1501–2	A Venetian-Hungarian naval crusading league ravages Turkish bases in the Ionian islands.
1505–10	The Spanish wage a crusading war of conquest in North Africa.
1516–17	The Ottoman sultan Selim I defeats the Mamluks and conquers Egypt.
1518	Martin Luther's *Explanations of the Ninety-five Theses* states that Ottoman attacks on Europe are God's punishment for Christians' sins, and so the Church authorities should not resist them with arms, only with prayer.
1522–23	Rhodes falls to the Ottoman Turks, commanded by Süleyman the Magnificent.
1529	The first Ottoman siege of Vienna. The Ottomans are repulsed.
1530	The Hospital of St. John moves to Malta.
1551	The Turks recapture Tripoli (North Africa).
1565	The Hospital of St. John defends Malta against the forces of Süleyman the Magnificent.

1571	Cyprus is conquered by the Ottoman Turks. Battle of Lepanto: a victory for the Catholic Christian Holy League against the Ottoman Turks, but Cyprus is not recaptured.
1578	A Portuguese crusade against Morocco is defeated at al-Qaṣr-al-Kabīr (Alcazar el-Kebir).
1588	The Spanish Armada: a Spanish Catholic Christian crusading expedition against Protestant Christian England. The fleet is scattered by storms, and the invasion fails.
1645–69	The Ottoman siege of Crete: Crete falls to the Ottomans.
1683	The second Ottoman siege of Vienna: the Ottomans are repulsed.
1684–97	The formation and operations of the Holy (Crusade) League.
1685–87	The Venetians conquer the Morea (Peloponnese) from the Ottomans.
1707	Spanish Oran (North Africa) is captured by the Muslims of Algiers.
1714–15	The Ottoman sultan Ahmed III attacks Venetian territories in the Greek islands and recaptures the Morea.
1750–92	France, Spain, and Venice launch attacks on North African Muslim cities that harbor pirates.
1784–92	The republic of Venice fights a war against Tunis.
1798	The Hospital of St. John on Malta surrenders to Napoleon.

INTRODUCTION: DEFINITIONS AND MOTIVATIONS

When did the crusades begin? The answer to this question depends on the definition of "crusade." Some historians would argue that the first crusade was the campaign of Spanish Christians against the Muslim-ruled city of Barbastro in the Iberian Peninsula in 1064. This campaign included Christian warriors from outside the peninsula and may have had the support of the pope (although historians do not agree whether it did). In 1087 a naval force from the Italian maritime cities of Pisa and Genoa and others attacked and plundered the North African coastal city of al-Mahdiyyah. Contemporary Christian descriptions of the campaign depicted it in similar terms to the later crusades—as a holy war led by Christ, fighting against the godless Muslims. The Pisans wore a pilgrim's badge, whereas the later crusaders wore a cross. If to be a "crusader" one must wear a cross, then these campaigns were not crusades, but they certainly foreshadowed the later campaigns in their personnel and their motivation.

Most scholars agree that the crusades began in November 1095 when Pope Urban II preached a sermon at the Church Council of Clermont in southeastern France. Exactly what he said is not known, but the result was an expedition against the Turks of Asia Minor, which recovered territory that had until recently belonged to the Byzantine emperor. It went on to capture additional fortresses and towns in Syria and Palestine, culminating in the capture of the city of Jerusalem in July 1099. The crusaders set up new Christian states in Syria and Palestine. These came under attack from neighboring Muslim rulers, who finally conquered them in 1291. However, the island of Cyprus remained in western European hands, and crusaders continued to operate in the eastern Mediterranean for many centuries.

Other "crusading fronts" included the Iberian Peninsula (now Spain and Portugal), where Christian warriors fought to capture territory that had been ruled by Christians until the eighth century; the Baltic area, where Christian warriors fought in defense of Christian territory and to persuade pagan peoples—whose religious beliefs are not now known—to convert to Christianity; wars between popes and their enemies in Italy; and wars against heretics—Christians who rejected the authority of the institutionalized Church. The word "crusade" is still used to mean a campaign against injustice or evil. Modern scholars of the crusades do not usually use the term "crusade" for military campaigns after the sixteenth century, although some would argue that crusades of a sort were still in progress up to the end of the eighteenth century. Again, some scholars would argue that the "crusade mentality" was important in the voyages of exploration and conquest of the New World in the sixteenth century.

WHAT WERE THE CRUSADES?

Scholars do not agree on one definition. Some recent works by leading crusade scholars have divided the different opinions into four general categories. These can be summarized as follows:[1]

1. The *generalists* define a crusade as any Christian religious war fought for God, and see the modern attempts to define a crusade as artificial and misleading. They would argue that in arguing over precise definitions of this medieval undertaking, modern scholars are trying to impose modern points of view and forms of thinking on a society that had a very different worldview.

2. The *popularists* regard the crusade as essentially a religious undertaking for the masses and/or for warriors (not for the clergy).

3. The *traditionalists* believe that the crusades were military-religious expeditions that set out to recover or defend Jerusalem.

4. The *pluralists* look at how crusades were recruited and organized, and argue that any military campaign that fits that pattern of re-

cruitment and organization was a crusade, while those that do not, were not crusades.

Those who hold these differing opinions do agree on certain points. They would regard the crusades as essentially a phenomenon of the Middle Ages: crusading was less common by 1500, and had almost disappeared by 1600. They would generally agree that those who went on crusades believed that taking part in a crusade was a form of penance. The crusaders were Latin Christians and believed that God was angry with them because of their sins—their disobedience to God (such as killing other Christians). They believed that if they did not do penance for their sins before they died, they would be punished severely after their death. One form of penance was to go on a pilgrimage, a journey to a particularly holy place. Jerusalem was a common goal of pilgrimages, for Christians believe that Jesus Christ died, was buried, and rose again from the dead in Jerusalem, and the Christian faith began in Jerusalem. Therefore, a crusade to Jerusalem was a form of pilgrimage.

Scholars also generally agree that a crusade was a holy war: a religious war fought for God, to advance what the crusaders believed to be God's plan. Typically this would involve defending Christians who were under attack from non-Christians (as in Asia Minor), but it could mean trying to recover Christian territory that had been conquered by non-Christians (as in the Iberian Peninsula). It could also involve groups of Christians who did not agree on some points of their belief fighting each other (as in the Hussite Crusades).

Those who took the vow to go on these expeditions sewed a cross onto their clothing as a symbol of the vow. The terms "to be signed by the cross" or "to take the cross"—*se croisier* in medieval French, and *crux suscepit*, *crux accepit*, or *crucizo* in medieval Latin—were already being used by writers during the twelfth century. The earliest known use of the term "to be signed with the cross" dates from 1097, less than two years after the First Crusade was called.[2] From these terms, the words "crusade" and "crusader" developed. According to the *Oxford English Dictionary*, the earliest use of the word "crusade" in English was in 1577, but the equivalent word *croisade* appeared in France more than a hundred years earlier.[3] In the Middle Ages, then, people "took the cross," but they did not start referring to "a crusade" until these expeditions had been taking place for over three hundred years. Up to the fifteenth century, the expeditions were often called pilgrimages, even though fighting was involved (traditional pilgrims did not fight). Not only military expeditions to Jerusalem were called pilgrimages, but also any sort of war against an evil enemy, anywhere in Christendom. The expeditions were also called "passages" (meaning voyages or journeys) and "Christ's business." This fluid terminology does suggest that the concept of crusading in the Middle Ages was broad.

So it is true, as the generalists say, that it is difficult to be precise over what a crusade was in the Middle Ages. The popularists are also correct in saying that many ordinary people from western Europe went on crusade—that is, people who were not nobles. In fact, contemporaries quickly noticed that one of the peculiarities of the crusade was that it offered a way for people who were on the sidelines of religion to win God's favor. Guibert of Nogent, one of the monks who wrote about the First Crusade after it happened, described it as follows: "in our time God has ordained holy wars, so that the knightly order and the wandering crowd—who had previously been engaged in slaughtering each other, like their ancient pagan forebears—could find a new way of earning salvation."[4] Because the crusade involved fighting, the clergy was not supposed to get involved. Priests were not supposed to shed blood, and monks and nuns were not supposed to go on crusade because their religious vows committed them to remaining in one place instead of traveling. In actuality, many priests, monks, and nuns did go on crusade.

There were also many other people who accompanied the expeditions to the Holy Land to visit the holy places rather than to fight. The large numbers of nonfighters caused a problem to crusade leaders in the twelfth century. As the expedition was a pilgrimage as well as a military undertaking, anyone and everyone could go on crusade—not simply warriors and their servants but the old and the young—men, women, and children—from every social class. Wealthy noblewomen accompanied their husbands, as Eleanor, duchess of Aquitaine, accompanied her husband King Louis VII of France on the Second Crusade, and Berengaria of Navarre accompanied King Richard I of England on the Third Crusade. Other wealthy noblewomen traveled without their menfolk and financed warriors from their own resources.[5] Poorer noncombatants could act as support troops, collecting and preparing food, looking after the sick, and bringing water to the troops on the battlefield. Both men and women acted as traders, selling food to the army, or as craftspeople, making armor and weapons. The noncombatants also gave spiritual support, praying for the warriors. However, they had to be fed and protected on the march and were a large drain on military resources. Popes and preachers tried to discourage noncombatants from going on crusade, but without success. In 1213 in his bull *Quia maior*, Pope Innocent III (see biography) tried to reorganize recruitment for crusades so that everyone could get the benefits of crusading but only warriors would go. Other people who "took the cross" and promised to go on crusade would be asked to give a sum of money instead—to *commute* their vow. They were told that they would receive the same reward from God as if they had gone on crusade: all the punishment due for their past sins would be wiped out. The payment counted as the penance they should have done.

Theologians disagreed over whether simply going on crusade was enough to wipe out all the punishment that was due for a person's sins, but Pope Innocent III declared that it was. Having all this punishment wiped out by going on crusade was called an "indulgence," and the system of paying instead of going on crusade was also called an indulgence. In later years, crusade preachers were accused of selling crusade indulgences in order to make money for the pope rather than to help the cause of the crusade. In 1265, a brother of the military religious order of the Temple, Brother Ricaut Bonomel, composed a song in which he criticized papal crusading policy:

> . . . The pope is very generous with his indulgences
> Against Italians, to Charles [of Anjou] and the French,
> But he makes great profits out of us,
> For he pardons for money people who have taken our cross;
>   And if anyone wishes to swop the Holy Land
>   For the war in Italy
> Our legate allows them to do so
> For he sells God and indulgences for cash.[6]

Brother Ricaut was complaining that the pope was diverting potential crusaders and money to Italy to fight his own enemies instead of sending these resources to fight the Muslims who were attacking the Holy Land. In the sixteenth century, the monk Martin Luther argued that the pope was wrong to claim that God had given him the power to remove the punishment for sins, and that the crusading indulgences and taxes had caused great heartbreak and misery in Christendom.[7] This argument over whether indulgences could be valid was one of the differences that led to the Protestants splitting off from the Catholic Church in the six-teenth century.

Motivation for Crusading

Did the people who went on crusade during the Middle Ages see the crusade as a religious undertaking, as the popularists maintain, or was religion just an excuse to fight? The Church gave the warriors and their companies a reason for going on a military campaign and gave them crosses to wear, but what if the warriors themselves did not think that the religious reasons were very important? Many warriors had no choice in going; they had to follow the lord who employed them. So why did their lords go?

Some historians have pointed to economic motives for going on cru-sade. The eleventh century saw population growth in western Europe, and as a result there was famine, since there was not enough food being produced to feed the growing population. Young nobles wanted land, because land was wealth and land gave them status, but there was not enough to go around. There were various customs of inheritance in use in western Europe, but all of them presented problems. Primogeniture, whereby all a family's inheritance went to the eldest son, left the other sons looking for an alternative career. If the whole family held land in common (*fraternitia*), typically only one son would be allowed to marry, so that the land would not have to be divided among many children. Some of the sons might prefer to leave the family inheritance and seek their fortune elsewhere.[8]

It is true that some landless nobles won great benefits from crusading. During the First Crusade, Bohemond, a Norman noble from southern Italy, won the important city of Antioch in Syria (now Antakya in Turkey) and made himself prince there. When he died, his nephew Tancred, who accompanied him on the crusade, succeeded him. On the same crusade, Baldwin of Boulogne, youngest son of Count Eustace of Boulogne and Ida of Lorraine, captured the city of Edessa (now Urfa in Turkey). He later became king of Jerusalem.

But most of the crusaders did not stay in the East. Even if they had set off with ideas of winning their fortune, when the expedition was over, they came home. In fact, crusading was very expensive. It was a prolonged military campaign in a far-off country, where it could be difficult to obtain food and water, or to replace lost armor, weapons, or horses. It seems unlikely that many warriors outside the nobility expected to make much money out of it.

Another possible motivation for crusading was the hope of winning glory and honor. Crusading was an honorable activity for a warrior. The Muslims in particular were regarded by western Christians as skilled and formidable warriors, and any warrior who went to fight them would win a great reputation at home. Honor and glory—the respect of their peers and of society as a whole—were enormously important to the warrior classes. They would rather lose everything else than their good name, and they would go to great lengths to increase their good reputation as warriors.

Overall, then, there were many reasons why warriors chose to go on crusade. The religious motivation was important, but it was not the only factor. In around the middle of the fourteenth century, the French noble knight Geoffrey de Charny wrote (among other things) a poem about how a warrior could win honor in deeds of arms. He urged young knights to go on crusade to win a name for themselves:

> Where do you wish to go?
> To Granada, or Overseas [to the Middle East]
> To damage God's enemies?
> That is a good life.
> In Prussia or in Lombardy,
> Or in the land of Romania [the Byzantine Empire]?
> Take care in choosing
> Where you wish to go overseas.
> "If I may find a Christian somewhere
> Who wishes to perform deeds of
> Arms to occupy themselves
> And do harm to God's enemies
> I will stay there;
> I will serve God as best as I can;
> To serve Him in the best way I will reach
> That height of achievement
> That is called 'noble prowess'

Which makes its home in valiant hearts."
Now, put your efforts into that.[9]

Geoffrey de Charny depicted the two motivations—serving God and winning honor—as being inextricably linked. To take another example, the biographer of Jean le Maingre, called "Boucicaut" (marshal of France and governor of Genoa; died 1421), tells us that in August 1407 Boucicaut sent messengers to Janus of Lusignan, king of Cyprus, to press for a campaign against the Muslims of Alexandria in northern Egypt. Boucicaut's first justification for the attack was that it was for love of God and to benefit Christianity, and the second was that it was to benefit his soul. So far this seems to have been a purely religious expedition. However, Boucicaut's third and fourth justifications were that all knights should use their youth and strength in doing good deeds for which they would win praise forever, and that all knights and gentlemen should continually exercise themselves in warfare to win honor and renown.[10] So in fact Boucicaut expected participants to have a mixture of motives for the campaign.

So a crusade was a military/religious expedition. It was called "a pilgrimage" although it involved fighting. Some of these expeditions went to the Holy Land, but many went to other frontiers of Christendom or fought enemies within Christendom. Historians do not agree whether people in the Middle Ages believed that the expeditions to the Holy Land were the most important, or whether all expeditions against the enemies of Christendom were equally prestigious. However, pluralist historians of the crusade argue that in defining a crusade, we should also consider how these expeditions were organized. What was special about the organization of a crusade, which set it apart from other military expeditions?

Organization of Crusades

Pluralist historians argue that in order for an expedition to have been a crusade, it must have shown the following features. First, the pope must have launched it, either by preaching or by issuing a general letter called a "papal encyclical," which was addressed to all Christians (see Document 5 for an example). He would have authorized members of the clergy to preach about the crusade and encourage people to take part, and would have appointed specific men to preach the crusade. Second, those taking part must have taken a vow that they would join the expedition, and sewed a cross onto their clothing as a symbol of this vow. This vow was like the vow that pilgrims took. Third, those who had "taken the cross" in this way must have been given certain privileges by the Church, so that their outstanding debts were held over until they returned, and their families and property were under Church protection; again, pilgrims used to receive the same protection. Crusaders also received the crusade indulgence, which has already been described.

There are problems with this definition. Not everyone who was on a crusade expedition would necessarily have "taken the cross," because a leading noble would bring his knights and other warriors with him on the expedition whether or not they had taken the vow. Those who remained at home did not always respect the protection given to crusaders' families and lands; for example, King Richard I of England and King Philip II of France set out on the Third Crusade together in 1189, but they quarreled and Philip II returned to France, where he launched attacks on Richard's lands in France. What is more, as was noted previously, it was possible to obtain a crusade indulgence without going on crusade. Yet overall, these features mark expeditions that we can call crusades.

By defining crusades by who started them and how they were organized, modern pluralist historians of the crusades define some expeditions as crusades that historians in the past did not, while disregarding other expeditions that used to be called crusades. For example, by this definition, expeditions to the Baltic region of Europe against pagans, those to the Iberian Peninsula against Muslims, those against heretics (such as the Albigensian and Hussite Crusades), and the wars in Italy between the pope and the Hohenstaufen rulers of Sicily in the thirteenth century were all crusades. Expeditions to the eastern Mediterranean after the loss of the crusader states in Syria and Palestine were still crusades even though Jerusalem had been lost, as were expeditions to the Balkans against the Ottoman Turks, and expeditions to North Africa against Morocco, Tunis, and Algiers. Naval campaigns against Muslim rulers were a form of crusading too, meaning that the "Holy Leagues" involving the Italian naval powers of Venice and Genoa in the sixteenth and seventeenth centuries were also a form of crusading. In the pluralist sense, crusading of a sort continued until 1798, when the naval campaigns by the Knights Hospitaller of Malta against Muslim pirates in the Mediterranean were halted by Napoleon's capture of Malta.

On the other hand, pluralist historians of the crusades would not regard the "Children's Crusade" of 1212 as a true crusade because it was not launched by the pope, there was no papally approved preaching, and there were no official Church privileges or crusade indulgences. Again, the so-called "Shepherds' Crusades" of 1251 and 1320 were not crusades for the same reason, nor were small expeditions to the East such as the Venetian expedition of 1122–24 and the pilgrimage of Duke Henry the Lion in 1172. Yet scholars who see the crusade as essentially a religious undertaking for the masses and/or for warriors would call these true crusades and argue that the campaigns of the Knights Hospitaller and the Holy Leagues were not really crusades because they only involved a small number of warriors.

Again, pluralist historians would not call any expedition a crusade that was not organized by Latin Christians. They argue that as the pope played an essential part in the organization of the crusade, any expedition not started by the pope cannot be a crusade. Hence the Byzantines could not launch crusades, as they were Orthodox Christians, not Latin, and did not acknowledge the spiritual authority of the pope. Likewise, Protestants could not launch crusades, as they had rebelled against papal authority. Any campaigns these Christians fought that might resemble crusades have to be labeled "holy war" rather than "crusade."

In the same way, non-Christians cannot launch crusades. The cross is an essential part of a crusade, from which the movement gets its name. So a holy war by members of another religious group has to be simply a holy war, not a crusade.

Where do all these definitions lead us? They certainly show how difficult it can be for us to define movements in the past. Seeking a definition can be useful because the process of definition forces us to try to understand what people of the past were doing and what they hoped to achieve. However, if we try to impose a single, strict definition on a broad and changing movement, we can overlook important factors. So scholars who insist that a crusade had to have Jerusalem as its ultimate aim exclude other forms of "Christ's business" within Europe, such as the war against pagans in the Baltic, while those who insist that a crusade had to be started by a papal crusading bull exclude popular movements such as the "Children's Crusade." In fact, most crusading scholars no longer insist on one definition of crusading; they use one definition as a guideline but include expeditions that do not exactly fit their definition.

As this book is intended to introduce readers to the crusades, it adopts a wide definition of the subject and tends toward the generalist view of crusading, so as to include as many crusades and aspects of crusading as possible. It begins with an overview of the crusades to the Holy Land, and then moves on to consider other crusading fields.

NOTES

1. Jonathan Riley-Smith, *What Were the Crusades?* 3rd ed. (Basingstoke: Palgrave Macmillan, 2002), pp. xi–xii; Giles Constable, "The Historiography of the Crusades," in Angeliki E. Laiou and Roy Parviz Mottahedeh, eds., *The Crusades from the Perspective of Byzantium and the Muslim World* (Washington, DC: Dumbarton Oaks, 2001), pp. 1–22, here pp. 12–15.

2. Christopher Tyerman, *The Invention of the Crusades* (Basingstoke: Palgrave Macmillan, 1998), p. 21, citing Heinrich Hagenmeyer, *Epistulae et chartae ad historiam primi belli sacri spectantes: Die Kreuzzugsbriefe aus den Jahren 1088–1100* (Innsbruck: Wagner'sche Universitäts-Buchhandlung, 1901, reprinted, Hildesheim and New York: G. Olms, 1973), p. 142; Charles Du Fresne Du Cange, *Glossarium mediae et infimae latinitatis* (Paris: Firmin Didot, 1840–50), vol. 2, p. 680 ("crux assumere"); *Le Robert Dictionnaire de la langue française*, 2nd ed., vol. 3 (Paris: Robert, 1992), pp. 64–65.

3. *Le Robert Dictionnaire*, vol. 3, p. 64.

4. Guibert of Nogent, *The Deeds of God through the Franks: Gesta Dei per Francos*, trans. Robert Levine (Rochester, NY: Boydell, 1997), p. 28 (amended).

5. On women and crusading, see James M. Powell, "The Role of Women in the Fifth Crusade," in Benjamin Z. Kedar, ed., *The Horns of Hattin* (Jerusalem and London: Yad Izhak Ben-Zvi and Variorum, 1992), pp. 294–301; Helen Nicholson, "Women on the Third Crusade," *Journal of Medieval History* 23 (1997): 335–49; and the articles in Susan B. Edgington and Sarah Lambert, eds., *Gendering the Crusades* (Cardiff: University of Wales Press; New York: Columbia University Press, 2001).

6. Antoine de Bastard, "La colère et la douleur d'un templier en Terre Sainte: 'I're dolors s'es dins mon cor asseza'," *Revue des Langues Romaines* 81 (1974): 333–73, here 357, French translation 359. English translation by Helen Nicholson.

7. Martin Luther, "Explanations of the Ninety-five Theses" (1518), Helmut

T. Lehmann, ed., *Luther's Works*, vol. 31, Harold J. Grimm, ed., *Career of the Reformer* (Philadelphia: Fortress Press, 1957), pp. 91–92; "On War against the Turk" (1529), in James Atkinson, ed., *Luther's Works*, vols. 44–47, *The Christian in Society*, vol. 46, ed. R. C. Schultz (Philadelphia: Fortress Press, 1967), p. 186.

8. Hans E. Mayer, *The Crusades*, trans. John Gillingham, 2nd ed. (Oxford: Oxford University Press, 1988), pp. 21–23.

9. Arthur Piaget, "Le *livre* Messire Geoffroi de Charny," *Romania* 26 (1897): 394–411, here 403–4, lines 329–47.

10. *Le Livre des Fais du bon Messire Jehan le Maingre, dit Bouciquaut, Mareschal de France et Gouverneur de Jennes*, ed. Denis Lalande (Geneva: Droz, 1985), bk. 3, ch. 15, p. 351.

CHAPTER 1

CRUSADING EXPEDITIONS TO THE HOLY LAND, 1095–1291

THE FIRST CRUSADE

Background

In November 1095, Pope Urban II gave a speech at a Church council that he had convened at Clermont in southeastern France. No text of his speech survives, but later accounts say that he urged his listeners to take part in a war in the service of God. They would be fighting Muslims in the East. They would free the Christians living in the East from oppression, and free the holy places where Christ had lived, died, and risen again. He probably said that the goal of the expedition was to recapture Jerusalem, which had been conquered by a Muslim army in 638. He also told them that anyone who set out on this expedition would not have to do any penance for their crimes against God, provided that they went for pious reasons only, not to win prestige or money.

To understand why the leaders of Christendom regarded Islam as such a danger, we need only compare the history of the two faiths. Christianity began in Palestine in the first century of the Roman Empire. By the year 400, it had spread to include not only the Roman Empire but also Ethiopia, and there were also some Christian communities in central Asia. The religion continued to spread slowly, so that by the late eleventh century, Eastern Europe, northern Germany, and Scandinavia had been converted, but not the Baltic coast or Finland. The Islamic religion spread much more quickly. It began in Arabia around six hundred years after the beginning of Christianity. Its founder, Muḥammad, died in 632. Three centuries later, Islam covered not only Arabia, Syria, Palestine, Mesopotamia, Persia, and what are now Pakistan and Afghanistan, but also northern Africa and most of the Iberian Peninsula, Sicily, and the Balearic Islands. The south coast of what is now France was briefly conquered, and in the first half of the eighth century, Arab generals led armies north from Spain and raided deep into Frankish (now French) territory. Christians believed that Islam was a false religion, inspired by the devil rather than by God, and they feared that it would conquer the whole of Christendom and destroy the Christian faith.

In 732 Charles Martel ("the Hammer"), commanding the Franks, defeated a Muslim army near Poitiers in central France. Many more battles were fought between the Franks and their Muslim neighbors, and were immortalized in epic verse. The victories and losses of the Emperor Charlemagne (d. 814) and of Duke William of Toulouse (d. 812) in their wars against the Muslims were very well known to the French warrior nobility throughout the Middle Ages through these epic poems. Some of these stirring accounts were translated into other languages and became popular throughout Europe. This meant that in the late eleventh century, the warriors of western Europe had preconceived ideas about the Muslims, drawn from the epic accounts that they listened to in their leisure hours. They believed that the Muslims intended to conquer the whole of Christendom (after all, they had nearly done so in 732!); that they were skilled warriors, very brave and determined; and that their religious beliefs were a strange distortion of Christianity, with three pagan gods rather than a holy Trinity. They believed that God wanted Christian warriors to defeat the Muslims and either convert them to Christianity or, if this were not possible, kill them.

So the pope's call to wage war on the Muslims fit the Christian warriors' beliefs. It is more difficult to understand why the warriors of western Europe were concerned about penance. In the early Christian Church, Christians who committed a crime against God (a sin) had to confess that they had done so and put right the wrong in some way (penance). They believed that until they had done this, God would reject them; and Christians who had sinned could not worship with other Christians (the Church). However, if Christians had committed some terrible crime, such as killing many innocent bystanders in a war, it would be a long time before they were able to put right what they had done, if ever; and until then, they would be excluded from the Church. Yet this did not seem to fit the Christian belief that the Christian God is loving and merciful. So Christian clergy gradually changed their approach to dealing with sin. By the eleventh century, the Church's system of dealing with wrongdoings had been amended so that as soon as a wrongdoer had confessed and begun penance, he or she would be absolved of the wrongdoing by a priest and reconciled to God and the Church, on the understanding that the penance would eventually be completed. Usual forms of penance were saying certain prayers, giving to charity, or going on a journey to a holy place (a pilgrimage). If joining a military expedition to the East could replace all other forms of penance, this would seem very attractive to the warriors of western Europe, who believed that their function in society was to fight. According to the pope, they could win God's approval and have their wrongdoings put right by taking part in their own proper activity.

Although warriors would obviously welcome the opportunity to fight for God, it may seem odd that the pope should encourage Christians to fight. Yet in fact when Pope Urban II called the crusade, the idea that the Church in western Europe could employ warriors to fight on God's behalf was already familiar to his hearers. The Christian Church had always accepted warfare, but only in certain defined circumstances. In the Gospels, Jesus made various statements implying that God's people should not fight, telling them to turn the other cheek rather than retaliate to blows, and not to use violence (Matt. 5:39; 26:52). Yet elsewhere in the Gospels, soldiers are not told to stop fighting. John the Baptist did not tell soldiers to stop fighting, but to be content with their pay; Jesus praised a centurion as having more faith than anyone he had met in Israel (Luke 3:14; Matt. 8:10). In the Old Testament, God's people were depicted fighting on God's behalf, to carry out God's will. So while some early Christians believed that Christians should not fight, others considered that, as in the time of the Old Testament, it was acceptable to fight with God's approval. For example, Bishop Augustine of Hippo Regius in North Africa (now Annaba or Bône in Tunisia) (d. 430), condemned war, but wrote that it is necessary to wage war to protect those who cannot protect themselves.

On this basis, the Christian emperors had a duty to wage war to protect the Roman Empire, for God had appointed them as emperors in order to protect his people. After the dissolution of the western Roman

Empire during the fifth century c.e., the remaining Christian authorities in the West continued to believe that they had a duty to fight to defend their subjects. Warriors who fought for them had a just cause for fighting, although they would have to do penance if they killed anyone in battle.[1] If the local lord was not able to defend the people, then the Church itself had to step in. In the late tenth century in the south of France, Church leaders assembled councils that tried to stop warriors from attacking noncombatants such as monks, nuns, and peasants. Local lords were asked to give their support to these councils' decrees and use force against anyone who broke the peace. This "peace of God" movement spread to the north of France and the Rhineland during the eleventh century. Some historians have seen it as a forerunner to the crusade movement, because Church leaders were trying to control war and were encouraging warriors to use force to carry out Church decrees. In addition, by controlling warfare within Christendom, the councils encouraged Christian warriors to go outside Christendom to fight. Other historians have noted that many of the crusaders came from areas where there was no "peace of God" to control warfare, and so there was no direct connection between the "peace of God" movement and the crusade.[2] However, the fact that the Church authorities were trying to control and direct violence does echo the concept of the crusade.

In the introduction it was noted that some scholars have argued for the Latin (Catholic) Christian campaigns against Barbastro in the Iberian Peninsula (1064) and al-Mahdiyyah in North Africa (1087) being precursors of the crusades. Another striking precedent for the crusade appeared in the policies of Pope Gregory VII (1073–85). Pope Gregory wanted to reform the Christian Church to make it more spiritually pure. He believed that in order to achieve his aim he must free the clergy from the control of nonclergy such as kings. The most active opponent of his policies was King Henry IV of Germany (1056–1106), who believed that it was his duty as a ruler appointed by God to guide and protect the Church. Pope Gregory and his supporters urged all warriors to fight against the king as the pope's enemy. Pope Gregory argued that by serving the pope, warriors would be serving God, because the pope was the heir of St. Peter, and he ruled everything in Christendom on God's behalf. According to his enemies, Gregory VII claimed that fighting for the pope wiped out all sins, and that anyone who killed a Christian in this cause would be forgiven, apparently not needing to do any penance.[3] This concept of war on behalf of the Church was very like the idea of the crusade: fighting that was authorized by the pope and that replaced penance. Gregory also planned an expedition to Constantinople (now Istanbul in Turkey) in 1074 to help the Byzantine Greeks against the Turks, but this never took place.

In short, by 1095, most Christians in western Europe accepted that Christians could and should fight against the enemies of Christendom on God's behalf. Theologians and Church lawyers would continue to discuss when war was legal and when it was not, but those who went on crusade believed that this was legal war, approved by God through the pope.

Why did the pope call the crusade in 1095? It had been over 450 years since Jerusalem fell to the Muslims; and almost a century since the Fatimid Caliph al-Hakim Bi-amr Allah had destroyed the Church of the Holy Sepulchre, the most sacred site in Christendom, and persecuted Christians in his domains. In 1095 there was no immediate provocation for war. However, we must remember that because most people in western Europe in the late eleventh century could not read or write and so could not read any written records that set out the passage of history over the centuries, they had no real sense of time beyond their own lifetimes. They had heard about the city of Jerusalem in the time of Christ, as it was in the New Testament, and therefore believed that it should still be a Christian city. For them, the stories of Jesus in Jerusalem and of Christian warriors fighting Muslim invaders in the eighth and ninth centuries, which they had heard told by priests or by traveling entertainers, were as real and current as any other news that they had heard yesterday.

For the better-educated members of society, there was another reason for launching an expedition in 1095. Western Christendom was more peaceful and the economy more buoyant than since the fall of the western Roman Empire in the fifth century. In contrast, Islam was divided. It was divided in religion, between the orthodox Sunnis, whose caliph was in Baghdad, and the Shi'ites, whose caliph was in Egypt. It was true that Christendom was also divided, between the Latin Christians of the West, whose religious leader was the pope in Rome and whose leading secular figure was the western or German emperor, and the orthodox

Greek Christians in the East, whose supreme leader was the Byzantine emperor. However, in the late eleventh century, these two groups were on good terms, whereas the Islamic religious divisions were not.

In the late eleventh century, the Middle East was divided between two Islamic empires: the Sunni Seljuks, who ruled Syria, Arabia, Mesopotamia, and Persia, and who had been advancing into Asia Minor over the previous half-century, and the Shi'ite Fatimids, who ruled Egypt and Palestine. The Seljuks had defeated the forces of the Byzantine Empire at the Battle of Manzikert in 1071, and in 1084 they captured the Byzantine city of Antioch in Syria. But in the early 1090s, a series of disasters hit both empires. The caliphs of both Egypt and Baghdad, the grand viziers of both empires, and the sultan of the Seljuk Empire died in quick succession, leaving both empires in political and religious confusion.

The Byzantine emperor, Alexios Comnenos (1081–1118), saw that this confusion offered him the opportunity to recover former Byzantine territory in Asia Minor and Syria from the Seljuks. In spring 1095 he sent ambassadors to a Church council that Pope Urban II had assembled at Piacenza in Italy, asking for aid against the Turks. He probably hoped that some armies of westerners would come to Constantinople from the West to join his own army. In the past, the Byzantine emperors had extensively employed western European warriors in their armies, and it was only to be expected that Alexios would try to recruit warriors from western Europe for a big campaign against the Turks.

When Pope Urban II received Emperor Alexios' request, he took it up enthusiastically. He was very anxious to bring about change and reform in the western Church. He hoped that by assisting the emperor, he could heal relations between the Church of Constantinople and the Church of Rome, uniting Christendom. By calling a holy war against the Muslims, he would also be acting as the supreme ruler over all Christians in the West. Traditionally the emperor had led holy wars to defend Christendom, but the emperor was at this time involved in wars in northern Italy, giving the pope the opportunity to take over that role. So at the Council of Clermont in November 1095, Pope Urban II called the First Crusade.

The Course of the Crusade

Nobles and their warriors in France, the Rhineland, and Italy responded to the pope's call and the clergy's preaching, and from spring 1096, several armies set off for Constantinople in four major groups. The first set off too early in the year, before the harvest had been brought in, and so was short of food. Some crusaders pillaged and murdered Jews in the Rhineland, on the excuse that the Jews were responsible for Christ's death. They took the Jews' money and tried to force them to convert to Christianity. Their atrocities were condemned by contemporary Christian writers. This first wave of crusaders pillaged their way to Constantinople and crossed into Asia Minor, where they engaged a Turkish army and were heavily defeated.

The later groups of crusaders set out in August 1096. The second group consisted of the Normans, led by Duke Robert Curthose of Normandy, son of William the Conqueror of England, and the northern French, led by Count Stephen of Blois, Duke Robert's brother-in-law; those from the Low Countries, led by Count Robert of Flanders, Count Eustace of Boulogne, and his youngest brother Baldwin; and the Rhinelanders, led by Eustace and Baldwin's brother Godfrey of Bouillon, duke of Lower Lorraine. The third major group consisted of the southern French, led by Count Raymond of St. Gilles, and the fourth group was made up of Italian Normans, led by Bohemond (sometimes incorrectly called "of Taranto"; see biography) and his nephew Tancred. Most of the crusaders came from parts of Europe populated by the Germanic people called "the Franks" and so the crusaders were called "Franks." The pope was represented by his legate or representative Adhémar of Monteil, bishop of Le Puy, who was associated with Count Raymond. Apart from the papal legate there was no overall leader.

The crusaders reached Constantinople, where they met the Emperor Alexios. After negotiation, the crusading leaders agreed on terms by which they would assist the emperor in recovering his territory from the Turks. The emperor would give them assistance, such as naval support and food, and the crusaders would act as the emperor's loyal people. The crusaders then crossed into Asia Minor and with the emperor's assistance besieged and captured the city of Nicaea, which had been conquered by the Seljuks from the Byzantines around ten years earlier. As agreed, the recaptured city was handed over to the emperor. The crusaders then proceeded across Asia Minor, the different leaders taking different routes, capturing fortresses and towns as they went. The Christians of Cilician Armenia in southern Asia Minor helped them. One of the [7] prominent nobles in the crusade, Baldwin of Boulogne, took his force east to the important city of Edessa, which was ruled by the Christian Armenians but was threatened by the Seljuks. Baldwin took over the city and drove off a siege by Kerbogha, Muslim ruler of Mosul. So Edessa and the area around it became one of the "crusader states"—the states founded by the crusaders.

In October 1097 the rest of the crusading forces reached the city of Antioch in Syria. As it was too large a city to be captured by assault, the crusaders had to besiege it (see Figure 7). While the siege was in progress, they negotiated with the vizier (or chief minister) of Egypt, al-Afḍal, who was hoping to employ them to help recapture Fatimid territory in Palestine. The Seljuks did very little to help Antioch because the two leading Seljuk princes, Barkyaruq and Muḥammad, were fighting in Iran and had little interest in the Christian conquests in the west of their empire.[4] The local princes tried to relieve Antioch but the crusaders defeated them. At last Kerbogha of Mosul set out to relieve the city and arrived in late June 1098, just after the crusaders had succeeded in taking Antioch. He engaged the crusaders in battle and lost. The crusaders were so surprised at defeating this great warrior that they believed their victory miraculous—St. George and the heavenly host had been helping them (see Document 2).

After this victory, Bohemond took over the administration of the city of Antioch and the area around it. In January 1099, most of the army pushed south to Jerusalem. Individual rulers of the towns and fortresses that they passed negotiated with them; some paid the crusaders to leave them alone. The Fatimids had recently recaptured Jerusalem from the Seljuks, and none of the Seljuks were prepared to help the Fatimids against the crusaders. The crusaders reached Jerusalem in June 1099, and after a fiercely fought siege, assisted by supplies of timber brought by Genoese ships to the port of Jaffa (now in Tel Aviv Yafo, Israel), the city fell by assault on July 15, 1099. The inhabitants were massacred, as was general practice when a city fell by assault.[5] An Egyptian army arrived in August to recover the city, but the crusaders defeated it.

The crusaders were now in control of much of Palestine and part of Syria. They were extremely surprised at their own success, and supposed that God must have brought it about. They believed that they were fulfilling biblical prophecy—they were the new Israelites, reconquering the Promised Land like Joshua in the Old Testament. However, modern historians point to other reasons why the First Crusade succeeded.[6]

First, the crusade had one united, clear aim that captured the imagination and aroused enthusiasm—to recapture Jerusalem. This was backed by religious conviction. Second, leadership was important. The First Crusade was led by an alliance of the Church and the lay princes, and the lay princes controlled their troops and worked together. Third, the crusaders were adaptable, changing their military tactics to deal with the Muslims, learning as they went along.

Fourth, the crusaders were helped by the Byzantine emperor. For example, Alexios had a fleet based at Cyprus, which brought supplies to the crusaders while they were besieging Antioch. The First Crusade was a joint enterprise between the Byzantine emperor and the western forces whom he had enlisted to help him. The crusaders also had help from other Christians in the Middle East. Fifth, Islam was divided. The Seljuk leaders were otherwise engaged. The Muslims did not understand what the crusaders were doing and there was little reaction to the fall of Jerusalem. In the east of the Seljuk Empire, when people heard about the fall of Jerusalem they thought the Byzantines had captured it.[7]

Yet although the First Crusade was successful in capturing Jerusalem, its original purposes were only partly achieved. Christendom was not unified; East and West remained divided. The Byzantine emperor recovered territory in Asia Minor, but the crusaders did not return Antioch or the territory they captured in Syria and Palestine. Instead, the crusaders set up new lordships and established the kingdom of Jerusalem.

THE CRUSADES FROM 1100 TO 1291

Crusades to the Holy Land between 1100 and 1291 can be divided into three stages:

- 1100–1193: The recovery of Muslim unity and Muslim aggression

- 1193–1260: Muslim disunity, Frankish recovery

- 1260–1291: Muslim unity under the Mamluks: the Franks lose the Holy Land

Stage One: Recovery of Muslim Unity

After the capture of Jerusalem in 1099, expeditions continued to come out from Europe to support the new states. These frequent expeditions were necessary because, as very few of the people who had accompanied the First Crusade actually settled in the East after Jerusalem was captured, the new lordships had very little fighting power. Since the nineteenth century, historians have given the larger expeditions numbers and referred to the smaller expeditions as pilgrimages. Modern scholars have kept these numbers for most of the crusades even though they are misleading. There were only two expeditions to the East in the twelfth century that were large enough for modern historians to give them a number: the so-called Second Crusade, which set off in 1147, and the Third Crusade, which set off in 1189. Both of these were prompted by a threat from a single, powerful Muslim leader.

Very quickly the Latin Christian settlers in the East (known as the "Palestinian Franks") lost one of their main advantages over the Muslims—their unity. While the Muslims were divided, the Franks could play them off against each other. When they were united, the Franks were quickly driven back.

In 1127–28 a new Muslim power arose to fill the power vacuum in northern Syria: 'Imād al-Dīn Zengi, ruler of Mosul and Aleppo (now Halab in Syria). In 1144 he captured the Christian city of Edessa. Zengi was a brilliant and ruthless military leader, whose Islamic contemporaries regarded him as fighting holy war against nonbelievers (*jihād*). After Zengi was murdered in 1146, his lands were divided between his two sons. His younger son, Nūr al-Dīn, took over the government of Aleppo and concentrated on expanding his power in Syria, capturing the important city of Damascus (now Dimashq in Syria) in 1154. Nūr al-Dīn was a very religious man as well as a skilled general, and he depicted his wars against the Christians as holy war, part of his duty as a Muslim. After Nūr al-Dīn's death in 1174, Saladin (see biography) became sultan of Egypt and Damascus, surrounding the crusader states. Saladin continued Nūr al-Dīn's policy of holy war and strove to unite Islam behind him in holy war against the "polytheist" Christians (called polytheists by the Muslims because they worship a Trinity of gods, "three-in-one," while Muslims worship a single god: "there is no god but Allah").[8]

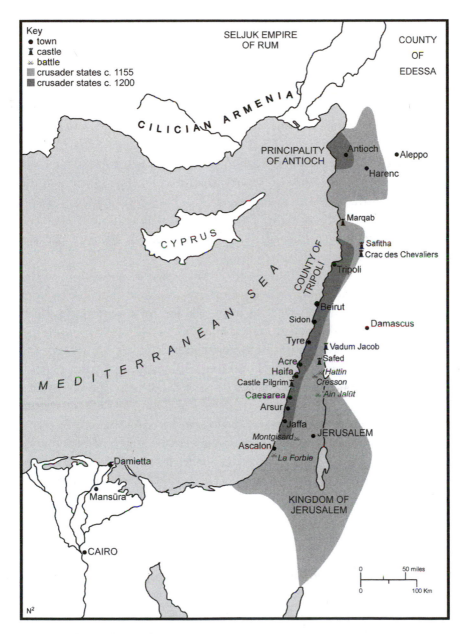

SELJUK EMPIRE
OF RUM

COUNTY
OF
EDESSA

CILICIAN ARMENIA

PRINCIPALITY
OF ANTIOCH

● Antioch

● Aleppo

● Harenc

CYPRUS

♜ Marqab

♜ Safitha
♜ Crac des Chevaliers

● Tripoli

COUNTY OF TRIPOLI

● Beirut

Sidon ●

● Damascus

Tyre ●

♜ Vadum Jacob

Acre ●
Haifa ●

♜ Safed

⚔ *Hattin*
Cresson

Castle Pilgrim ♜

Caesarea ●

⚔ *Ain Jalūt*

Arsur ●

● Jaffa

JERUSALEM ●

Montgisard ⚔

Ascalon ●

⚔ *La Forbie*

● Damietta

KINGDOM OF
JERUSALEM

MEDITERRANEAN SEA

● Mansūra

● CAIRO

0 _____ 50 miles

0 _____ 100 Km

N²

Map 1. The Holy Land, 1099–1291

The Second Crusade was launched in response to the victories of Zengi and Nūr al-Dīn. Two large expeditions set off to the Holy Land in 1147, led by the kings of France and Germany. Other military expeditions during the same period fought Muslims in the Iberian Peninsula or pagans in North Germany on the coast of the Baltic Sea. Only the expeditions in the Iberian Peninsula achieved anything.

The Second Crusade failed in the Holy Land largely because of bad planning. The crusaders went overland to Constantinople, where they quarreled with the emperor. Then the armies crossed Asia Minor, where they were cut to pieces by the Turks. Too few warriors reached the Holy Land to wage a field campaign against the Muslims. The few remaining crusaders and the Palestinian Franks tried to capture Damascus, to prevent Nūr al-Dīn from taking it. The siege was a failure, and in 1154 the people of Damascus welcomed Nūr al-Dīn as lord of the city because they wanted protection against crusaders.

Christians in western Europe were disillusioned by the failure of the Second Crusade, and for a whole generation, no large expeditions went to the East. Even the clear threat from Saladin, ruler of Egypt and Damascus after 1174, did not prompt a crusade.

The Third Crusade did not begin until after Saladin's conquest of the kingdom of Jerusalem in 1187. This crusade did achieve a truce (1192), which returned some territory on the coast of Palestine to the Christians. During the course of the crusade, the island of Cyprus was captured from its Byzantine Greek ruler, and was settled by the crusaders and Palestinian Franks from the kingdom of Jerusalem. They set up lordships on the island, which was an important center of trade, and it became a vital staging post for crusaders. The islanders also supplied the crusader states of the mainland with food. The crusaders did not, however, recapture Jerusalem, because they knew that even if they captured it, they could not hold the city against unified Islam.

The Third Crusade also suffered from bad luck and problems of rivalry between the leaders of the crusade. It was led by Marquis Conrad of Montferrat (in Italy), King Philip II of France, Emperor Frederick Barbarossa of Germany, and King Richard I of England—now known as Richard the Lionheart. The Emperor Frederick died on the way to the Holy Land, in Cilician Armenia; he drowned while he was crossing a river. Conrad of Montferrat was assassinated—some said instigated by

Richard of England. Philip II of France and Richard of England quarreled, and Philip went back to France, leaving Duke Hugh III of Burgundy in charge of the French contingent. The duke and King Richard quarreled—the duke complained that Richard would not lend him money—and they sang insulting songs about each other. Eventually, after making a truce with Saladin and (although they had no Jerusalem to rule), arranging a marriage between Queen Isabel of Jerusalem and Count Henry of Champagne—respectively Richard's cousin and nephew—Richard went back to England.

The kingdom of Jerusalem that was restored in 1192 was much smaller than before 1187 (see Map 1). It comprised a stretch of coastline, and its capital was the port of Acre (now 'Akko in Israel).

Stage Two: Muslim Disunity, Frankish Recovery

From the death of Saladin in 1193 until 1260, the Muslim powers that bordered the crusader states were divided. At first Aleppo, Damascus, and Egypt were ruled by different members of Saladin's family (the Ayyūbids) who were constantly at war with each other; as a result, the Franks played them off against each other. In 1250 there was a change of government in Egypt when the Mamluks, elite slave warriors who had served the sultan, seized power (see biography of Shajar al-Durr). As Aleppo and Damascus were still ruled by the Ayyūbids, the Franks could still play the rival powers off.

So between 1193 and 1260 there was a repeating pattern of a truce, followed by a crusading expedition that tried to recover new territory, followed by another truce.

Some of these expeditions were more successful than others. The Fourth Crusade of 1202–4 was sidetracked to Constantinople, where the crusaders set up a Latin, or Catholic, Christian emperor ruling a "Latin Empire of Constantinople." Whatever the reason for the diversion (which has been debated ever since the crusade took place), the leaders of the crusade told the pope, Innocent III, that control of Constantinople would assist the crusader states in the Holy Land. In fact, the Latin empire was soon reduced to a small area around Constantinople, and in 1261, the city fell to Michael VIII Palaeologos, who reestablished the Byzantine Empire. The "Children's Crusade" of 1212, what we would now call a popular movement of young people and adults from northern France and the Rhineland, broke up before it reached the Holy Land. The Fifth Crusade of 1218–21 was initially successful, but its chances of success were destroyed by quarrels between the papal legate—the pope's representative who was trying to run the crusade—and the secular princes who thought they should be running it. In 1228–29 the Emperor Frederick II recovered Jerusalem by negotiating with al-Kāmil, sultan of Egypt, rather than fighting (see biography of Frederick II). He was excommunicated at the time, which meant that he was cut off from Christian society, and that the military leaders in the Holy Land were not allowed to associate with him. Some of them doubted that his truce was in their interests, and in fact some modern historians believe that Frederick was more interested in protecting the commercial interests of his kingdom of Sicily than in protecting the Holy Land.

Ten years later, two more expeditions came out to the East and again ended with truces that secured territory for the Palestinian Franks. Roughly ten years later another crusade came to the East, under King Louis IX of France.

It is striking that during this period, crusade leaders were shifting their strategy from simply defending the Holy Land to attacking Egypt. This policy had originated under King Amaury of Jerusalem in the 1160s. Richard the Lionheart had planned to attack Egypt in 1192 but had been unable to persuade the whole crusade army to accompany him. The leaders of the Fifth Crusade and Louis IX believed that if they could conquer Egypt, they could hold the Holy Land securely. However, although individual fortresses or cities could be captured, no crusade was successful in Egypt.

The Franks in the Latin East suffered some very serious reverses during this period. In 1244 they lost Jerusalem for good, and an Egyptian army destroyed the Frankish army in a battle at La Forbie in the south of the kingdom of Jerusalem. Yet in general the Franks were in a strong position. The kingdom of Jerusalem was rich from the trade that passed through the kingdom's ports en route between the Far East and Europe. The Frankish rulers could afford to hire mercenaries and build fortresses, the towns and cities flourished, and merchants came every year from western Europe to trade.[9]

Stage Three: Muslim Unity under the Mamluks

In the first half of the thirteenth century the Mongols, nomads from what is now Mongolia, had swept across central Asia and attacked eastern Europe. In 1258 they captured Baghdad, and early in 1260 they captured Aleppo and Damascus. The Christian rulers in their path had to decide whether to negotiate with the Mongols or risk being destroyed by them. The Christian King Hetoum of Cilician Armenia had started negotiating with the Mongols in 1247 and had visited the Mongol Great Khan at Karakorum (or Qaraqorum: in Mongolia) between 1253 and 1256. In 1254 King Hetoum's daughter Sybilla married Prince Bohemond VI of Tripoli (now Tarābalus in Lebanon) and Antioch, who then also came to terms with the Mongols. In contrast, the leaders of the kingdom of Jerusalem decided to remain neutral, not assisting either the Mongols or the Mamluks. However, in September 1260 the Mamluk sultan of Egypt, Qutuz, defeated the Mongols at 'Ain Jālūt in Galilee. This decisive victory saved the crusader states and Egypt from the Mongols, but it also enabled the Mamluks to take over Aleppo and Damascus, which had previously opposed them. The crusader states were now surrounded, and over the next three decades the Mamluk generals captured fortress after fortress and city after city, until the crusader states were reduced to a few fortified cities along the coastline.

The kingdom of Jerusalem was already suffering financial decline. Wars between the Italian merchant cities of Genoa, Venice, and Pisa from 1256 onward damaged trade, the lifeblood of the crusader states. Trade was further disrupted by Mongol conquests in central Asia. It became too dangerous for merchants to travel through Syria, and so they traveled farther north, via the Black Sea.[10] The Mamluks' repeated campaigns destroyed the agriculture and infrastructure of the crusader states. They adopted a scorched-earth policy, destroying everything so that the Franks could not regroup and recover as they had in 1189–92, during the Third Crusade. Unlike Saladin, who used to allow the Christian defenders of a castle or town to go in peace if they surrendered, the Mamluks would routinely kill the defenders of the castles and towns they captured. Saladin's policy had been intended to encourage quick surrenders. The Mamluks relied on their superior siege machinery to capture fortresses quickly, and aimed at destroying their enemy completely.

Figure 1. Marqab (Margat) castle, Syria. Bought by the Hospitallers of St. John of Jerusalem in 1186. Saladin did not even attempt to besiege it in 1188, regarding it as impregnable; it was eventually captured by Sultan Qalawun of Egypt in 1285. Copyright Denys Pringle.

* * *

In May 1291, Acre—the capital of the kingdom of Jerusalem—fell to the troops of the Mamluk sultan al-Ashraf Khalīl. Some of those in the city managed to escape by sea to Cyprus, but the rest were either killed or taken prisoner. Cyprus remained an independent Christian kingdom until the Ottoman Turks conquered it in 1571, but the mainland was lost for good. Many plans were drawn up to recover the Holy Land, but these all came to nothing.

WHY DID THE CRUSADES TO THE HOLY LAND FAIL?

Although the First Crusade was successful, no crusade to the East was ever as successful again. The main reason was that never again could crusaders take advantage of the divisions that had existed in Islam during the 1090s. In a sense, the First Crusade took Islam by surprise. After

1100 the Islamic powers in the East were more prepared for attack from the West. Strong leaders such as Nūr al-Dīn and Saladin unified the various peoples under their command and urged them to fight the invaders in the name of God, to defend their own faith. After 1260, when both Aleppo and Damascus fell under Mamluk control and the Mamluk sultan Baibars took over power in Egypt (see biography) the crusader states could not survive in the face of Baibars' strong generalship and determination.

In contrast, the Palestinian Franks were divided and lacked strong leadership. The cooperation between the leaders of the First Crusade was never achieved in later crusades, particularly in the Third Crusade. Between 1225 and 1268 the king of Jerusalem did not reside in the East. Crusade armies that came to the East were often under divided leadership, or their leaders did not have the experience in the politics and military realities of the area that was needed to counter Muslim military tactics. So, although crusaders were able to halt the advance of Saladin in 1189–92 and recapture some territory at various times, they were unable to make long-term gains.

The First Crusade had received the active support of the Byzantine emperor, but during the Second Crusade (1147–49), the crusaders distrusted the Byzantine emperor, and during the Third Crusade (1189–92), the Byzantine emperor was in alliance with Saladin—one reason why the Fourth Crusade (1202–4) attacked Constantinople. After the Fourth Crusade, the Greek emperors in exile wanted to weaken rather than help the Latin states in the East because they wanted to recapture Constantinople.

However, it is also true that there was less support in western Europe for the crusader states, especially after 1250. The crusader states in the East were always short of warriors. Their supply lines were long; they could be self-supporting in some products, such as sugar, but the Palestinian Franks preferred to import other necessities, such as warhorses, from Europe. After 1250, trade was disrupted, and by the late thirteenth century, fewer people were going on crusade to the East. This was not because people were turning against crusades—crusades continued to attract support throughout the Middle Ages. But there were other crusades to join. For example, the papacy was involved in wars in Sicily. The popes from 1250 onward believed that they had to deal with the difficult political situation in Sicily before sending another army to fight the Muslims, so they declared that their wars in Sicily were crusades, and encouraged would-be crusaders to go to Sicily rather than to the East.

At the same time, the kings of western Europe who had traditionally been interested in crusading were involved in more pressing problems closer to home. The kings of England had quarrels with their barons during the thirteenth century, which prevented them from leaving the West, as well as disputes with the king of France over territory. So although, for example, King Edward I was able to go on crusade before he became king, he was not able to lead any more crusades afterward. King Louis IX of France led two crusades against the Muslims, but neither of his successors did.

There was also a problem in deciding which strategy to adopt in the East. After the failure of King Louis IX's first crusade of 1248–54, it was clear that large expeditions to the Holy Land did not work, and so western Europeans were unwilling to pour more money into them. They preferred to send smaller expeditions, but these could not achieve much in the face of Muslim unity, the larger Muslim armies, and the superior Muslim siege equipment. For some years before 1300 there were hopes that the Mongols would help the Latin Christians recover their territory in the Holy Land, but the two sides were unable to coordinate their campaigns.[11] Because it was believed that all human affairs were controlled by God, Christians in the West blamed their fellow Christians in the Holy Land for the Muslim successes, saying that they must be sinners and that God had deserted them.

Crusading continued after 1291, but it became more diverse, and its achievements were less dramatic than the crusades before 1291. The chapters that follow consider these other crusading fields.

NOTES

1. On the ideal of just war and legal war in the Middle Ages, see Frederick H. Russell, *The Just War in the Middle Ages* (Cambridge and New York: Cambridge University Press, 1975); Maurice Keen, *The Laws of War in the Late Middle Ages* (London: Routledge, 1965).

2. H.E.J. Cowdrey, "The Peace and Truce of God in the Eleventh Century," *Past and Present* 46 (1970): 42–67. See also, for instance, Marcus Bull,

Knightly Piety and the Lay Response to the First Crusade: The Limousin and Gascony, c. 970–1130 (Oxford and New York: Oxford University Press, 1993), pp. 21–69.

3. Ian S. Robinson, "Gregory VII and the Soldiers of Christ," *History* 58 (1973): 169–92. See also H.E.J. Cowdrey, "Pope Gregory VII and the Bearing of Arms," in Benjamin Z. Kedar, Jonathan Riley-Smith, and Rudolf Hiestand, eds., *Montjoie: Studies in Crusade History in Honour of Hans Eberhard Mayer* (Aldershot, Hants., and Brookfield, VT: Variorum, 1997), pp. 21–35.

4. Carole Hillenbrand, "The First Crusade: The Muslim Perspective," in Jonathan Phillips, ed., *The First Crusade: Origins and Impact* (Manchester and New York: Manchester University Press, 1997), pp. 130–41, here pp. 134–35.

5. For an assessment, see John France, *Victory in the East: A Military History of the First Crusade* (Cambridge and New York: Cambridge University Press, 1994), pp. 355–56.

6. On these reasons for the success of the crusade, see France, *Victory in the East*, pp. 367–73.

7. Hillenbrand, "The First Crusade," pp. 134–36.

8. Carole Hillenbrand, *The Crusades: Islamic Perspectives* (Edinburgh: Edinburgh University Press, 1999), pp. 112–95.

9. Peter Edbury, "The Crusader States," in David Abulafia, ed., *The New Cambridge Medieval History*, vol. 5, *c. 1198–c. 1300* (Cambridge and New York: Cambridge University Press, 1999), pp. 590–606, here pp. 596–97.

10. Edbury, "Crusader States," pp. 602–3.

11. Silvia Schein, "*Gesta Dei per Mongolos* 1300: The Genesis of a Nonevent," *English Historical Review* 94 (1979): 805–19.

CHAPTER 2

EXPEDITIONS IN THE IBERIAN PENINSULA

The crusades in the Iberian Peninsula originated in the *reconquista*, the "reconquest" of the peninsula from the Muslims. It is clear that the rulers of the Latin (Catholic) Christian kingdoms in the Iberian Peninsula used the concept of "reconquest" to win their own subjects' support for their military action against the Muslims and also to win support from outside the peninsula. As Christian ideals forbid aggressive warfare, the war had to be depicted as a reconquest, a recovery of land that used to be Christian. If the kings had said that they were fighting an aggressive war, they could not have won the support of the Church, which helped them recruit so many Christian warriors.

From a modern point of view, this was not a reconquest, in that when Alfonso VI of Castile (d. 1109) began his wars of conquest in earnest, it was more than three hundred years since the Christian Visigoths had been defeated by the invading Muslims of North Africa. Yet in the Middle Ages, Christians in western Europe believed that this was a war of reconquest, in the same way that they believed that the Holy Land truly belonged to Christians.

THE BACKGROUND TO THE "RECONQUEST"

The Visigothic Inheritance

The Iberian Peninsula had been part of the Roman Empire and was converted to Christianity in the fourth century with the rest of the Roman Empire. From the second half of the fifth century it was ruled by the Visigoths—a group of Gothic tribes from eastern Europe. They had been driven out of their own territory and entered the Roman Empire as refugees. After many travels, they conquered the Iberian Peninsula and set up their own government, ruled by a king with his capital at Toledo.

The Visigoths founded their own royal dynasty, with their own art and culture. There was peace under their rule; learning continued and great works were composed. The great scholar Isidore of Seville (d. 636) flourished under Visigothic government. Yet initially there was a major division in society. The Visigoths were Arian Christians, not Catholics; they did not believe that Christ and the Holy Spirit are equal to God the Father. Most of the people in the Iberian Peninsula were not Visigoths but of Hispanic-Roman descent and Catholic. The Visigoths ruled Spain as a military heretical elite, controlling the Catholic, Roman population. Eventually they saw the political advantages of conversion to Catholicism; if they could work with the Church rather than against it, they would have far more control over the people. In 587 King Reccared became a Catholic. The Catholic bishops happily worked with the Catholic kings, and as a result, the Visigothic government was unusually stable for western Europe during the seventh century.

Archaeological evidence gives a picture of a peaceful, prosperous era that ended suddenly with destruction. The written sources do not give much indication of what went wrong. Some historians now think that reports of factional infighting between the Visigoths were invented by later writers, although there are hints of a war between two Visigothic kings in the early eighth century.[1] In any case, in around 711, Arabs and Berbers from North Africa, new converts to Islam, invaded the Iberian Peninsula. The Visigothic king Roderic was killed in battle, and Visigothic government collapsed. The Arab invaders seized Toledo and set up their own government. Having established themselves, they moved farther north into Gaul, but they were defeated in battle and eventually settled only in the Iberian Peninsula. They called this area "al-Andalus."

The Arabs continued government much as the Visigoths had done. Learning continued, and many Christians and Jews formed part of the government. Christians and Jews were allowed to carry on their faith, although they had to pay taxes from which Muslims were exempt. They adopted Muslim customs but did not convert. From 756 al-Andalus was independent from the rest of Islam, and from 929 the Muslims of al-Andalus had their own caliph, a religious leader with political authority.

However, the north of the Peninsula was never conquered. The Christian kingdom of Asturias remained. This was a mountainous area, which the Visigoths had not been able to control completely, and which the Muslims could not overrun. Between Christians and Muslims lay a frontier zone—an area that belonged to neither side, over which no king could claim control.

The Early Expansion of the Christian States

At first the Christian rulers in the north had neither the money nor the armies to attack the Muslims, while the Muslims could not easily attack the Christians because they were protected by mountains. However, the Christians could move into areas that the Muslims did not control, settling on unsettled land. By the year 900 they had expanded their territories south to the River Duero. The Christian settlers built castles and fortified towns to defend this line, and there the frontier remained for a century (see Map 2).

These Christian kings justified this expansion southward on the basis that they were the heirs of the Visigoths. The Visigothic kings had been valid holders of authority in medieval eyes, for they had been given their authority by the Roman emperors. By establishing a link between themselves and the Visigoths, the Latin Christian rulers of the peninsula could present themselves as valid rulers of the Iberian Peninsula. "We are new Visigoths," they would claim, "continuing the Visigothic government, cultured and brilliant as it was." These claims were being written down by Christian Spanish writers by the later ninth century. The Visigoths had been defeated, they wrote, but the new kingdoms in the north of the peninsula continued their traditions, and were the natural successors of the Visigoths. It was God's will that the Muslim invaders be expelled from the peninsula, and God would help the Christians do this.

In fact, the kingdoms in the north were not Visigothic; their kings were descended from the Astures and the Sueves, who had opposed the Visigoths. But claiming descent from the powerful Visigoths gave them more validity as kings, and encouraged their subjects to support them, believing that God would make them victorious.[2]

In the early eleventh century, the great rulers of al-Andalus died without leaving capable successors. The vizier Muḥammad al-Mansūr .

ibn Abi Amir, who had led many successful military campaigns deep
into Christian territory in the north, died in 1002, while his son 'Abd
al-Malik al-Muzaffar died in 1008. The office of caliph that they served
and in whose name they ruled did not possess the necessary power and
prestige in itself to hold the country together. In 1031 a revolt drove
the caliph out and none replaced him. Muslim Spain split into *Ta'ifah*
states—"party states" identified with different ethnic groups, such as the
Berbers on the south coast. Each little state had its own king. These
were all rivals, so there was no united front against the Christian attack.

The Christian rulers took advantage of this rivalry. They allied themselves with the Muslim rulers and charged them tribute, called *parias*, in
exchange for assisting them against their enemies or in return for not

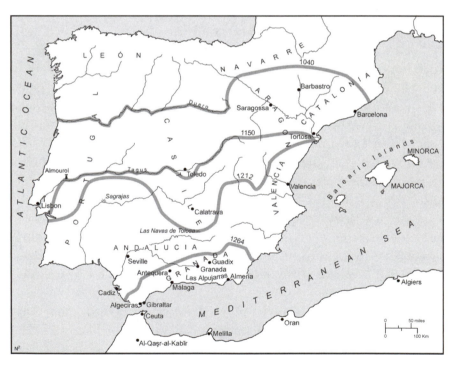

Map 2. The Iberian Peninsula during the "Reconquest," showing the
approximate frontier lines between the Christian and Muslim regions in
1040, 1150, 1212, and 1264, after Angus MacKay, *Spain in the Middle Ages:
From Frontier to Empire, 1000–1500* (Basingstoke: Macmillan, 1977), p. xiv.

attacking them. The system of *parias* has been aptly termed "a protection racket."[3] It was an important source of income for the Christian rulers, and they used it to build saints' shrines, churches, and monasteries. On the other side, the costs of paying *parias* forced the Muslim kings to tax their subjects heavily, so that their subjects grew restless and revolted.

This situation had some similarities with the Middle East, where Frankish lords would ally with Muslim lords for mutual advantage. As in the Middle East, Christian rulers in the Iberian Peninsula would also ally with Muslim rulers against other Christians. There was also a good deal of cooperation between the different religions within the Christian and Muslim kingdoms of the Iberian Peninsula. The Muslim rulers did not force Christians to convert to Islam. When Christian kings conquered Muslim territory, they usually allowed the Muslims to keep their religion and their own laws, and mosques remained open. The Christian kings had to be tolerant toward their Muslim subjects because there were not enough Christians to populate all the newly conquered land. The Franks had the same problem in the crusader states.

RECONQUEST

By the eleventh century, the main Christian kingdoms in the Iberian Peninsula were León, Castile, and Aragon. There were also the independent counties of Portugal and Barcelona. The weakness of the Muslim states gave the rulers of these Christian countries the opportunity to push south, yet they themselves were involved in dynastic disputes within their own territories.[4] The expansion southward was therefore organized by powerful individuals within Christian Spain: bishops, barons, abbots, and so on, who took over land and organized colonization programs.

In the 1070s the king of Castile, Alfonso VI, began to organize colonization programs of his own. These programs were organized so that the settlements could be defended against Muslim attack, and the settlers could take part in military action against the Muslims. He also began military campaigns to conquer territory from the Muslims. He depicted this conquest as a reconquest because the lands had been Christian before 711. In 1085 Alfonso VI captured Toledo, which had been the Visigothic capital before the Muslim invasion. This was an important propaganda gain as well as a territorial victory. By becoming ruler of Toledo, Alfonso could depict himself as the successor not only of the Visigoths but of the Roman emperors who had allowed the Visigoths to establish themselves in the Iberian Peninsula. He moved his capital to Toledo and took the title "emperor." He encouraged scholars to come to Toledo from all over western Europe to use the classical library there. Scholars flocked to Toledo to read the Arab translations of ancient Greek works and the Arab works of science and philosophy that were in the library, translating them into Latin so that they could be read by western European Christians.[5] Alfonso VI was able to establish himself as a great European ruler, bringing in western European culture and religious practices to replace the antiquated Visigothic customs and the Spanish customs that had been "contaminated" by Muslim government.

The Crusade

Support from popes also speeded up "the reconquest," as it helped to recruit warriors for campaigns in Spain. The oldest surviving example of papal support has been connected with the expedition against Barbastro in 1064. Pope Alexander II wrote a letter stating that those who were intending to journey to Spain were to confess their sins but would not have to do any penance because the expedition to Spain would be their penance. Historians, however, do not agree on whether this letter was referring to the Barbastro campaign,[6] yet the letter does indicate that the pope supported Christian warriors going to Spain. Barbastro was captured with the aid of Normans, Aquitanians, and Burgundians and other French warriors, showing that western Christians from outside the Iberian Peninsula were getting involved in "the reconquest."

After the First Crusade (1095–99), Pope Paschal II decided that those who fought the Muslims in the Iberian Peninsula should have their penance remitted, just as if they had gone to Jerusalem. He did this because the kings in the peninsula complained that their warriors were going on crusade to the Holy Land when they were needed on the frontier at home. So Pope Paschal banned Spanish knights from going on crusade while the Muslims were a danger in Spain. With the encouragement of the pope, in the first few decades of the twelfth century, the Spanish frontier came to be generally acknowledged by western European Christians as a crusading area.

Papal support also enabled the Christian rulers of the Iberian Peninsula to draw in additional military aid. From the 1120s, rulers of Portugal, Castile, and Aragon tried to persuade the new military religious orders—the Templars and Hospitallers—to come to the Iberian Peninsula and take over the defense of strategic castles. They also wanted these religious orders to supply troops to assist them in their campaigns against the Muslims. The Orders of the Temple and Hospital did become involved in the Iberian Peninsula and did take command

Figure 2. Almourol castle, Portugal. Built on an island in the River Tagus, in the twelfth century it was entrusted to the Templars so that they could guard the area against Muslim attacks. Copyright Joan Fuguet Sans.

of many castles, but they were not able to supply enough troops for the Christian rulers' needs. So the Christian rulers of the Iberian Peninsula set up or approved local military religious orders—the most famous being the Order of Calatrava and the Order of Santiago. These religious orders worked with the Christian rulers, supplying troops and money, and were closely controlled by the kings.

The kings of the Iberian Peninsula organized their campaigns to involve crusaders who were passing the peninsula on their way to the East. For instance, in 1147 Afonso I Henriques of Portugal took advantage of the large numbers of crusaders sailing around the peninsula to go to the Holy Land for the Second Crusade to attack the Muslim-held city of Lisbon. The attack was a success. In 1189 Sancho I of Portugal took advantage of the Third Crusade in the same way.

Rulers of the Iberian Peninsula also became involved in crusades in the Holy Land. King James I of Aragon (see biography) set out on crusade (although he turned back), and his illegitimate sons reached the East and campaigned there. So the rulers of the Iberian Peninsula established themselves in the eyes of other European Christians as being closely involved in crusading and being at the heart of God's wars against God's enemies.

Muslim Resurgence: The Almoravids and Almohads

After the loss of Toledo in 1085, the Muslim ruler of Seville called in help from the Berber Almoravids of North Africa. These were pious, radical Muslims who were determined to fight infidels. The Almoravids took over al-Andalus (Muslim Spain), defeated Alfonso VI at Sagrajas, and halted the expansion south. They also succeeded in imposing some unity on the Muslims of al-Andalus but by the 1140s they were losing control, and al-Andalus was fragmenting again. The Almohads replaced the Almoravids in al-Andalus. They were a Berber confederation, founded by a religious leader named Ibn Tumart in what is now Morocco. Ibn Tumart preached about the need for moral reform—he had very puritanical views on lifestyle. He also stressed the unity of God, in contrast to the Christian concept of three-gods-in-one. He began by waging war against the Almoravids, seeing them as corrupt and worldly. The Almohads, his followers, defeated the Almoravids and in 1147 destroyed their state in North Africa. They then invaded al-Andalus, where in 1154 they conquered Granada. Their caliph forced the Almoravid ruler of Seville to surrender to them, and in 1172 they took over the government of al-Andalus. The Almohads went on to win victories against the Christian kings of the peninsula, halting Christian advance and recovering territory from the Christians. As Berbers and outsiders, however, they were not well loved in al-Andalus.[7]

In 1212 the forces of al-Andalus, commanded by the Almohad caliph al-Nāsir, were defeated by a Christian Spanish coalition force at Las Navas de Tolosa. Almohad control of al-Andalus was broken and rapidly disintegrating as individual Muslims turned to Christian lords for military aid against the Almohads, while rebellions in North Africa destroyed their empire in the south.

The "Reconquest" after 1212

Following their victory at Las Navas de Tolosa, the Christian kings of the peninsula were able to expand their authority south rapidly. Between 1229 and 1240 King James I of Aragon (1213–76) conquered the Balearic Islands and Valencia—"the best and most beautiful country in the world," as a contemporary described it (see Document 8), a wealthy kingdom with prosperous, well-fortified cities. By 1248 the kingdom of Aragon-Catalonia controlled most of the Spanish Mediterranean coastline, and Aragon-Catalonia went on to become a great Mediterranean sea power, both in military terms and in trade. The kings of Portugal had captured the Algarve before 1250. In 1243 the Muslim king of Murcia became a vassal of the king of Castile, and in 1246 the emir of Granada followed suit, although the kingdom of Granada remained self-governing and in practice was independent. In 1248 the king of Castile conquered Seville, in 1250 the famous port of Cadiz was captured, and by the 1260s Andalusia was conquered. By 1300 the Christian rulers of the Iberian Peninsula had conquered the whole of the peninsula except Granada (see Map 2).

Granada might be forced to pay tribute, but it could not be conquered. It had good military forces and a defensive system of castles and watchtowers to restrict Christian raiders. It is a mountainous region and was relatively remote from the capitals of the Christian rulers of the peninsula, though could be easily supplied from North Africa. Military aid came from Tunisia and Morocco. Between 1308 and 1310, the kings of Castile and Aragon launched a crusade against Granada, but it was an embarrassing failure. Yet the kingdom of Granada had positive uses for the Christians of the Iberian Peninsula. The emirs of Granada sometimes allied with the Christians against the North African Muslims, as in the 1270s, when the emir allied with Castile against Morocco. They also allied with Christians against Christians, as in 1293–1303, when the emir of Granada allied with King James II of Aragon against their mutual enemy Castile.

Arab pirates were a serious threat along the Christian-controlled coast, raiding and taking prisoners who could be sold as slaves. The king of Castile, Alfonso X ("the Wise," 1252–84), set up a new naval military religious order (the Order of Santa Maria) to fight them. The Arabs of North Africa also suffered from Christian piracy, and the two sides often made treaties, promising to prevent their own people from preying on the other. These treaties do not seem to have been very effective.

Raids and counterraids continued along the Castilian-Granadan frontier. In the 1320s the Granadans invaded Castile and took many prisoners. The emir of Granada made an alliance with Morocco, which was also on the offensive against Castile. King Alfonso XI of Castile launched a counteroffensive in 1339, fighting both on land and at sea, and made significant gains. His campaigns were promoted as crusades with papal approval, and crusaders came from all over western Europe to take part. In 1340 he won an important victory at Salado, essential for maintaining control of the Straits of Gibraltar and therefore sea traffic. He went on in 1344 to capture the city of Algeciras after a two-year siege. Alfonso died in 1350 while besieging Gibraltar, which was held by the kingdom of Morocco. Granada came under attack again in 1407. The Christians' military efforts were hampered by the political upheavals within Castile, but they did succeed in capturing the town of Antequera.[8]

Coexistence

Although conflict continued, within Christian Spain there was also coexistence between Christians, Muslims, and Jews. Muslims were allowed to keep their faith and mosques remained open. The kingdom of Valencia remained mainly Muslim, even after the Aragonese conquest. The Muslims were not always happy with Christian government and there were revolts; many left the peninsula and went to North Africa. In the 1260s the Muslims of Andalusia revolted and were evicted from the peninsula. Yet there was also cooperation. For example, when Alfonso X's nobles wanted to exert pressure on him, they went to Granada and asked the Muslim king for shelter. Alfonso himself took an interest in Arab learning. The historians he employed to write the history of Castile used Arab sources as well as Latin sources. The astronomical and scientific works produced for him were based on Arab works. Christian mercenaries fought for Muslim kings, and Muslim mercenaries for Christian kings.

While there was fighting along the Christian-Muslim frontier, it was hardly ever all-out war. Instead there were raids and skirmishes. Latin Christian knights could come to Spain to fight the Muslims and win honor and forgiveness of their sins—it was a much easier crusade than going all the way to the eastern Mediterranean. In the late fourteenth century, the English poet Geoffrey Chaucer imagined that his "knight" character in *The Canterbury Tales* would have gone to fight the Muslims of Granada, and the chronicler Jean Froissart wrote that Granada was one of the places that good Christian knights meet.[9] There were many stories of heroic deeds against the Spanish Muslims, although the Castilian nobles spent as much time fighting each other and their king as fighting the Muslims.[10]

Christians and Muslims lived on both sides of the frontier; the frontier was not a tidy line between two religions. The two were in conflict, but they also learned from each other and benefited from each other. The Spanish frontier was an area of assimilation as well as division.[11]

Holy War?

To what degree was the war in the Iberian Peninsula a crusade in the same way as the war to the Holy Land was a crusade? Both Islam and Christianity hold that believers have a religious duty to resist when their faith is under threat. However, not all the warfare in the Iberian Peninsula can be called holy war. There were volunteer fighters on the Muslim side who came to fight the Christians as a religious duty, but they were not the main part of the fighting force. The Almoravids and Almohads promoted the war as a holy war, as did the Christian kings— many of the large campaigns were preached to Christians as crusades, and the participants were given the crusade indulgence. Yet warriors on both sides fought not only for the glory of God but also to win and control land. Settlement operated alongside military activity.

The End of the War

After 1410, Granada suffered no serious military action until 1460, although raiding continued. Portugal, which since the mid-thirteenth century had not had a frontier with Islam, took the crusade ideal into the Atlantic and North Africa.

From the 1340s the kings of Portugal wanted to conquer the recently rediscovered Canary Islands (known to the ancient Romans, but since forgotten). The kings of Castile also claimed the Canary Islands, maintaining that they had belonged to the Visigoths—which was untrue—and should therefore now belong to Castile—a claim that the Portuguese disputed. Popes granted crusade indulgences to the expeditions of conquest. In the early fifteenth century, a French expedition with Castilian help established a colony in the Canary Islands. Its justification was the need to convert the native islanders to Christianity. The islanders were called "Moors," the term used for Spanish Muslims, although in fact they were not Muslims but pagans. The islanders were either killed or deported as slaves. The Portuguese then again took up conquest and colonization, launching expeditions to capture the islands. The main instigator of these expeditions was the Infante Dom Henrique, known in English as "Prince Henry the Navigator" (d. 1460). Although he claimed that his main intention was religious, to convert the pagan islanders, modern historians believe that his real desire was to control the African gold trade.[12] Under Henrique's encouragement, Portuguese explorers sailed south along the west African coast, looking for gold. Henrique also sponsored Portuguese colonization of the island of Madeira and the Azores.

In 1415 the Portuguese besieged and captured the city of Ceuta on the north Moroccan coast. Participants in the campaign received the crusade indulgence. These campaigns could be regarded as a reconquest because northwest Africa had once been Christian—it had been part of the Roman Empire and was conquered by the Muslims in the seventh and eighth centuries. The conquests also enabled the Portuguese to gain control of the gold trade. The Portuguese went on to capture other towns on the North African coast, including Tangier in 1471.

Because of political upheaval within their kingdom, the kings of Castile did little in terms of holy war between 1410 and 1460. In times of peace, expeditions were launched, and the kings continued asking popes to acknowledge their campaigns as crusades so that they could raise funds from crusade indulgences. In 1456 Pope Calixtus III, a native of the Iberian Peninsula, allowed people to buy crusade indulgences for the dead, whose souls were believed to be in purgatory. Catholics believed that with the aid of the indulgence, part of the time that they were due to spend in purgatory could be reduced. Sales were enormous; the money raised was to be applied to the war against Islam.[13]

In times of internal upheaval, war against Christians was more important than crusade. The Castilian civil war of 1474–79 involved not only the Castilian nobility but also King Afonso V of Portugal, the betrothed husband of Queen Juana, one of the claimants to the Castilian throne. The war spread into the Canary Islands, where Portugal and Castile had been rivals in colonization and conquest, and between 1478 and 1496 the Castilians conquered the islands. In 1479 Castile made peace with Portugal, and Isabella of Castile and her husband Ferdinand of Aragon succeeded to the thrones of Castile and Aragon. With political stability restored, in 1482 they began a military campaign against the Muslim emirate of Granada. The pope granted the campaign crusade status, which assisted in both financing and raising troops. The war culminated in the capture of the capital city of Granada in 1492 (see biography of Boabdil). Isabella and Ferdinand then embarked on a policy of religious repression against all non-Catholics in Spain.

The Spanish crusade did not end with the fall of Granada; North Africa remained to be conquered. The kings of Castile believed that North Africa, too, had belonged to the Visigoths (in fact it had been conquered by another Germanic people, the Vandals), and if North Africa could be conquered, it would be possible to reach and win Jerusalem. Isabella urged her husband in her will (1504) to conquer North Africa for Christendom. Campaigns were waged until 1510, capturing important towns such as Oran and forcing Algiers to pay tribute. But in 1511 Ferdinand called off the campaigns, in view of the threat posed by France to the kingdom of Naples (another of Ferdinand's domains). It was difficult for the kings of Spain to expand their North African possessions further because the Ottoman sultan in Constantinople sent naval aid to the Muslim powers of North Africa. The Portuguese still harbored ambitions in the area, which ended in a serious defeat at al-Qaṣr-al-Kabīr (Alcazar el-Kebir) in Morocco in 1578. Holy war in North Africa would continue, but it would be fought mostly at sea, with bombardment of North African ports. Spain held Oran until 1707, while at the time this book was written, Ceuta and Melilla, on the North African coast, are still Spanish possessions.

The fall of Granada also marked the beginning of another form of expansion from the Iberian Peninsula—into the New World. In 1492 Christopher Columbus set out sailing westward to find a westerly route to India and Jerusalem, financed by Isabella and Ferdinand of Castile-Aragon. Since ancient times, educated Europeans had known that the world is a globe, and the existence of other, unknown continents was guessed at, but clearly the "New World" that Columbus and his successors discovered could not be claimed by reconquest. Instead, the Castilians and Portuguese believed that these lands had been given to them by God. The conquerors had visions of St. James of Santiago, a saint particularly associated with the "reconquest" in Spain. They claimed that it was their duty to win the pagan Americans to Christianity. Although the exploration and conquest of the New World was not a crusade, historians have seen similarities to the crusades in the justifications used for the campaigns in the New World and the mind-set of the conquerors.[14]

CONCLUSION: THE IMPACT OF THE CRUSADES ON THE PENINSULA

King Alfonso VI of Castile, conqueror of Toledo in 1085, had claimed that his dynasty had been chosen by God to do God's will in the reconquering of the Iberian Peninsula. Therefore, he had a duty to continue the war, and his subjects had a duty to help him. This propaganda or belief (depending how one interprets it)—that the king of Castile, or the rulers of the peninsula as a whole, had been chosen by God—continued throughout the Middle Ages. This belief inspired Isabella and Ferdinand to conquer Granada and send Christopher Columbus across the Atlantic. It inspired the conquest of the New World and the persecution of Jews, Muslims, and Protestants in Spain after 1492. Through the "reconquest," the rulers of the Iberian Peninsula looked outward to the rest of Europe and encouraged the rest of Europe to look to the peninsula as a center of culture and learning, Christian piety, and military power.

Hence, "the reconquest" was an essential part of the development of the modern states of the Iberian Peninsula. But the concept has misled historians. Historians in the past thought that the Spanish Christians were recolonizing empty land with Christians, that they wiped out the Muslims, and that they were always at war with the Muslims. More recent studies have shown that this was not so; we have been fooled by the rhetoric of the age. Though it is true that the Christian rulers carried out some colonization, many of the Muslims remained where they were, and were absorbed into the Christian kingdom. The Christians worked alongside the Muslims. The great Spanish hero "El Cid" (d. 1099) served King Alfonso VI of Castile, but when they quarreled, he went to serve a Muslim king instead. Christian Spanish kings negotiated with the Muslims and the Muslims became tributaries of the Christian kings. What happened in the "reconquest" was not the wholesale conquest of one religious group by another but more a matter of changing one lord for another: the Muslim kings lost power to the Christian kings. It was not until the beginning of the sixteenth century that the Iberian Peninsula became a wholly Catholic Christian region.

NOTES

1. Roger Collins, *Early Medieval Europe, 300–1000*, 2nd ed. (Basingstoke: Macmillan; New York: St. Martin's Press, 1999), pp. 157–61.

2. Eduardo Manzano Moreno, "The Creation of a Medieval Frontier: Islam and Christianity in the Iberian Peninsula, Eighth to Eleventh Centuries," in Daniel Power and Naomi Standen, eds., *Frontiers in Question: Eurasian Borderlands, 700–1700* (Basingstoke: Macmillan; New York: St. Martin's Press, 1999), pp. 32–54, here pp. 42–43.

3. Angus MacKay, *Spain in the Middle Ages: From Frontier to Empire, 1000–1500* (Basingstoke: Macmillan, 1977), p. 15.

4. On what follows, see Manuel González Jiménez, "Frontier and Settlement in the Kingdom of Castile (1085–1350)," in Robert Bartlett and Angus MacKay, eds., *Medieval Frontier Societies* (Oxford and New York: Oxford University Press, 1989), pp. 49–74, here pp. 53–57.

5. MacKay, *Spain in the Middle Ages*, pp. 81–87.

6. Marcus Bull, *Knightly Piety and the Lay Response to the First Crusade: The Limousin and Gascony, c. 970–1130* (Oxford and New York: Oxford University Press, 1993), pp. 72–78.

7. MacKay, *Spain in the Middle Ages*, pp. 27–29.

8. J. N. Hillgarth, *The Spanish Kingdoms, 1250–1516*, vol. 1, *1250–1410, Precarious Balance* (Oxford: Oxford University Press, 1976), pp. 339–44, 406–7; Norman Housley, *The Later Crusades: From Lyons to Alcazar, 1274–1580* (Oxford and New York: Oxford University Press, 1992), pp. 280–81, 283–84.

9. Geoffrey Chaucer, *The Canterbury Tales*, general prologue, lines 49–67; Jean Froissart, *Chroniques: livre 1: le manuscrit d'Amiens, Bibliothèque municipal no. 486*, ed. George T. Diller, 5 vols. (Geneva: Droz, 1991–98), vol. 2, p. 384, ch. 494, lines 46–48.

10. Hillgarth, *The Spanish Kingdoms*, vol. 1, *1250–1410*, pp. 59–60.

11. See, for example, Angus MacKay, "Religion, Culture and Ideology on the Late Medieval Castilian-Granadan Frontier," in Bartlett and MacKay, eds., *Medieval Frontier Societies*, pp. 217–43.

12. Felipe Fernández-Armesto, *Before Columbus: Exploration and Colonisation from the Mediterranean to the Atlantic, 1229–1492* (Basingstoke: Macmillan, 1987), pp. 185–92. For the conquest of the Canary Islands in general, see pp. 171–222.

13. Housley, *Later Crusades*, p. 293.

14. On this, see Fernández-Armesto, *Before Columbus*, pp. 212–17; Housley, *Later Crusades*, pp. 308–12.

CHAPTER 3

THE "CRUSADE" IN NORTHEASTERN EUROPE

The Baltic crusade played a very significant role in the history of Europe. Through the activities of the military religious Teutonic Order during the crusade, the Prussian state was formed. After the dissolution of the order in Prussia in the sixteenth century, Prussia became a secular state, and by the seventeenth century, its name was a byword for military efficiency. In the nineteenth century, Prussia led German reunification, and in the twentieth century, conflicting German and Polish claims to Prussia played their part in causing two world wars.

In contrast, the Teutonic Order did not set up an independent state in the northeastern Baltic, but played a significant role in the development of national feeling—a national feeling completely opposed to Russia. Since the collapse of the USSR and the reestablishment of the Baltic States of Estonia, Latvia, and Lithuania, these states have been able to appeal to their historic links with western Europe as justification for their being considered European states and in support of their applications to join the European Union.

The Baltic crusade was fought on two fronts. The first front was in the area now called the Baltic States. At the beginning of the thirteenth century, the land on the east coast of the Baltic Sea was either marshy or densely forested and was inhabited by a variety of pagan tribes, notably the Livs, the Letts, and the Ests. The second front was in the land of Prussia, on the south coast of the Baltic. Like Livonia, this was flat, marshy, and forested land, crisscrossed by rivers and inhabited by pagan tribes—the Prussians. The isolation of this area was reflected in the fact that even at the beginning of the thirteenth century it was still pagan,

Map 3. Northeastern Europe during the Baltic Crusades

and Christian missionaries had not even touched it. Missionaries were working in distant Finland to the north, but not here.

Like the Spanish crusade, the Baltic crusade was, strictly speaking, not a crusade, although it certainly enjoyed the appearance of being a crusade. From the time of Pope Innocent III (1198–1216), the pope allowed the religious leaders in the area to preach the crusade on an annual basis without having to refer back to the pope for a new crusading bull. So every year the bishops in the Baltic area would send their messengers to the bishops of Germany, the Netherlands, and even France and England, asking them to preach to their congregations and promise them remission of their penance for their sins if they would take a vow to go on pilgrimage to the Baltic and fight the unbelievers in the name of Christ. And every year the crusaders went to the Baltic area. In Prussia they were welcomed, housed, and entertained by the Teutonic Order—a Latin Christian religious order whose brothers not only took the three monastic vows of poverty, chastity, and obedience but also undertook to defend Christendom and to care for the sick poor. The crusaders and the Latin Christian warriors of Prussia and Livonia would campaign against the local pagans, particularly the Lithuanians, and against the Rus' (who were schismatics, being Russian Orthodox) and then go home. By the late fourteenth and early fifteenth centuries, the Teutonic Order had transformed the war in Prussia into a sort of "crusade experience"—or organized tour, like a modern "package deal"— which guaranteed knights from the West the opportunity to fight pagans, win renown in the field, and enjoy feasting, along with the chance to win the prize given for the most valiant knight in battle. The knights' arms would be hung in the Teutonic Order's hall at its central convent at Marienburg, so that all who came would see them.

Yet despite all the crusading paraphernalia—the vow, the remission of sins, the imagery of taking the cross, the crusading language of pilgrimage—this was more of a holy war than a crusade. As the land was not and never had been Christian, the war could not be a pilgrimage in the strict sense. The region was claimed by the pope on the basis that heathens cannot legally hold any land and that all land legally belongs to Christians. At base, this was a war inspired by commercial and territorial interest, added to the need for self-defense against the local bandits and pirates, and a desire to win converts for Christianity.

Given the complexity of the events in these crusading campaigns, this survey will begin by setting out the main players in the campaigns, followed by a chronological summary of events.

THE PLAYERS IN 1200

In the year 1200, various peoples had interests in the Baltic region (see Map 3). Those within the region were the pagan peoples of the Baltic and the Christian Rus' and Poles, who had been Christian for several centuries by the time the crusades began. Latin Christian powers from outside the area also had ambitions there, including the rulers of Bohemia, Sweden and Denmark, and the north German merchant towns. The Germans and the Poles would bring in military religious orders to support them—orders that later became major players in their own right.

The pagans are sometimes called "the Balts" or "the Baltic tribes"; the most famous were the Prussians, the Lithuanians, the Livs, and the Letts (in what is now Latvia). Strictly speaking, the Ests (to the north of the Livs and Letts) are not Balts. The Zemgalians and Selonians of Samogitia and the Jatwingians were distinct Baltic tribes, although their territorial areas were lost after conquest by the Lithuanians or the Teutonic Order, and they are not associated with a single modern state. Other tribes also existed. These peoples were all pagans, but in fact we know hardly anything about their beliefs; they may not have had "gods" in the western sense at all. Certain areas and objects were regarded as holy and there were certain religious customs, but there was no single, centralized religion. Their chiefs could perform religious rites, but they may also have had shaman-like holy men. Otherwise, most of what was written about these people's beliefs by Latin Christians appears to be invention, based on Christianity and classical Roman and Greek paganism. Under the pressure of the crusades, the princes of Lithuania apparently tried to centralize and reorganize their pagan religions to counter the "German god" that the crusaders were trying to foist on them.[1]

More is known about Lithuanian pagan political organization than the pagan societies of the other Baltic peoples because it survived longer, and because the Lithuanian princes had diplomatic and military relations with Christian powers that enabled contemporary writers to observe their society and comment on it. Although Baltic society was not literate, the Lithuanian princes quickly adopted writing as a means of recording agreements in their negotiations with the crusaders. A Lithuanian prince was "acclaimed" by his people in a ceremony acknowledging him as prince, and his people gave him oaths of allegiance. The same procedures were followed in many western European kingdoms.[2] The pagan tribes were well organized and were good warriors. They built fortresses—called "castles" by the crusaders—with defensive ditches and high fortifications that were able to withstand a siege of several days by western Europeans.[3] Until the crusades began, the pagans had withstood all invasions by the supposedly more advanced Christian nations around them.

As to the Christian states in the region, Poland was a large and wealthy kingdom. The rivers Vistula and Oder flow through it, forming major trade routes across northeastern Europe. Poland's lack of natural geographical frontiers left the kingdom open to attack from Germans in the west, Pomerania in the northwest, Bohemia in the south, and the pagans to the north and east. Yet the lack of natural frontiers also meant that Polish rulers could easily expand their authority outward. After 1138, Poland was divided into several dukedoms, with no overall king: Silesia, Greater Poland, Little Poland, and Cujavia-Masovia. If one of those dukes could win the aid of the emperor or the pope and either wage a war against the Prussians or persuade them to convert to Christianity as his subjects, he would gain territory, money, and power, and would perhaps be able to establish himself as supreme in Poland.

In the east, the land of the Rus' was divided into many principalities. Although they were united in religion—being Orthodox Christian with religious links to Constantinople and with a single archbishop, based at Kiev—the Rus' did not regard themselves as a single nation. During the twelfth century, individual cities gained importance, such as Novgorod "the Great" on the River Volkhov in the north and Galich (now also called Halych, Halicz, or Galicz, in the Ukraine) and Volyn' (now Vladimir Volynsky, in the Ukraine) in the southwest, bordering with Poland.[4] Novgorod in particular was an important trading center, ruled by an oligarchy and a city assembly that made decisions and elected a prince to lead the city in battle. If the oligarchy did not agree with the prince's policies, he would be "shown out," or deposed, and a new prince elected.

In the early thirteenth century, Prince Roman Mstislavich united the cities of Galich and Volyn' in one principality and conquered the great city of Kiev, taking the title "grand duke of Kievan Rus." His son Daniil (Danylo or Daniel), called "Daniel of Ruthenia" by western writers, wanted to take over the pagan lands to the north and west of his territories. In 1253 he accepted a crown and the title of "king" from the papal legate (representative) in return for his help with the war against the pagans. But he remained Russian Orthodox, to the frustration of his Latin Christian allies.

To the northwest of the area lay Pomerania, whose Latin Christian princes wanted land and control of the valuable trade that passed down the River Vistula.

The interested powers outside the region should now be considered. To the southwest of Poland lay Bohemia. Technically part of the western

Empire and subject to the emperor, from 1198 onward it was ruled by its own king, who was anxious to extend his power and authority. The political divisions within Poland made it an obvious target for the ambitious Bohemian kings. Přemysl Ottokar II (1253–78) joined the Teutonic Order in the Prussian crusade and paid for the construction of its castle in Königsberg (now Kaliningrad). Clearly he was hoping to gain power in Prussia at the expense of the Polish dukes. His son Waclaw (Václav) succeeded in making himself king of all Poland in 1300.

In the north, both the kings of Denmark and Sweden hoped to win territory in the eastern Baltic. In the twelfth century, the kings of Denmark were involved in crusades against the Wends, who were their pagan neighbors and notorious pirates. Having established control of these areas, they looked further afield, and in the early thirteenth century, Danish fleets attacked Finland, Estonia, the island of Ösel, and Prussia. In 1219 King Valdemar II sent a large expedition to assist the Christian mission in Estonia, and built the fort of Reval (Tallinn), which was garrisoned with Danes. However, when he claimed control over the whole of the Livonian mission, the different national groups among the crusaders quarreled. Finally King Valdemar was given jurisdiction over Estonia, while Livonia remained under the control of its German bishop. Danish sea power made Danish support extremely valuable to the crusaders, but after Valdemar's death in 1241, his successors had too many problems at home in Denmark to come eastward. Estonia remained a Danish possession, and in 1318 King Eric VI told his vassals in Estonia to help the Teutonic Order, but did not bring any assistance himself.

The Swedes' major reason for becoming involved in the east Baltic was to set up trading links and control trade routes. The kings of Sweden sent and led raids to the eastern Baltic coasts throughout the twelfth century, though not as a crusade. As the historian Eric Christiansen wrote, "These were old-fashioned Viking raids."[5] Yet Pope Innocent III, writing to Sweden in the early thirteenth century, seems to have regarded Swedish campaigns against the pagan Finns as holy wars, although these campaigns were not official crusades. King Johan Sverkersson of Sweden (d. 1222) became involved in the campaigns in Estonia, building in 1220 a fort at Leal, opposite the island of Ösel. The Swedes were soon driven out of this fort, and after this failure they concentrated on converting and colonizing Finland. Here they were in competition with the city of Novgorod the Great, which already had control over the Karelians (who lived to the south and east of Finland) and the Vods (who lived on the southeast coast of the Gulf of Finland). In the early thirteenth century, the prince of Novgorod was organizing missions to convert the Karelians to Russian Orthodoxy. In their desire to win religious and political control of the Finns, the Swedes were drawn into conflict with Novgorod. In 1240 a Swedish military expedition was defeated on the River Neva by Prince Alexander Nevsky of Novgorod. The Swedes sent further expeditions to Finland and Karelia in 1249 and 1292. These were not official crusades, because the pope had not granted crusade indulgences to those taking part. Yet the Swedish warriors who took part regarded them as honorable wars, fought for the glory of God and to save the souls of the Finns by winning them to Latin Christianity.[6]

The German merchant cities were also interested in the east Baltic. In the late twelfth century, German traders came to the area of Livonia south of the River Dvina to trade in furs, metal ore, and timber. They were anxious to convert the local tribes—the Letts and the Livs—to Christianity partly to ensure their own safety and partly to control them. If the Letts became Christians, the Germans would be able to trade with them and make agreements with them on equal terms; trading with non-Christians was always risky because, it was believed, they could not be trusted (they were "faithless" in every sense). The German merchants also wanted to stop piracy by the Ests, the Kuronians of Kurland, and the people of Ösel island, which was damaging trade in the Baltic. It was Archbishop Hartwig II of Bremen, one of the leading German merchant cities, who initiated the mission in Livonia and who in 1195 initiated the Livonian crusade.

The political situation in eastern and northeastern Europe at the beginning of the thirteenth century was, then, very fluid, with various players jockeying for position. Having identified the main interests in the region, it is now possible to consider how the crusades began and developed.

THE BEGINNING OF THE CRUSADE

The crusade began in Livonia in the late twelfth century, when German traders arrived to trade with the pagans. Archbishop Hartwig II of Bremen sent missionaries to preach to the local pagans. The mis-

sionaries had some success, but the Letts and Livs refused to stay converted.

In 1195 Hartwig persuaded Pope Celestine III to authorize full crusading privileges, so that all who went on pilgrimage to the River Dvina
would receive a full crusade indulgence for their sins. Clearly Hartwig
intended to provide an armed protection for his missionaries. Perhaps
he thought that when the Letts and Livs saw the military strength of
the West, they would convert to Christianity to gain the protection of
this great god. Alternatively, perhaps he thought that the converts were
relapsing to paganism because they were afraid of their pagan neighbors
and needed military protection.

In 1198 Pope Innocent III confirmed Celestine's authorization. He
made this a continual crusade, which would be preached in Germany
every year with no need for a new crusading bull. In 1200 Hartwig sent
his nephew, Albert of Buxtehude, to be bishop of the area and lead the
mission, and in 1201 the merchants founded a trading port at the mouth
of the Dvina called Riga, which acted as a base for the missionaries and
the crusades. This town is now the capital of Latvia. Bands of crusaders
came to Livonia each year, and by the 1230s what is now Latvia and
southern Estonia and the island of Ösel had been conquered by the
crusaders, and Christian missionaries were in the process of converting
the people. This rapid progress in Livonia contrasted with the lack of
success that the missionaries were having further south, in Prussia.

The Prussians were a dangerous threat to the Polish frontier, and
attempts at missionary work had failed. The Polish dukes wanted to
crush the Prussians, both to safeguard Poland and to gain land. However,
despite various military expeditions in the twelfth century, no headway
had been made against the Prussians. The Prussians were well organized
and well led, and there were a lot of them. In addition, the marshy,
heavily forested terrain was difficult for cavalry. No single Polish duke
was able to deal with the Prussians alone, so the duke of Cujavia-
Masovia, whose lands bordered Prussia, asked for papal aid. Pope Innocent III sent Abbot Gottfried of Lekno to preach to the Prussians,
but he gave up by 1209. In 1217 a Cistercian monk named Christian
was appointed to lead the mission with Polish backing, but he, too, made
little progress. Clearly military aid was needed.

Military Religious Orders

Both in Livonia and in Prussia, the missionary bishops decided to set up military religious orders to support their missions of conversion. Crusaders could give only limited support because they came east for a short period. A military religious order would give continual support. In the first years of the thirteenth century, Bishop Albert of Riga set up a military religious order based on the Order of the Temple that had been founded in Jerusalem in 1120. The brothers wore a white mantle with the symbol of a red cross with a red sword underneath. Their official name was "the knights of Christ of Livonia," but they were known as the Swordbrothers.

In around 1225 Bishop Christian of Prussia formed a military religious order to help his own mission. Duke Conrad of Cujavia-Masovia gave it his castle at Dobrin, so it became known as the Order of Dobrin. Its symbol was a red star with a red sword.

Neither order lasted beyond the 1230s, as they both lacked land and other sources of wealth and their recruiting ground was limited to a few north German towns. In Livonia the Swordbrothers quarreled with the bishop of Riga over the division of land, were accused of oppressing the new converts (in particular, by chopping down their bee trees), and in 1229 quarreled with the papal legate, Baldwin of Aulne. Baldwin accused them of besieging a Cistercian monastery, Dünemünde, which had supported him, and piling up the defeated dead in a heap instead of burying them. When their enemies said that they would appeal to the pope, the Swordbrothers drew their swords and said: "This is our pope." On the other hand, Baldwin of Aulne seems to have gone out of his way to throw his weight around and offend the Swordbrothers and the people of Riga. Pope Gregory IX summoned everyone to Rome to sort out the matter. The Swordbrothers were cleared, but their reputation was tarnished. They applied to join the Teutonic Order, which, having sent an investigation team to look at them, declared that they did not want them: "Their rule is not good and they do not keep it well." Then in 1236 the Swordbrothers were almost wiped out by the Lithuanians at the battle of Saule. The remaining few applied again to join the Teutonic Order and were accepted.

The Teutonic Order

The Teutonic Order, in full "the Hospital of St. Mary of the Teutons," was a military religious order originally founded in the Holy Land during the Third Crusade. It had never had much territory there because by the time it was founded, the Palestinian Franks were losing territory. The order had tried to acquire lands, but failed. In 1226 Duke Conrad of Cujavia-Masovia offered the order the land of Kulm (Chełmno) in Prussia, to the northwest of Conrad's lands. Being part of Prussia, this land was not in fact his to give. Conrad's gift of Kulm was purely for defense against the pagans; there was no mention of converting pagans. The master of the order, Hermann von Salza (see biography), asked Emperor Frederick II to approve the grant, which he did. Frederick II's charter stated that he himself wanted to convert the pagans, but the Teutonic Order's task would be to fight pagans—not to convert them.

Hermann von Salza also asked Pope Gregory IX to confirm Duke Conrad's grant. The pope did—yet it appears that what he confirmed was not what Conrad had granted. His confirmation (1234) gave the order an independent lordship in Kulm and whatever it could conquer, and it stated that Conrad had promised never to evict the order. Conrad had promised no such thing in 1226.

In any case, what the pope confirmed was what the order did. The brothers came into Kulm and set up a base; they also set up a castle at Thorn (Toruń) to cover their rear. They advanced down the River Vistula, fighting and defeating the pagans and building castles of timber and earth as they went, some of them just wooden forts in trees. (There is no building stone in Prussia, so later castles were built of brick.) If the brothers were defeated in battle, they could fall back on their forts. They used the river as a road through Prussian territory, and the Prussians were quickly defeated. At the same time, the Teutonic Order had effectively removed Bishop Christian from power. He had been captured by the Prussians in 1234, and the Teutonic Order neglected to ransom him. The order took over the bishop's lands, and absorbed the Order of Dobrin. By the 1240s, the order was effectively in control of Prussia.

From 1237 the order was also involved in the Livonian crusade, although it was never as powerful in Livonia as it was in Prussia. In 1240 the brothers in Livonia began a campaign east into Rus' territory, which they called a crusade (because it was against schismatics)—the excuse being that the Rus' had never tried to convert the pagans, simply taking tribute from them. The brothers' main motivation was actually trade, intending to control the rivers along which traveled merchant boats carrying valuable furs, ore, and timber from central Russia. The Teutonic Order took possession of the Russian towns of Izborsk and Pskov, and continued to press eastward. In 1242 the brothers and their allies were defeated in a battle on the frozen Lake Chud (or Peipus) by Prince Alexander Nevsky and the people of Novgorod. After this defeat, the order in Livonia abandoned ideas for going east and went south against Lithuania.

THE "CONTINUOUS CRUSADE" IN THE BALTIC

Although the Teutonic Order established itself in Prussia very quickly, this was not the end of the war. In Prussia there were two revolts, in 1242–49 and 1260–83. The Prussians were supported by the Christian dukes of Pomerania, who regarded the order as a dangerous threat to their interests. In 1249 the Treaty of Christburg gave the Prussians equal rights with Germans and allowed them to keep their customs, but after the second revolt, the Prussians lost their rights and were treated as serfs by the order—that is, with no legal rights. The Teutonic brothers said "Let Prussians stay Prussians," and would not allow them to convert to Christianity.

The order also found rivals in the Polish princes, who launched a rival crusade in the late 1250s in an attempt to take over the Jatwingians. The princes apparently accused the order of preventing pagans from converting to Christianity and of attacking new converts. They claimed that the Jatwingians had appealed to them for help against the Teutonic Order. The order was able to get the crusade stopped by appealing to the pope. These sorts of accusations against the Teutonic Order resurfaced at the Council of Constance in 1414–18.

The Teutonic Order was initially successful in Prussia because it had a large resource base, with property in Germany, eastern France, and Italy, as well as in the Holy Land and Greece. It used a more carefully thought out strategy than its forerunners in the area. The order also had valuable allies, such as the emperor Frederick II, the papacy, and various secular princes. Most notable of these was the pagan Mindaugas of Lithuania, who allied with the order in 1251. He promised to convert to

Christianity if the pope would acknowledge him as king of Lithuania. He was crowned, and a bishop was sent to lead a Christian mission to convert the Lithuanians. Mindaugas, however, reverted to paganism. Two other valuable allies were Prince Daniil of Galich-Volyn' and Přemysl Ottokar of Bohemia, who have already been mentioned. The Polish princes were rivals, and the order could simply play them off against each other.

So in the short run, the order was successful in establishing itself and winning territory; however, in the long run, the order was not successful. In the fourteenth century, having played a praiseworthy role in the last battle to defend Acre in 1291, the Teutonic brothers moved their headquarters to Venice, and from there to Prussia in 1309. The order was now committed to the crusade in the Baltic area rather than the Holy Land, but rather than winning great territories for Christ, the order became bogged down in the politics of the area.

In 1298, 1300, and 1305, the archbishop and people of Riga appealed to the pope against the Livonian branch of the Teutonic Order. They accused it of perpetrating offenses against the Church in Livonia, impeding the trade of Riga, not defending Livonia against the pagans, selling weapons to the Lithuanians, and preventing missionary work. When pagans did convert to Christianity, the brothers' tyranny caused the new converts to revert to paganism. They were also heretics: they burned the bodies of their dead (a pagan practice), allowed mercy killing of badly wounded brothers, ate meat during Lent, took no notice of the pope, and practiced witchcraft. Pope Clement V launched an investigation against the order in Livonia, but the order fought it with determination, denying all charges, and eventually the investigation was dropped.[7]

Meanwhile in Prussia, the order became involved in war with both Poland and Lithuania. In 1295 a king of all Poland was crowned, Přemysl II. He was assassinated in the following year. Władysław the short (Łokietek), duke of Greater Poland, tried to take over as king and failed. He finally succeeded and was crowned at Kraków, the Polish capital, in 1320. While he was struggling to win control of Poland, he made an alliance with the Teutonic Order, who conquered Gdańsk (Danzig) and eastern Pomerelia (Pomorze)—apparently on his behalf, or so he thought—and then refused to hand them over to him. Gdańsk was a vital port, and Władysław was determined to get possession of it. He appealed to the pope. In 1319 Pope John XXII ordered an investigation, which decided against the order in 1321. Yet the order refused to give up the city, and Pope John XXII could not force it to obey, as he needed its political support against the emperor, Louis of Bavaria. War between Poland and the order followed. This continued until 1343, when King Casimir III of Poland ceded Gdańsk to the order.

At the same time, both the Teutonic Order in Prussia and the kingdom of Poland were at war with the Lithuanians. The Lithuanians were well organized and excellent warriors. They were also happy to ally with Christian powers: the Lithuanian princes regularly allied with the Rus' city of Pskov against the Novgorodians. In 1331 Prince Gediminas of Lithuania (see biography) allied with the archbishop of Novgorod, sending forces to fight the Swedes in defense of Novgorod. He also allied with other Russian cities, giving them military assistance against their enemies, and had a long-standing alliance with the archbishop and people of Riga against the Teutonic Order. The Teutonic Order waged annual military campaigns against Lithuania, but the Lithuanians returned the compliment.

Each year the order launched two campaigns, one setting out on the Assumption of the Blessed Virgin Mary (15 August) and the other on the Purification of the Blessed Virgin Mary (2 February). These dates were originally chosen because they were the most important feast days of the order's patron saint. The campaigns were conducted with cavalry and foot soldiers, including crusaders from Germany, Britain, and France. The war was very attractive to would-be crusaders from northern Europe because campaigns took place every year, and as the Lithuanians were known to be a dangerous pagan foe, there was much honor to be won in fighting them. In addition, this crusading front was easier to reach than Granada or the eastern Mediterranean.

Travel across the countryside was difficult, so river transport was used to carry supplies, reinforcements, siege machines, and horses. Having reached enemy territory and set up a base, the order's forces conducted raids on a daily basis, moving on to a new area after each raid, and then withdrawing before the enemy's army could arrive to engage them.[8] The aim of the campaign was not only to take booty and prisoners, but also to weaken the enemy so that in the long term, Lithuanian territory could be taken under the rule of the order. However, because of the nature of the terrain (forested or marshy), it was difficult to win long-term gains in any one campaign. Eric Christiansen has noted that the Teutonic Order's campaigns were unsuccessful as a war of attrition—while the order grew stronger, so did the Lithuanians.[9] Any improvements to weapons, armor, or siege machinery enjoyed by the Teutonic Order was quickly matched by the Lithuanians. The result was stalemate.

Well aware of the futility of the continuing contest, Gediminas of Lithuania attempted to make peace. In 1322 he wrote to Pope John XXII, asking for peace and saying that he would be happy to allow Christian missionaries into his kingdom and to convert to Christianity himself, provided that the Teutonic Order was not involved. He asked for papal legates to be sent, to enable the frontiers of his kingdom to be agreed. The Livonians agreed to a treaty, but the Teutonic Order attacked Gediminas' overtures, declaring that his offers were fraudulent. Their main objection was that he would not accept baptism from them. The pope, however, took Gediminas' offers seriously, and he told the brothers to keep the peace while negotiations took place. Yet the order was clearly not willing to agree to a peace, and—as in 1321—Pope John XXII could not afford to offend the order. Gediminas was unwilling to commit himself absolutely to becoming a Latin Christian when he could obtain as good terms or better for converting to Russian Orthodoxy and allying with a Russian prince. So although Gediminas did succeed in making an alliance with King Władysław Łokietek of Poland, the war continued.[10]

After 1350, the Teutonic Order's situation began to improve. The order constructed lines of castles to defend its borders in Prussia and Livonia from attack by the Lithuanians. More crusaders were coming east on crusade. Meanwhile, the rulers of Poland and Lithuania were distracted in the southeast, mopping up what was left of the principality of Galich-Volyn', or Ruthenia, after the murder of its prince in 1340. Their excuse for their intervention was the need to prevent the Mongols from conquering it. The ruling dynasties of Lithuania and Poland both claimed the area. The pope agreed that King Casimir III of Poland's war in Ruthenia was a crusade, and allowed him to tax the clergy to pay for it. Casimir was able to conquer most of Ruthenia, which became part of Poland.[11]

THE END OF THE CRUSADE

The Teutonic Order never conquered Lithuania, but its war against Lithuania helped to persuade the Lithuanians to convert to Christianity. In 1386 Queen Jadwiga of Poland (see biography) married Duke Jagiełło of Lithuania as part of an alliance against the Teutonic Order. Jagiełło accepted baptism, and the Lithuanians became Christians. The Teutonic Order claimed that the conversion was a fraud and continued the war against the Lithuanians until 1410, when a Polish-Lithuanian army defeated the Teutonic Order at Tannenberg/Grunwald. After this, the Teutonic Order's fortunes declined. The order came under attack at the Church Council of Constance in 1414–18, the supply of crusaders dried up because the knights of Latin Europe were involved in either the Anglo-French wars or the war against Hussites in Bohemia, and in 1454 the Prussian cities revolted against the Teutonic Order. By the Second Treaty of Thorn, 1466, the Teutonic Order in Prussia lost west Prussia, including its capital of Marienburg (now Malbork in Poland), and became a vassal of the king of Poland. So the crusade in Prussia ended. The order continued to exist in east Prussia until 1525, when the grand master, Albert of Brandenburg-Ansbach, became a Lutheran Christian and dissolved the order in Prussia.

The crusade in Livonia continued until the sixteenth century, but now against the increasing threat from the grand princes of Moscow. In 1501 the master of the Teutonic Order in Livonia allied with the Lithuanians against Grand Prince Ivan III of Moscow, but the Lithuanians failed to appear and the Russians broke into Livonia and ravaged it. Although the brothers became Protestant Lutherans in 1526, they continued to follow their monastic lifestyle, and their order continued to play a role in the government and defense of Livonia.

Yet the increasing aggression of Moscow could not be met alone, and in 1559, Poland, Sweden, and Denmark moved into the area to divide up Livonia and Estonia among them. In 1561–62, the Teutonic brothers became simply a secular order, and their master became Duke of Kurland-Semigallia, a vassal of the king of Poland. It was not until the 1580s that the Poles would drive Grand Prince Ivan IV back from threatening Livonia.

The Teutonic Order continued to exist as a military religious order in Germany, where it became involved in the war against the Ottoman

Turks. Today it is a charitable order, running hospitals and schools in Germany and Austria.

From the point of view of the crusaders, the Baltic crusade was successful in that it drew the Balts into a Catholic European ambit, rather than allowing them to move into a Russian and/or Orthodox milieu. However, this was achieved at great cost to human life and through the destruction of local cultures and identities. Conflicting western European and Russian claims to this area persisted into the late twentieth century. In 1991, with the dissolution of the USSR, Latvia, Estonia, and Lithuania again became independent countries. In 2002 the applications from these Baltic States for entry into the European Union were accepted for admission in 2004, making these countries once again oriented toward the West.

NOTES

1. Endre Bojtár, *Foreword to the Past: A Cultural History of the Baltic People*, trans. Szilvia Rédey and Michael Webb (Budapest and New York: Central European University Press, 1999), pp. 128–63, 233–342; Stephen C. Rowell, *Lithuania Ascending: A Pagan Empire within East-Central Europe, 1295–1345* (Cambridge and New York: Cambridge University Press, 1994), pp. 137–39, 147–48.

2. Rowell, *Lithuania Ascending*, pp. 139–47.

3. *The Chronicle of Henry of Livonia*, trans. James A. Brundage (Madison: University of Wisconsin Press, 1961), pp. 127–28.

4. For straightforward information about the Russian principalities in the Middle Ages, the Library of Congress's Country Studies are very useful. See http://lcweb2.loc.gov/frd/cs/rutoc.html.

5. Eric Christiansen, *The Northern Crusades*, 2nd ed. (London: Penguin, 1997), p. 114.

6. Christiansen, *Northern Crusades*, pp. 113–22.

7. Norman Housley, *The Avignon Papacy and the Crusades, 1305–1378* (Oxford and New York: Oxford University Press, 1986), pp. 267–71.

8. Christiansen, *Northern Crusades*, p. 171.

9. Christiansen, *Northern Crusades*, p. 167.

10. Rowell, *Lithuania Ascending*, pp. 189–228.

11. Norman Housley, *The Later Crusades: From Lyons to Alcazar, 1274–1580* (Oxford and New York: Oxford University Press, 1992), pp. 346–47.

CHAPTER 4

CRUSADES AGAINST HERETICS: THE ALBIGENSIAN CRUSADES AND THE HUSSITE CRUSADES

The previous two chapters considered crusades to areas outside the Holy Land but on the frontiers of Christendom, where Latin (Catholic) Christians fought people with different religious beliefs in defense of Christendom. The crusades considered in this chapter were against "the enemy within"—heresy.

In the writings of the New Testament, heretics are described as pseudo-Christians who hold false, destructive beliefs that will lead many Christians astray and bring down eternal destruction on themselves (for instance, 2 Pet. 2). In the Middle Ages, Christians believed that heresy was a real danger to Christian society, and would destroy it from within like a cancer or some other hidden disease. They believed that heretics lived immoral lives and even ate their own babies. Christian priests believed that they were answerable to God for the souls of those in their care, and so they must protect their people from heresy. Indeed, if the Church authorities did not try to destroy heresy, they themselves would be punished by God for failing in their duty.

However, there were many reasons why Christians might become heretics. They might reject the teachings of the Latin Church because they believed that the Latin Church did not follow biblical teachings, as did the Hussites. They might have reinterpreted the Bible, as did the Cathars. They might be disillusioned by the wealth and power, or the ignorance and immoral lives, of the Latin clergy, in contrast to the life of poverty preached by Christ and the apostles in the New Testament. They might reject Church political authority, as a form of social protest. As a result, heretics did not acknowledge that they were heretics; as far as they were concerned, they were good Christians and it was the Latin Church that was heretical. In fact, heretics were generally extremely pious people who clung to their beliefs in the face of persecution, believing that God was testing them as God had tested the early Christians. This meant that heresy was very difficult to stamp out. From the early thirteenth century, popes resorted to violence as a means of crushing heresy. They called crusades against heretics, promising those who took part in the campaigns the same privileges as those who went to fight the Muslims in the Holy Land. However, these crusades were not very successful in ending heresy. The two most famous crusading campaigns against heretics were the Albigensian Crusades (1209–26) and the crusades against the Hussites (1420–31), and these will be considered in this chapter.

THE ALBIGENSIAN CRUSADES

The Cathar Heretics

The Albigensian Crusades were launched against Cathar heretics in the Languedoc, now southwestern France. The word "Cathar" probably comes from the Greek word "Καθαροι" (katharoi), which means "pure ones," and would have been what the heretics called themselves. They would have used a Greek name because their beliefs originated with the Bogomil heretics of the Byzantine Empire, who spoke Greek. The Cathar leaders were also called "Good men" by their followers.

The Cathars held dualist beliefs, which means that they believed in two opposed gods—one good god of light and an evil god of darkness. The good god, they believed, created everything spiritual, which cannot be seen or felt with the bodily senses, while the evil god created everything physical—including human bodies, the earth, the stars, sun, and planets. The Cathars accepted the Christian Bible as a holy book, but according to them, the god who appears in the Old Testament is the evil god, and Jesus in the New Testament is an entirely spiritual being who only appeared to have physical form. The Cathars would have called themselves "pure" because they believed that they were separate from the evil physical world and belonged to the pure, perfect world of spirit. As dualists, the Cathars were following in a long line of dualist religions, and their contemporaries confused them with the Manichaeans, dualists who had been active in the ancient Roman Empire.

The Cathars believed that human souls, which are spirits, are trapped through no fault of their own in physical bodies made by the devil. The spirit has to pass from one physical body to the next in a continual cycle. This is transmigration of souls—souls migrating from one body to another. Their belief in the transmigration of souls meant that they should not kill any human or other animal, should not consume anything from an animal (meat or milk products), and despised sex and childbearing. Some devout Cathars called babies "demons," because when a woman became pregnant, she was perpetuating the cycle of trapped souls. This attitude encouraged their enemies to believe that Cathars murdered babies and ate them.

Unlike some religions that believe in transmigration of souls, the Cathars did not believe that the spirits could escape back to Heaven, to the good god, by becoming progressively better in each lifetime. Their behavior in one lifetime would affect what sort of body they had in their next life, but there was no way to escape from the cycle unless one became a "perfect." Once the human had undergone the correct rituals and been made a perfect, it could escape from the cycle of death and rebirth when it died. So ultimately salvation depended on ritual rather than personal behavior.

Members of the Cathar Church were divided into the perfect, or elect, who were full members of the Church; the believers, who had undergone the initial rituals but were not yet full members; and the hearers, who were on the edge of the Cathar Church. The most important ceremony, the means of becoming a perfect, was the *consolamentum*—the consoling. Cathars believed that this ceremony removed a believer from the control of the devil and returned him or her to God's control. Only then was that believer a true Christian, allowed to call God "Father." So only a consoled Cathar was allowed to say the Lord's Prayer. After being consoled, the perfect had to live a full Cathar life—not digging the ground, eating only the permitted food, not having sex, wearing a black robe, and repeating the Lord's Prayer frequently. If perfects committed a major sin, they lost their relationship with God and had to be reconsoled. In addition, if the bishop who had consoled them committed a major sin, all the people he had consoled also fell from grace and had to be reconsoled.[1] Cathars studied the Bible and their own holy books, and they also actively spread their religion, either by preaching or by simply talking about their faith.

Most Cathars remained believers, supporting a relatively small number of perfects. The believers would be consoled only on their deathbeds, and would then live a perfect life until they died. Some elected not to eat at all after being consoled, starving themselves to death. When the dying person was an unweaned baby, it would not be allowed to drink milk after being consoled and so would die of starvation—although it was far too young to understand why.

In theory, male and female perfects were equal, so both could preach or become bishops. In practice, there were no known female Cathar bishops, Cathar deacons were always male, and the female perfects were seldom found walking the roads preaching, although they did teach. There were houses of Cathar perfect women, where the daughters of Cathar families were sent to be educated. These seem to have been very similar to Latin Christian nunneries.

Reactions to Cathars

Cathar beliefs were so different from Latin Christians that arguably the Cathars followed a new, non-Christian religion. Many uneducated Catholics did not know the difference between Cathars and Latin Christians and believed that the Cathars were very pious people who followed a lifestyle like that of the early Christians. In fact, they admired them. However, more educated Latin Christians found the Cathars' belief in transmigration of souls utterly horrible (see Document 6). They were angry at how the Cathars reinterpreted the Bible to suit their own beliefs, claiming that the devil made the world; claiming that Jesus was only a spirit, not a physical being (in contradiction of Luke 24: 36–43); and forbidding marriage and eating only certain foods (a prohibition that 1 Tim. 4:3 condemned as a lie). They were angry that the Cathars rejected the authority of the Latin Christian Church, claiming that they alone could reach God, while the Latin Church was trapped by the devil.

Catharism became widespread in areas of trade and rapid city growth, such as the Rhineland, the south of France (the Languedoc), and northern Italy. These were wealthy areas, where merchants were constantly on the move from place to place. They were areas of cultural activity, where new ideas circulated and were debated. They were also areas where there was no single strong central authority, so there was no single person to initiate and coordinate actions against the Cathars. In these areas, the Latin Church had failed to keep up with the needs of Christians, not building enough churches or educating clergy to answer the questions posed by their increasingly educated flocks. Catharism was not the only heresy to develop in these areas. The evangelical Waldensian sect began in Lyon and spread into Italy, where it still survives, while in the late thirteenth century, the spiritual Franciscans, dedicated to radical poverty, were widespread in the Languedoc and Italy. Some secular lords admired the Cathars' piety and learning and protected them. It may seem odd that the nobles were supporting this world-hating religion at the same time as they were embracing the new ideals of knighthood ("chivalry") and courtly love—both of which Catharism would condemn—but perhaps Catharism offered a counterbalance to the bloodshed of chivalry and the obsession with sexual activity that underlay courtly love. Because Catharism rejected traditional earthly figures of authority, such as bishops and the kings the bishops supported, it could also become a focus for local pride and independence. In this way, Catharism became a regional movement rather than a religious one.

Some historians have argued that Catharism was particularly attractive to women, because in theory Cathar women could hold exactly the same offices as Cathar men. Some leading noblewomen did become Cathars, perhaps because Catharism enabled them to escape from marriage and childbirth. Yet most ordinary women were repelled by the fact that Cathars condemned human love, marriage, and having babies.[2]

The Cathars became so influential in the Languedoc that devout Latin Christians became afraid that Catharism was going to replace Latin Christianity in that area. Because Cathars did not acknowledge the authority of the Latin Church, and rejected everything in this world as stemming from the devil, they were potential revolutionaries. In theory, Cathar perfects would acknowledge no power but their own bishops and refuse to pay taxes, to swear oaths of allegiance, or to do military service. They were therefore a threat to government and law and order in the region.

In 1178 Count Raymond V of Toulouse sent an appeal for help
against heretics to King Louis VII of France and to the monastic Cistercian Order. The Cistercians answered Count Raymond's appeal and
sent a preaching mission to the Languedoc, with an armed escort to
protect it. But the Cistercian preachers made little impact. The problem
was that they were outsiders who did not speak the local language (Oc-
citan), were rich and represented the north French king's authority
(which was not acknowledged in the south), and did not preach at a
level that ordinary people could understand.

In contrast, military force had some success. In 1181 the abbot of
Clairvaux, a leading Cistercian abbey, led an army to capture heretics
in the castle of Lavaur in the county of Toulouse. This castle belonged
to Roger Trencavel II, who was accused of protecting heretics and was
an enemy of Count Raymond V of Toulouse. The castle surrendered,
and the heretics confessed their faults and were reconciled to the
Church.

Raymond V died in 1194 and was succeeded by his son, Raymond
VI, who was far less worried about heretics. Pope Innocent III (1198–
1216) tried to win the Cathars back to Latin Christianity by peaceful
means. He believed that one reason that the heretics had been winning
converts was because ordinary Christians did not know enough about
their faith. He sent out Cistercians to preach the faith, although they
did not make much progress. In 1204 Innocent appointed the abbot of
Cîteaux (the leading house of the Cistercian order), Arnold Aimery, as
his legate in the Languedoc and to oversee preaching. In 1206 two
Spanish clerics arrived in the Languedoc to help Arnold Aimery: Bishop
Diego of Castile and one of his canons, the priest Dominic. Their idea
was to preach by example as well as with words, going about barefoot
like the apostles and living very austerely, like the Cathars. They tried
to preach at the level of their listeners, and did have some success.
Although in 1209 their preaching was superseded by the crusade, Dominic continued to preach, and his group became the Dominican friars.

The Origins of the Crusade

In 1207 Peter of Castelnau, one of the Cistercian papal legates in the
Languedoc, set up an association, or league of warriors, to fight against
heretics and asked Count Raymond VI of Toulouse to join. When the

count refused, the legate excommunicated him, saying that he suspected the count of harboring heretics. Meanwhile Pope Innocent III kept trying to persuade King Philip II of France (1180–1223) to send military intervention into the Languedoc, but Philip refused to do anything. Count Raymond VI was technically his vassal and he had not been found guilty of heresy; in addition, Philip had more urgent military commitments in northern France.

In 1208 Peter of Castelnau was murdered. Innocent assumed that Raymond VI of Toulouse was responsible, although this was never proved. He sent letters to kings, barons, and the people of France, urging them to take up the sword, confiscate the lands infested with heresy, and populate them with faithful Christians. He authorized the Cistercians to preach the war as a crusade. Everyone who took part for forty days would be given full clearance from all the sins they had confessed, there would be a moratorium on their debts, and their vassals and the clergy would be encouraged to contribute toward their expenses.

King Philip II still refused to get involved in the Languedoc. Yet it was in his interest to support the crusade because it would enable him to enforce his authority over the south of France, which had been effectively independent of the French king since 987. So he allowed 500 knights from northern France to take the cross for the crusade.

Around the same time, Pope Innocent also started using the threat of military force against heretics in Italy.[3]

The Course of the Crusade

The campaigns are called the Albigensian Crusades because the area where they took place is the Albigeois; Albi is right in the center of the area.

There were very few pitched battles during the crusades. The crusade commanders preferred to concentrate on laying waste the land (burning crops and destroying houses) to starve their opponents out, and on besieging towns and fortresses. Whenever they captured a town or fortress by surrender, the terms for surrender would usually allow the Latin Christian knights to go free, but heretics were taken prisoner, interrogated, and (if they would not repent) burned to death. Burning to death was a traditional method of dealing with heretics, going back at least to Old Testament times; it was believed that fire would destroy the evil of heresy. Sometimes all the prisoners were burned to ensure that heresy was destroyed.

At towns and fortresses that fell to a military assault, everyone was killed. It was normal military practice to kill or take captive every person in a fortress that was taken by assault, or "storm," but it was not usual to go to the lengths that were later reported about the assault on the town of Béziers in July 1209. The papal legate was said to have advised the crusaders to kill everyone without question in order to destroy the heretics completely. It did not matter that most of the people in the town were actually Latin Christians because God would know his own (see Document 6). When the town of Lavaur was captured in 1211, Lord Aimery of Montréal and his knights were executed as suspected heretics and supporters of heretics while Aimery's sister, the Lady Giraude (or Guirauda), known as a leading Cathar, was thrown down a well and stoned to death (see biography). These were clearly terror tactics, intended to arouse maximum alarm among the local population and encourage them to surrender quickly rather than resist.[4]

First Stage: 1209–15

The crusaders arrived in the Albigeois late in June 1209. They began by attacking the lands of Raymond Roger Trencavel, viscount of Béziers and Carcassonne, a known Cathar sympathizer. In July they besieged and captured Béziers and killed everyone. In August they besieged and took Carcassonne. Those captured included Raymond Roger himself, who later died in prison. Most of the noble crusaders went home to the north for the winter. The remaining crusaders chose Simon de Montfort as leader of the army.

Simon de Montfort was a minor noble from northern France. He had a claim to the earldom of Leicester in England through his mother, and his son Simon later became earl of Leicester and one of the opponents of King Henry III of England (1216–72). He was a pious man who had already been on the Fourth Crusade, where he was one of the few who had actually reached the Holy Land. But he also wanted land, as his own estates were small. He continued military activity throughout the winter of 1209–10. New crusaders came south in spring and the campaign continued, burning crops and capturing fortresses.

Count Raymond VI at first helped the crusaders, but after the capture

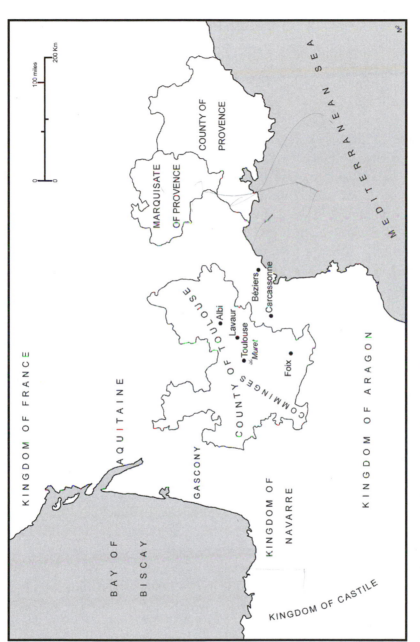

Map 4. Southern France during the Albigensian Crusades

of Carcassonne, he left the army and was then suspected of heresy. In early summer 1211 the crusaders marched to besiege Toulouse. They failed to capture it, but Raymond saw that he needed help. He asked King Peter II of Aragon for assistance.

Peter II was Raymond's brother-in-law (Raymond had married Peter's sister Eleanor), and had territorial interests in southern France. Raymond Roger Trencavel had been his vassal. In July 1212 he was one of the Christian leaders of the army that defeated the Almohads at the battle of Las Navas de Tolosa, winning himself a great reputation as a defender of Christianity. King Peter took Raymond under his protection and asked Pope Innocent III to make a peaceful settlement in the Languedoc. It was clear that what had begun as a war against heresy was becoming a war for land, and many of those who were suffering or who had died were not heretics but good Christians. The pope ordered the crusaders to stop their advance and make peace, but they refused, saying that Count Raymond was a heretic. Seeing that his interests and his allies could not be protected in any other way, Peter II then invaded the Languedoc with an army. Count Raymond and the counts of Foix and Comminges joined him, and in August 1213, they engaged the forces of Simon de Montfort and the crusaders at Muret. They were defeated, and Peter II was killed.

With no one left who could stand in his way, Simon de Montfort conquered the northern part of the county of Toulouse and went on northward into Gascony, attacking any town or fortress where he had heard there were heretics. In 1215 Lord Louis, son of King Philip II, also took the cross and came south to join the crusade, but did not make any gains.

The first stage of the crusade ended in November 1215 at the Fourth Lateran Council, convened by Pope Innocent III at Rome. Count Raymond VI was formally deprived of his county because he had sheltered heretics, and Simon de Montfort was confirmed in his conquests. Raymond's son Raymond VII was made count of Toulouse in his father's place, but he had lost most of his lands to Simon de Montfort. He was given the marquisate of Provence, which had not been conquered by the crusaders.

Second Stage: 1216–29

In 1216 King Philip II of France accepted Simon de Montfort's homage as count of Toulouse, duke of Narbonne, viscount of Béziers and Carcassonne. But Raymond VI and his son gained support in Provence and started to fight back. In autumn 1217 Toulouse rebelled. Raymond VI got into the city and became a focus of revolt against de Montfort.

Pope Honorius III ordered the preaching of a new crusade. Simon de Montfort besieged Toulouse, but on June 27, 1218, he was killed by a stone hurled from a stone thrower inside the town. The "Song of the Albigensian War" states that a local carpenter had made the stone thrower and a group of women, teenage girls, and children were operating it.[5] The Albigensians saw de Montfort's death as an act of God. Without Simon de Montfort's leadership, the crusaders gave up—his elder son, Amaury, lacked his father's reputation as a leader and had no money. Philip II of France refused to help in person, although he sent his son, the Lord Louis. Louis arrived in May 1219 with an army but went home in August without having achieved a great deal. So the rebels were left in possession of the city and much of the county of Toulouse.

This was the end of the crusade, but not the end of the war.

In August 1222, Count Raymond VI died, and his son Raymond VII became count of Toulouse. In 1223 Philip II of France died, and his son became King Louis VIII. Louis VIII led a new expedition against Raymond VII in 1226. He captured Avignon, and many of the nobles of Provence and the Languedoc surrendered to him, but he had to withdraw from the area because he was ill. He died in November 1226, on his way back north. Since his only son, Louis IX, was a child, his widow, Queen Blanche, acted as regent. The war continued, the crusaders using a "scorched earth" policy so that the Albigensians' resources were gradually destroyed. In 1228 Raymond had to negotiate for peace.

In 1229, in the Peace of Paris, Raymond VII surrendered two-thirds of his county of Toulouse to the king of France and kept one-third for life. His daughter Jeanne was to marry Alphonse, count of Poitou (King Louis IX's younger brother) so that when Raymond VII died (in 1249), his county of Toulouse passed into the control of the French royal family. Raymond had to give some castles to the king and destroy others. He had to surrender the county of Provence to King Louis IX and the marquisate of Provence to the Church, but he later recovered this land. He had to promise to obey the Church and to help seek out heretics. Finally, he had to take the cross, go to the Holy Land, and fight the Muslims there for five years—but he did not go.

Historians disagree over whether these terms were "good" or harsh. On parchment they appeared harsh. Whatever happened, the county of Toulouse would pass to the family of the King of France's brother and lose its independence from French royal authority. Raymond lost territory, and his severe penance (five years in the Holy Land) indicated that he had been found guilty of sympathizing with heretics, although he had not. But in fact some of the terms were not enforced; he did not go to the East, and he recovered some of his land. The terms of 1229 were more lenient than those of 1215, which had aroused great anger and resentment in the south and had proved to be unenforceable.[6]

Although the peace of 1229 marked the end of the Albigensian Crusades, hostilities continued. One by one the castles held by the Cathars' supporters were captured and the Cathars killed. But the activities of the investigators of heresy (called *inquisitores* in Latin) angered local people, and there were some attempts at resistance. In May 1242 an armed band set out from the castle of Montségur near Toulouse to the village of Avignonet, where they found a team of investigators and killed them. The lord of Montségur was a Cathar sympathizer, and his mother had been a Cathar perfect. In reprisal for these murders, the king of France's representative in the area led an attack on Montségur and captured it, destroying it as a base of Catharism.

The Results of the Albigensian Crusades

The crusade was not successful in destroying the Cathars, for the Cathar religion survived into the fourteenth century. However, it did destroy the network of secular lords who supported and protected the Cathars. With their protectors gone, the Cathars were reduced to being fugitives in hiding. Many fled to northern Italy.

The crusade also began the reestablishment of the authority of the French king in the Languedoc, which would lead to the decline of the distinctive culture of the region. Although it was prompted by religious disputes, at base, the Albigensian Crusade—like the crusade in the Iberian Peninsula—turned out to be a war about territory and authority.

In the Languedoc today, the Cathars are widely regarded as representing the spirit of the region. They are seen as a symbol of Languedocian culture, and as martyrs crushed by the heavy hand of the north. This romanticized view acknowledges the political and territorial basis of the Albigensian Crusade. But it overlooks the fact that the Cathar religion would probably have declined in any case in the late Middle Ages. The Cathars' religious beliefs, which condemned everything physical, including human love and family life, were opposed to the prevailing beliefs of the thirteenth and fourteenth centuries, which celebrated the body of Christ and promoted human love as a reflection of God's love. The Cathar belief that made the individual's connection to God dependent on the behavior of the Cathar bishop was completely opposed to the thirteenth- and fourteenth-century emphasis on the individual's close personal relationship with Christ, without any intermediary. Even if there had been no crusade, it seems unlikely that Catharism would have survived as a fanatical, world-hating religion. The fact that Catharism became so widespread before the crusade suggests that most believers were not actually very interested in its fundamental religious beliefs, and were attracted more by its rejection of worldly authority and wealth.

THE HUSSITE CRUSADE

The Hussite Heresy

The Hussites were very different from the Cathars. They were more like a radical form of Latin Christianity than a heresy. Like most medieval European heretics, the Hussites were literate and produced their own literature, and their beliefs were defined in a manifesto published in April 1420. This manifesto contained what became known as "The Four Articles of Prague," which state:

1. The Word of God (the Gospels) should be freely preached.

2. Communion should be in both kinds for everyone (both = *utraque* in Latin, so the Hussites are called "Utraquists"). That is, all Christians should receive both the bread and wine at communion. At this time, laypeople usually received only the bread. Everyone

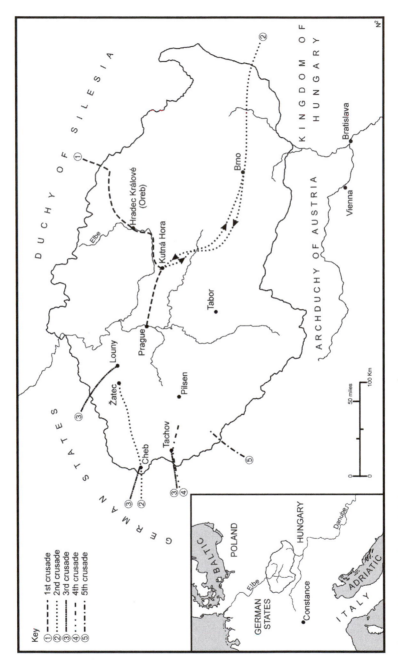

Map 5. The Kingdom of Bohemia and the Hussite Crusades

should be able to receive communion as soon as they are baptized, and take it at least once a week.

3. The clergy should be directed to follow Jesus' lifestyle, living in poverty and without simony (that is, not buying and selling Church appointments and sacraments).

4. All sins should be repressed.

These four Articles remained a fundamental basis that both moderate and radical Hussites could agree on. They were an important unifying element.

However, Hussitism was more than this. It was a nationalist, philosophical, and academic movement bound together by a sense of outrage at injustice—nationalist, because it was a Czech movement, a reaction against the strong German influences in Bohemia; philosophical and academic, because it was linked to the writings of the philosopher John Wycliffe and sprang from the University of Prague and, in particular, the preachings of John Hus; bound together by outrage, because the movement flared up after the martyrdom of John Hus, who was burned as a heretic by the Council of Constance in July 1415. Within the movement there were many divergent schools of thought, so the Four Articles of Prague were essential in keeping the movement together.

The Origins of Hussitism and the Background to the Crusades

Hussitism appeared in Bohemia in the early fifteenth century. It had its roots in the friction between Germans who had settled in Bohemia and the native Czechs, and in the Church reform sponsored by King Charles IV (1346–78), the western Roman emperor. A series of reforming preachers flourished in the capital city, Prague. They infuriated the clergy by preaching against the wealth and immorality of the clergy, but were very popular with laypeople. They preached in Czech, the language of the people.

In Prague University there was also great interest in Church reform, based on the writings of the English reformer John Wycliffe (pronounced "Wick-cliff"). One of the academics who followed Wycliffe's ideas was John Hus, a native-speaking Czech who preached against corruption in the Church. In 1409 he was elected rector of the University of Prague.

Hus became involved in opposition to King Wenceslas (Václav) IV of Bohemia (1378–1419). He was eventually excommunicated for his opposition and for preaching against abuses in the Church, and he went into voluntary exile in southern Bohemia. Here he was able to develop his ideas, continue preaching reform in the country, and build up support among the Czech nobles.

In southern Bohemia a radical Christian sect developed, centered around a community on a mountain that was renamed Mount Tabor (a biblical mountain). This community aimed at a very austere, Bible-based Christianity, expecting Christ's imminent return to earth, and it became the militant wing of Hussitism.

In 1410 Wenceslas' younger brother, Sigismund, had been elected to be western emperor—he was the husband of Queen Mary of Hungary. In 1414 Sigismund summoned John Hus to the Church Council at Constance to answer questions about his preaching. He promised Hus that he would be safe. Yet when John Hus arrived, in late 1414, he was arrested and interrogated. Sigismund's need to promote himself as a leader of Latin Christendom (as western emperor) by repressing heresy was more important to him than keeping his promises to a suspected heretic. Despite protests from the Bohemian nobles, John Hus was condemned as a heretic by the Council of Constance and burned to death in July 1415.

The death of Hus caused outrage in Bohemia. The Czech nobles defied the Council of Constance and formed a league to defend Hussitism. At last in 1419 Wenceslas decided, far too late, that he must do something. He dismissed the town councilors of Prague New Town, because they were supporters of Hus' reforming ideas, and replaced them with traditionalists. There was a violent reaction; one of the Hussite radical preachers led a procession to the New Town Hall, where they demanded that Hussites who were being held in prison be released. When the councilors refused, the crowd broke in and threw thirteen councilors from a first-floor window. This event, the "Defenestration of Prague," marks the beginning of the war. The Hussites took over the town hall, and the king died shortly afterward.

His brother Sigismund succeeded him. The Hussites regarded him as the murderer of Hus, treacherous and untrustworthy. There were riots in Prague and the regent, Wenceslas' widow Queen Sophia, could not keep control. Within Bohemia, Catholics began to persecute Hussites;

at the silver-mining town of Kutná Hora, the German population killed Hussites by throwing them down mine shafts. It is possible that Sigismund could have taken Bohemia if he had moved at once, but he did not; when he finally did arrive, he continued the persecution. The papal legate in Bohemia then declared a crusade against the Hussites. As a result, the Bohemians refused to accept Sigismund. However, they would probably have had to surrender had it not been for the Taborites under their general John Žižka (see biography), who formed an effective and dedicated fighting force that Sigismund could not defeat.

The Campaigns against the Hussites

1420: First crusade Sigismund marched to attack Prague, which was defended by the city militia and by military forces from the radical Hussite communities of Tabor (in south Bohemia) and Oreb (in east Bohemia). Sigismund could have besieged the city much longer, but instead he withdrew (see Map 5).

It was during the siege that the Hussite leaders in Prague agreed on the Four Articles of Prague. Copies of the Articles were distributed far and wide in an attempt to win Catholics over to Hussitism. The Hussites in Prague tried to find a new king to replace Sigismund. Eventually Korybut, a relative of King Władysław Jagiełło of Poland and Grand Duke Witold of Lithuania, came to Bohemia and was recognized as regent. Yet he was never able to establish his position in the country. He tried to negotiate with the pope, but that only turned the radicals against him. At last in 1428 he was sent back to Poland.

1421: Second crusade The second crusade came in the autumn of 1421, fifteen months after the first one. It was a large expedition, but Sigismund was delayed, and rumors circulated that he did not want to suppress the heretics. The plan had been that Sigismund would attack from the east while the Germans attacked from the west, crushing the Hussites in a pincer movement. The Germans arrived and attacked Žatec, but the siege dragged on and the leaders started to quarrel. After two weeks they heard that a great Hussite army was coming, and fled.

Sigismund arrived in mid-October. He delayed at Brno, trying to win over Catholic Czechs. This gave the Hussites time to draw up their forces. Although Sigismund won the initial attack at Kutná Hora, the Hussites under Žižka rallied and forced him to withdraw from Bohemia.

1422: *Third crusade* Sigismund put Frederick of Hohenzollern in charge of the campaign. The crusaders were not enthusiastic, and Sigismund gave virtually no help. Eventually all Frederick could do was go to the relief of Karlstein, which was being besieged by the Hussites. Prince Korybut negotiated with Frederick, and while the negotiations dragged on, Karlstein surrendered. The crusaders withdrew.

After this, there were no crusades for a few years. In the meantime, the Hussite radicals and moderates fought between themselves, and during the winter of 1422–23, the Taborite general John Žižka left the radical community at Tabor and joined the community at Mount Oreb. The Hussites eventually united behind Prince Korybut and went on to the offensive, attacking Moravia in spring 1424, where John Žižka died. The Orebites chose a new leader, named Prokůpek (Prokop the Lesser). The new general of the Taborites was Prokop Holý, which means "Prokop the Shaven" or "Prokop the Bald." Originally a Taborite priest, he was a great general although not as outstanding as Žižka. He changed Hussite strategy; whereas Žižka had remained within Bohemia, Prokop took the war to the Catholics outside Bohemia, encouraging them to adopt Hussitism by demonstrating Hussite military strength. These raids were called "the magnificent rides" ("ride" = "raid").

1427: *Fourth crusade* Described as a "spiritual tournament" by the pope, this expedition was led by Frederick of Hohenzollern. The pope's representative, or legate, was Henry Beaufort, bishop of Winchester. Frederick had negotiated with the Hussites beforehand, trying to divide the moderates from the radicals. Beaufort sent a conciliatory letter to the Hussites, asking them to repent and return to Catholic unity: "Don't refuse us—come!"[7]

Yet when the army set out, it had only a very limited aim—to recapture a fortress. Frederick of Hohenzollern fell ill. The Hussites advanced and the crusaders fled, not stopping even when the papal legate unfurled the papal banner and shouted to them to come back.

Pope Martin V's reaction was immediately to start planning another crusade. He suggested raising an English army to fight the Hussites, arguing that the English had started Hussitism because Hus' ideas were based on John Wycliffe's writing. However, this expedition was diverted to France to fight Joan of Arc.

After the fourth crusade, the Hussites began what Thomas Fudge terms "an international propaganda campaign."[8] They sent out pamphlets across Europe, outlining the Hussite program. The Hussites had always wanted a full, public debate of their ideas, but Sigismund and the Catholic Church had never allowed them to have one. Now they were presenting their ideas to the public without the permission of king or Church. The Hussites were so successful that they forced the Catholic Church and Sigismund to enter into formal negotiations on the Hussites' terms. In 1429 negotiations began at Bratislava in Hungary. Nothing was resolved, but the Hussites could congratulate themselves for forcing the Church and Sigismund to the negotiating table through their military successes.

1431: Fifth crusade This crusade started after the failure of negotiations. The crusaders fled before the armies had even engaged. Cardinal Guiliano Cesarini, who was papal legate on that campaign, decided it would be better to revert to negotiations. The Hussites were invited to the Church Council at Basel in 1433. At the previous council, Hus had been burned as a heretic; now the Hussites were being treated as equals. Here at last they were allowed to put forth their case, but were disappointed to discover that the Catholic Church did not immediately convert to Hussitism. Meanwhile, the fighting in Bohemia went on.

The End of the War and the Hussite Legacy

In May 1434 the radical and moderate Hussite forces fought each other at Lipany. The moderates won; the two Prokops were killed, and the Taborites, Orebites, and militia of Prague New Town were destroyed. This was the real end of the Hussite crusades. The crusaders could not defeat the Hussites in battle; only the Hussites could defeat each other.

Negotiations began again. The moderates came to a settlement with Sigismund and with the Catholic Church, which allowed Hussites to continue to receive communion in both kinds. All other demands by the Hussites were dropped. Sigismund was finally accepted by the Czechs as king of Bohemia in 1436 and entered Prague with his empress, Barbara, in August of that year. He died in December 1437.

Sigismund's daughter and heir Elizabeth did not long outlive him, leaving an infant son, Ladislas. George of Poděbrady was made regent. When Ladislas died in 1457, the Czechs elected and crowned the regent George as king, and despite the hostility of Catholic Europe, he ruled as "Hussite king" of Bohemia until 1471.[9]

* * *

Hussitism continued in Bohemia until the early 1620s. In 1618 the Archduke Ferdinand, who had been elected king of Bohemia (Ferdinand II), tried to enforce Catholicism. He issued a decree forbidding Protestant meetings, which included Hussites. Some of the leading Protestants went to the palace in Prague and found the imperial regents, argued with them, and threw them out of the window in the second Defenestration of Prague. The Protestant nobles then rebelled against Ferdinand and called in to rule them the Protestant elector palatine, Frederick V, and his wife, Elizabeth, daughter of James I of England. (Their son was Prince Rupert, famous for his role in the English Civil War.) Yet Frederick received no help from his father-in-law, and in the Battle of the White Mountain in 1620, the Protestants were defeated. In the Thirty Years' War that followed, Protestantism in general and Hussitism in particular were crushed in Bohemia.

However, some Hussites escaped from Moravia and Bohemia to Saxony, where they set up the Moravian Church. In the eighteenth century, members of the Moravian Church went to America, where they preached Christianity to the North American natives. The Moravian Church is still very active in the United States. There are also Moravian churches in the British Isles. Modern Protestants in the Czech Republic trace some of their traditions back to the Hussites.

The Hussites' Achievements

The Hussite movement removed German influence from Bohemia, and Czechs took control of government. The Hussites secured the long-term independence of the Hussite Church—the Catholic Church could not destroy the Hussites and had to acknowledge their separate beliefs. Church property was secularized and tithes were abolished. The townspeople won more power; the Church lost a great deal of power. On the other hand, Bohemia became culturally and politically isolated.

How did the Hussites defeat the crusaders? Historians identify certain advantages that they held, and weaknesses among their opponents. First, the Four Articles of Prague held the moderates and radicals together. If the Hussites disagreed on everything else, they could at least agree on these. Again, Hussitism was very widespread in Bohemian society: Thomas Fudge has estimated that 50–60 percent of the population were

Hussite.[10] This meant that Bohemia was effectively a Hussite nation, and Hussitism became part of the institutions of Bohemia. Hence it was very difficult to eradicate. The radical communities of Tabor and Oreb were united and confident; they believed that they were God's army, ushering in the second coming of Christ, and that their enemies represented the Antichrist. Each victory gave them even more confidence. They were skilled and disciplined, and their generals were effective and imaginative leaders. As well as all this, the movement had intellectual backing from the University of Prague, giving it theological leadership and giving Hussite beliefs a firm, rational basis.

On the other side, there is no doubt that King Sigismund made serious errors. He was too slow in coming to Bohemia, allowing his opponents to establish themselves; he agreed to a crusade and persecuted Hussites, turning the whole country against him; and he allowed his soldiers to commit atrocities rather than keeping them firmly in check so as to convince people that he did care about the Czechs. He was disliked in Bohemia and seen as the betrayer of Hus, a foreigner and a lover of foreigners. Moreover he never seemed to realize the strengths of his opponents, as if he could not believe that the Czechs had rejected their rightful ruler and were serious about religious reform.

However, not all Sigismund's weaknesses were his own fault. He had too many other things to do; such as fighting the Ottoman Turks and keeping the peace between the Imperial princes in Germany. He was also anxious to go to Rome to be crowned emperor, so he wanted to please the pope by crushing heresy—hence he could not negotiate with the Czech heretics.

Sigismund was not the only person to underestimate the Hussites. The crusaders could not believe that non-nobles, inexperienced in war— a weak rabble—could repulse the crusades alone. They were told that the Hussites worshiped the devil, so they believed that the devil was helping the Hussites, and this made them terrified. The German princes lacked an effective leader who could devise a workable strategy and coordinate campaigns. Meetings to plan the crusade were poorly attended, and the German towns were unwilling to contribute money to the cause. Yet if the Germans did not go on crusade against the Hussites, there was no one else to go. The French and English were at war, and Joan of Arc distracted English military efforts from the Hussites to France. One of the reasons for going on crusade was to win honor and glory, and there was more honor and glory to be won fighting chivalrous wars in France than fighting supposed devil worshipers in Bohemia.

Arguably negotiation was a more effective tactic than war, for the Hussites were fundamentally divided. Whenever the pressure from outside relaxed, the nobles, the people of Prague, and the radical Taborites began to go their separate ways. For example, the Taborites wanted to burn down all magnificent churches and monasteries, partly to destroy idolatry but also because most Taborites were from a poor farming background and they hated displays of noble wealth. The people of Prague were proud of their architectural heritage, and the nobles did not want their monasteries destroyed. An intelligent enemy should have exploited those divisions. Yet military campaigns forced all the Czechs to unite against a common foe. In short, the crusade was the wrong weapon to use against the Hussites.

NOTES

1. Malcolm Lambert, *The Cathars* (Oxford and Malden, MA: Blackwell, 1998), pp. 49–53.

2. Malcolm Barber, "Women and Catharism," *Reading Medieval Studies* 3 (1977): 45–62; reprinted in Malcolm Barber, *Crusaders and Heretics, 12th–14th Centuries* (Aldershot, Hants., and Brookfield, VT: Variorum, 1995), no. III; Richard Abels and Ellen Harrison, "The Participation of Women in Languedocian Catharism," *Mediaeval Studies* 41 (1979): 215–51; Peter Biller, "The Common Woman in the Western Church in the Thirteenth and Fourteenth Centuries," in W. J. Sheils and Diana Wood, eds., *Women in the Church: Papers Read at the 1989 Summer Meeting and the 1990 Winter Meeting of the Ecclesiastical History Society; Studies in Church History* 27 (1990): pp. 127–57.

3. Norman Housley, "Politics and Heresy in Italy," *Journal of Ecclesiastical History* 33 (1982): 193–208.

4. Malcolm Barber, "The Albigensian Crusades: Wars Like Any Other?" in Michel Balard, Benjamin Z. Kedar, and Jonathan Riley-Smith, eds., *Dei Gesta Per Francos: Études sur les croisades dédiées à Jean Richard: Crusade Studies in Honour of Jean Richard* (Aldershot, Hants., and Burlington, VT: Ashgate, 2001), pp. 45–55.

5. *The Song of the Cathar Wars: A History of the Albigensian Crusade*, trans. Janet Shirley (Aldershot, Hants., and Brookfield, VT: Ashgate, 1996), p. 172.

6. Lambert, *Cathars*, p. 137.

7. G. A. Holmes, "Cardinal Beaufort and the Crusade against the Hussites," *English Historical Review* 88 (1973): 721–50, here 722–23.

8. Thomas Fudge, *The Magnificent Ride: The First Reformation in Hussite Bohemia* (Aldershot, Hants, and Brookfield, VT: Ashgate, 1998), p. 108.

9. Otakar Odložilík, *The Hussite King: Bohemia in European Affairs, 1440–1471* (New Brunswick, NJ: Rutgers University Press, 1965).

10. Fudge, *The Magnificent Ride*, p. 276.

CHAPTER 5

CRUSADES AGAINST THE OTTOMAN TURKS IN THE BALKANS

THE ORIGINS OF THE OTTOMANS

The Ottomans were Muslim Turks who first came to the notice of other nations at the beginning of the fourteenth century. The former Seljuk Empire had been broken up before the middle of the thirteenth century by the Mongol invasions, and by the start of the fourteenth century there was effectively a power vacuum in Asia Minor. The Īl khāns, Mongol rulers of what is now Iran, were no longer able to control an area so far to the west of their center of power; the Byzantine Empire could no longer protect its territories to the east of the Bosphorus. Asia Minor divided into a multiplicity of small Turkish lordships. One of these was the emirate of Osman, in what used to be Bithynia in the days of the Byzantine Empire (see Map 6).[1]

Osman's dynasty, the Osmanlı dynasty, gave its name to the Ottoman Empire. Osman and his descendants rapidly expanded their domains, conquering both Byzantine and other Turkish territory in Asia Minor. The Ottoman ruler did not govern all his lands directly, but subdivided his domains and appointed governors to rule on his behalf. These governors would be responsible for providing warriors for the army and collecting taxes. Those appointed as governors would typically be members of the ruling dynasty and trusted followers.

The Ottomans' warfare comprised not only formal campaigns but also raids into enemy territory, carrying off booty and prisoners. The prisoners were sold as slaves, and a certain levy was passed on to the sultan, who used slaves as administrators and warriors. As raids did not supply sufficient slaves, from the fourteenth century onward the Ottomans also levied a tax of slaves on their Christian subjects—even though this practice was forbidden by Islamic law. By Islamic law, Jews and Christians should have freedom of religion, provided they did not try to convert Muslims, and should not be enslaved. The Ottomans could have argued that the boys taken as slaves were educated, well housed, and clothed and could follow a good career in the sultan's service. This argument would overlook the fact that these children were forced to leave their homes, their families, and their religion. The levy of slaves, taking one boy in forty, was the cause of enormous grief and resentment among the Christians of the Ottoman Empire, and of horror among western Christians.[2]

Even in a violent age, the Ottomans acquired a reputation for treating their enemies savagely. This encouraged their terrified enemies to surrender quickly, but did them no favor in the eyes of posterity. Famous examples included Bayezid I's execution of almost all his prisoners after the Battle of Nicopolis in 1396 (contrary to contemporary practice, in which prisoners were normally held for ransom or enslaved); Mehmed II having 400 prisoners cut in two lengthways in 1462 after they had surrendered to him on his promise not to cut off their heads; the killing of defenders who had surrendered castles on the promise that their lives would be spared (contrary to contemporary custom, in which such promises were normally honored); and the sacking of the Italian city of Otranto in 1480, with "eight hundred martyrs," or Christians, slaughtered (such sackings were a normal part of warfare, but the attack was on a major Italian port, and uncomfortably close to Rome). Contemporary westerners regarded these actions as far worse than any atrocities committed by the crusaders, the Ayyūbids, or the Mamluks during the crusades to the Holy Land. Western Christendom was convinced that the Ottoman Turks were bloodthirsty barbarians.[3] In later centuries this reputation would stand against the Ottomans' attempts to win recognition as a European power.

OTTOMAN EXPANSION

The dynastic quarrels within the Byzantine imperial family gave the Ottomans an opportunity for expansion. In 1346 Osman's son Orhan

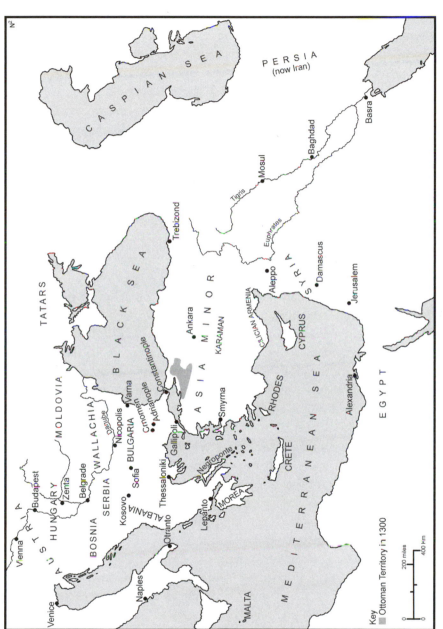

Map 6. The Balkans and the Middle East during the Ottoman invasions

made an alliance with one contender for the imperial throne, John VI
Kantakouzenos, by which Orhan would marry Kantakouzenos' daughter
Theodora in return for his military aid. Later Orhan was also granted a
fortress on the west bank of the Dardenelles, and his forces went on to
capture Gallipoli and other towns, with help from the Genoese. The
Ottomans were now established in Europe, and continued to raid and
conquer territory both in Europe and in Asia Minor.

Since the loss of the Holy Land in 1291, the crusading movement in
the East had been at a low ebb. The military religious order of the
Hospital of St. John, which since 1309 had been based on the island of
Rhodes, had been waging war on some of the Turkish emirates in Asia
Minor, and making alliances with others. The Venetians and Genoese
cooperated with each other and the Hospitallers in forming naval
leagues against the Turks. In 1344 one of these leagues succeeded in
capturing the important Turkish port of Smyrna (now Izmir), but in
1350 war broke out between Venice and Genoa, ending the naval
league.

In 1359 Pope Innocent VI ordered crusade preaching. His legate in
the Eastern Mediterranean, Peter Thomas, organized a naval force made
up of Venetian and Hospitaller ships. This was successful in recapturing
some of the Ottoman Turks' conquests, but had to be abandoned when
the Turks counterattacked. In 1366 another crusade came east, led by
Amedeo VI of Savoy, the cousin of the Byzantine emperor John V.
Working in cooperation with the Byzantines, this expedition succeeded
in recapturing Gallipoli.

The Ottoman threat was not yet critical. The most famous crusade
of the 1360s was not against the Ottomans but against the Mamluks of
Egypt; in 1365, King Peter I of Cyprus captured the Egyptian city of
Alexandria. The city was abandoned after a few days, and all Peter
seemed to have done was to win booty and disrupt Egyptian trade, which
in itself would benefit Cyprus. His deed was acclaimed in the West
although the warriors of western Europe were mainly involved in the
Anglo-French war at this time rather than thinking of crusades to the
East. In 1375, when the Mamluks conquered the Christian kingdom of
Cilician Armenia, no aid came from the West or even from Cyprus or
Rhodes.

However, in 1369 the Ottoman emir Murad captured Adrianople.
Constantinople was now surrounded by Ottoman territory. Murad

moved his capital to his new city. Although King Louis of Hungary did nothing, the Serbs attempted to fight the Ottomans. In 1371 an expedition led by two Serbian princes was defeated at Crnomen on the Maritza River near Adrianople. Pope Gregory XI tried to organize another crusade, but the Anglo-French war and another war between Venice and Genoa meant that Europe's warriors and rulers were distracted elsewhere. So instead the pope looked to the military religious order of the Hospital of St. John to lead a campaign. He ordered an inquest to be conducted into all the order's properties to see how they could best be used for the crusade in the East. The inquest only showed what the Hospitallers already knew: the Black Death of 1348–49 and increasing costs had reduced their personnel and wealth in the West so much that the order was unable to launch its own campaign against the Turks. But the pope did make the Hospitallers take over responsibility for the defense of Smyrna, and the order did take over the defense of the Morea (the Peloponnese, in southern Greece), hiring mercenary companies for the purpose. In 1377 the grand master of the Hospital of St. John, Juan Fernández de Heredia, a trusted friend of the pope, led an expedition to attack the Albanians, who were the Ottomans' allies. The expedition met with some success, but then disaster struck. The order's army was ambushed and Heredia was taken prisoner. The Hospital quickly ransomed him, but crusading efforts halted in 1378 on the death of Pope Gregory XI. Two popes were elected to succeed him, and the "great schism" that resulted continued until 1415.

Meanwhile Murad continued to expand Ottoman territories. He married Thamar, the sister of Tsar Shishman of Bulgaria, and the tsar became his vassal. In 1372 he invaded northern Greece; the city of Thessaloníki fell to him in 1387. By 1387 he had conquered southern Macedonia, and his forces moved north into Serbia, where he captured Sofia but had to withdraw after being defeated by the Serbian prince Lazar. Other forces pressed south, attacking the Peloponnese, but Murad then had to withdraw into Asia Minor to fight the Muslim emir of Karaman, who had attacked his eastern territories.

In 1389 Murad returned to Serbia, where his army met Prince Lazar's army at Kosovo Polje. Both Murad and Lazar were killed, and both sides suffered terrible losses. The Turks were left in possession of the field and therefore claimed victory, but it was at a great cost. Murad's son Bayezid succeeded his father. As the news of Kosovo spread, the Ottomans' Muslim neighbors in Asia Minor attacked Ottoman territory, and Bayezid's first few years were occupied in fighting them. He then moved back into Europe and continued to consolidate Ottoman authority and to expand his territory.

King Louis of Hungary had died in 1382 and was succeeded by his daughter Mary and her husband, Sigismund. Sigismund saw the danger from the Turks and began to organize a crusade. In the West, a truce had been made in the Anglo-French war in 1384, and Philip de Mezières, tutor to King Charles VI of France, had been campaigning for a crusade. In 1390 the Duke of Bourbon organized a crusade expedition to al-Mahdiyyah in what is now Tunisia. A large expedition made up of nobles from France and Burgundy set out for Hungary in 1396. The army joined King Sigismund and his army at Buda and marched south to meet Bayezid I's forces. They captured some Turkish-held fortresses, and then the two armies met at Nicopolis, on the River Danube (see Figure 3). The crusader army was resoundingly defeated. King Sigismund escaped, but a great many crusaders were captured, and Bayezid ordered their executions. Only a few were spared to be ransomed.

The contemporary sources do not make clear why the crusaders lost so badly. Obviously the Muslim army was better disciplined and better led, but that does not explain the extent of the defeat. It appears that the crusaders' tactics were somehow unsuitable; perhaps they began the battle with a cavalry charge (i.e., a charge on horseback), as was the custom in the West, while it might have been wiser to adopt a defensive strategy, with the infantry (foot soldiers) in the front rank to await the Muslim attack, or perhaps the crusaders were misled by a feigned retreat, which led them into an ambush. In any case, this defeat ended plans for a second, larger crusade from France and England.[4]

Bayezid, however, did not advance into Hungary. He went back to Asia Minor to deal with problems there, and spent the next few years campaigning in that region. Timur the Lame, otherwise known in the West as Tamerlane—a brilliant and ruthless military leader who had built up a Central Asian empire centered on Samarkand—advanced into Bayezid's neighborhood in 1400 and, in 1402, invaded Bayezid's domains. At the battle of Ankara, Bayezid was captured and later died in prison. Timur spent the next year ravaging Asia Minor before withdrawing to the East.

In the confusion after the defeat of Bayezid I and the breakup of his

Figure 3. Bayezid I routs the crusaders at the battle of Nicopolis, 1396. From a sixteenth-century Ottoman manuscript. Jerome Wheelock Fund. Bridgeman Art Library.

domains in Asia Minor, the Christians in Europe were able to force his heir in Europe, Süleyman, into surrendering some of his territories. For some years the Ottoman advance halted as Bayezid's sons warred against each other. Finally in 1413 the youngest son, Mehmed I, gained control of the Ottoman domains.

After Nicopolis, there were no more major expeditions to the Balkans against the Turks until the 1440s. Individual Christian powers, such as the Venetians, the kings of Cyprus, and the Hospitallers of Rhodes, kept up raids against the Turks at sea, and King Sigismund of Hungary campaigned against them on land, but these did not become full-scale campaigns. Even individual powers could do a great deal of damage; in 1416, a Venetian fleet destroyed the Ottoman fleet in a sea battle. Without a fleet, Mehmed I could not harass the Greek islands or coast, or attack Rhodes or Cyprus.

Mehmed I's successor, Murad II, besieged Constantinople in 1422, but withdrew due to problems elsewhere in his empire. He conquered territory in Asia Minor and in 1430 recaptured the city of Thessaloníki from the Venetians. He campaigned in the Balkans against King Sigismund of Hungary, both sides trying to control Serbia. In 1433 he took over Albania, by 1439 had conquered Serbia, and then began to advance into Hungary, where he was opposed by John Hunyadi (see biography). In 1443–44 a crusading army led by Hunyadi and Władysław III of Poland (elected king of Hungary as Ladislas the Jagiełłonian); Cardinal Julian Cesarini, papal legate; and George Branković of Serbia campaigned deep into Turkish territory, only withdrawing because of the winter weather. Late in 1444 Hunyadi and Ladislas/Władysław led a second army, which met the Turks at Varna. Although the battle was indecisive, the Christian army was destroyed, and Ladislas was killed.

Constantinople had been surrounded by Ottoman territory since 1369. Following the battle of Varna, it was unlikely to receive military assistance. In Hungary, the nobles were in dispute over the succession; in the West, only Duke Philip the Good of Burgundy showed an active interest in events in the East. In spring 1453 the young sultan Mehmed II (see biography) besieged Constantinople. The city was taken by storm on May 29 and sacked. Mehmed II cut short the sack and moved his capital to Constantinople. He allowed the Greek Orthodox Church to continue, appointing a patriarch and allowing Christians to worship. Ruling from Constantinople, Mehmed claimed to have taken over the Roman right to rule the world. He reorganized his government, codified law, and encouraged trade.

Western Europeans were horrified at the fall of the imperial city of Constantinople, fearing that Mehmed would invade Italy next. Yet despite active efforts by the popes, the duke of Burgundy, and the king of Aragon, no crusade was launched. Mehmed continued to campaign in the Balkans, consolidating his control over Serbia and pushing into Hungary. In 1456 he besieged Belgrade, but was repulsed by a crusading army led by John Hunyadi. This defeat did not prevent him from finally taking over Serbia in 1458. He conquered Wallachia in 1462 and Bosnia in 1463.

Mehmed also waged war at sea, capturing Genoese- and Venetian-controlled towns and islands, and former Byzantine territory, including the city of Trebizond (now Trabzon) in 1461. A Venetian counterattack on the Ottomans in 1463 failed to recapture Lesbos (Mitylene) from the Turks, but the Venetians did make an anti-Ottoman alliance with Uzun Hasan, who ruled the Akkoyunlu Empire in what is now Iran and Iraq.[5] Hungary also joined the alliance, but the Ottomans captured the big island of Negroponte (Euboea) from Venice in 1470, and defeated Uzun Hasan in battle in 1473. In the late 1470s, Mehmed began to raid Italy itself, culminating in 1480 with the capture of Otranto. In 1480 he also sent a naval force to besiege Rhodes, which failed to capture the island (see Document 12).

Mehmed died in 1481, at the start of another campaign. The Christians recaptured Otranto, and the Ottoman Empire was divided by a succession dispute between Mehmed's sons Bayezid and Jem. When Jem fled to Rhodes to seek help from the Hospital of St. John, Bayezid came to an agreement with the Hospitallers whereby he would pay them tribute and they would keep Jem out of his way. Although raiding continued along the frontier with Hungary and there was some campaigning within the Balkans, Bayezid II's reign was generally a time of peace between the Ottomans and western Christendom. Instead, he concentrated on the Mamluks, who were now his neighbors to the south.

In Hungary, King Matthias Corvinus (son of John Hunyadi) had been an effective general against the Ottomans. His death in 1490 left Hungary in political turmoil. Bayezid hoped to win some territory, but failed. In 1495 King Charles VIII of France took Jem under his protection and proclaimed a crusade to the East to place Jem on the Ottoman throne, but Jem died suddenly. Rumor said he had been poisoned by the pope, the Borgia Alexander VI, to prevent the French from using him against Bayezid, with whom (rumor said) Alexander had an alliance.[6]

After Jem's death, Bayezid could act more freely. King John Albert of Poland (d. 1501) was attempting to win control of Moldavia; Bayezid thwarted this attempt and, in alliance with the Tatars of southern Russia, launched a raid into Poland in 1498. At the same time he was building up his fleet, not only constructing his own ships but following the normal practice among the Christian naval powers of employing corsairs—licensed privateers—as part of his fleet. These corsairs could carry on the war against Christian powers even when Bayezid's own fleet was not at sea. War broke out between Bayezid and Venice, and the Venetians suffered heavy losses. Pope Alexander VI granted the Venetians crusade indulgences, but could not persuade other Christian powers to help against the Muslims. Other Italian cities were relieved to see the powerful Venetians on the losing side; Milan and Naples allied with Bayezid against Venice. The Venetians persuaded the Hungarians to support them, but they could make no progress against the Ottomans and both soon made peace—Venice in 1502 and Hungary in 1503.

THE SIXTEENTH CENTURY

With the start of the sixteenth century, the war between western Christendom and the Ottomans moved into a new phase. The idea of crusading was still very much alive in Europe; the wars against the Ottomans were publicized as crusades, and those who took part were promised the crusade indulgence. The Ottomans posed a great threat to Christian Europe, and the crusade still provided the best framework for meeting that threat. At the same time, however, the Ottomans were becoming an important force on the European political stage. Christian powers had always allied with Muslim powers in the Holy Land and in the Iberian Peninsula, while Poland and the Teutonic Order had allied with pagan Lithuania. In the sixteenth century, leading Christian nations such as France (in the 1520s under Francis I) and England (in the 1580s under Elizabeth I) began to make friendly diplomatic contact with the Ottoman Turks.

In 1512, Sultan Bayezid II abdicated in favor of his son Selim. Selim's first priority was to deal with his Muslim enemies in the Middle East. In 1516 he defeated the army of the Mamluk sultan Qansuh Ghawri at Marj Dabiq, north of Aleppo. The Mamluk sultan was killed and his army fled. Selim occupied Syria, Lebanon, and Palestine, and in 1517 he occupied Egypt. The Mamluk and Ottoman domains were now united under one sultan.

Selim died in 1520 and was succeeded by his young son Suleiman or Süleyman I, termed "the magnificent" by western Europeans (see biography). He attacked Hungary in 1521, capturing the city of Belgrade. In 1522 he led a naval force to besiege the island of Rhodes. The island surrendered, and the Hospital of St. John left at the beginning of 1523.

The German princes were very anxious about Süleyman's advance into Hungary, but it was clear that none of the great European Christian powers was about to launch a crusade. King Francis I of France was a prisoner of the emperor Charles V after being captured at the Battle of

Pavia in 1525. In Germany, the preaching of Martin Luther and his followers was arousing popular doubt over whether the pope could legally call crusades against non-Christians. Those princes who supported Luther would only grant military aid to the emperor to fight the Turks if he would agree to make religious concessions. Eventually the German Diet of Speyer of 1526 agreed to send money to help the Hungarians. But the Hungarian army was defeated at Mohács in 1526, and King Louis II (Lajos) killed. Süleyman occupied the capital, Buda. He then had to withdraw because of rebellion in Asia Minor, but Hungary was divided by political upheaval over who would succeed King Louis. King Francis I, who had sent naval forces against the Turks in 1518 and 1520 and who in 1526 was declaring that one of his main aims was to organize an expedition against the Turks, now began diplomatic contacts with Süleyman. He was far less worried about the Turks than about the threat to France from Emperor Charles V, who was ruler of Germany and Spain and dominant in Italy. Francis hoped to use the Turks to distract Charles V from attacking French territory.

In 1529 Süleyman returned to the Balkans, set up his ally John Zápolya as king of Hungary, raided Bavaria and Bohemia, and besieged Vienna. Germany was in a panic; both Catholic and Protestant princes united in sending military forces to relieve Vienna. Süleyman withdrew. He returned in 1532, but had to withdraw again.

THE END OF OTTOMAN EXPANSION

The Christian victory at Vienna was far from the end of the Ottoman threat to Christian Europe. Turkish ships and Turkish-sponsored corsairs continued to harass Christian shipping and settlements in the Mediterranean until well into the eighteenth century, disrupting trade and taking slaves and booty. Islands could be made uninhabitable by repeated raids; coastal ports were in constant danger. Süleyman's forces besieged Malta in 1565 but were rebuffed. The Ottomans captured Cyprus in 1571, accompanied by tales of appalling atrocities committed during the siege and after the capture. Crete was besieged between 1645 and 1669, finally falling to the Turks despite all the aid sent from Europe, while in 1683 the Ottomans besieged Vienna a second time. Catholic rulers set up holy leagues against the Ottomans. After several years without a base, in 1530 the Hospital of St. John accepted the island of Malta from

Emperor Charles V. From that base the Hospitallers continued to wage naval warfare against the Ottomans in the Mediterranean, while what was left of the Teutonic Order after the Reformation took part in the campaigns against the Turks in Hungary. The Teutonic knights were involved against the Turks in Crete in 1668, in the battle of Zenta in 1697, and at Belgrade in 1717. They also fought for the German emperor against the French.[7]

However, the Ottoman Empire never reached farther into Europe than Vienna. In that respect, the repulse of Süleyman's forces from Vienna in 1529 by a combined force of Catholics and Protestants is a suitable point at which to conclude this short survey. Protestant Europe would applaud victories over the Turks, such as at Malta in 1565 and Lepanto in 1571, but Protestants could not take part in crusades, for they did not accept the need for indulgences nor acknowledge the authority of the pope. After 1529 European Christians continued to fight holy wars against the Ottomans, but they were no longer wars fought by the united forces of western Christendom against a common enemy. With the coming of the Protestant Reformation, "the crusade" in the medieval sense had changed forever.

NOTES

1. On the origins and history of the Ottomans, see Colin Imber, *The Ottoman Empire, 1300–1650: The Structure of Power* (Basingstoke and New York: Palgrave Macmillan, 2002). Much of this chapter is based on Imber's study.

2. Imber, *Ottoman Empire*, pp. 128–37.

3. Imber, *Ottoman Empire*, p. 15; Kenneth M. Setton, *The Papacy and the Levant (1204–1571)*, vol. 2, *The Fifteenth Century* (Philadelphia: American Philosophical Society, 1978), pp. 238, 249, 327, 345.

4. Norman Housley, *The Later Crusades: From Lyons to Alcazar, 1274–1580* (Oxford and New York: Oxford University Press, 1992), pp. 76–78.

5. Imber, *Ottoman Empire*, pp. 32–34.

6. Abbé de Vertot, *Histoire des chevaliers hospitaliers de S. Jean de Jérusalem, appellez depuis chevaliers de Rhodes, et aujourd'hui chevaliers de Malte*, 5 vols. (Paris: Rollin, Quillau and Desaint, 1726), bk. 7, vol. 3, pp. 191–92.

7. Kenneth M. Setton, *Venice, Austria, and the Turks in the Seventeenth Century* (Philadelphia: American Philosophical Society, 1991); George Hill, *A History of Cyprus*, vol. 3, *The Frankish Period, 1432–1571* (Cambridge: Cambridge University Press, 1948), pp. 950–1040, especially pp. 1032–33, 1035, and note

also pp. 986–87; Helen Nicholson, *The Knights Hospitaller* (Woodbridge, Suffolk, and Rochester, NY: Boydell, 2001), pp. 121–29; Bernhard Demel, "Welfare and Warfare in the Teutonic Order," in Helen Nicholson, ed., *The Military Orders*, vol. 2, *Welfare and Warfare* (Aldershot, Hants., and Brookfield, VT: Ashgate, 1998), pp. 61–73, here pp. 70–72.

CHAPTER 6

CONCLUSION: THE IMPACT OF CRUSADING ON HISTORY

IMMEDIATE RESULTS OF CRUSADING

The results of crusading varied from area to area. In the Middle East, the Muslims won the crusades. The crusades to the Balkans were unable to prevent the Ottoman Turks from invading and conquering Eastern Europe from the fourteenth century onward. However, the crusaders did slow down Islamic advance. Saladin was never able to cross the Mediterranean and conquer Europe, as his friend Bāhā' al-Dīn ibn Shaddād believed he wished to do. When the Ottoman Turks advanced into the Balkans in the late fourteenth century, their advance was slowed by Albanian, Serbian, and Hungarian military action, including crusades. The Ottoman Turks did not reach Vienna until 1529, and were turned back by a crusade.

The Ottoman Empire ruled the Balkans, Egypt, and the Middle East until the nineteenth century. As the empire weakened, the western European powers supported it in the Balkans as a barrier to expansionist Russia. Egypt was occupied by the British in the 1880s, while France and Germany, and later Italy, showed an active interest in the affairs of northern Africa and the Middle East. After the destruction of the Ottoman Empire in the First World War, France and Britain played a central role in the creation of new states in the Middle East. The nations of western Europe justified their interventions in the Ottoman Empire on the basis that they were continuing their ancestors' crusading traditions. In fact, there was no religious or chronological continuity between medieval crusading and nineteenth- and twentieth-century imperialism.

The direct legacy of the crusades in the Middle East had another aspect. After the destruction of the kingdom of Jerusalem in 1291, the Muslim rulers of Syria and Palestine continued to allow Christian pilgrims to visit the holy places. Arguably, the threat of further crusades if pilgrims were hindered may have encouraged these rulers to allow unhindered access. The networks of European religious orders that existed in the Middle East to assist pilgrims dated from the time of the crusader states. Had the crusader states not existed, the pilgrims to the Holy Land would have found their journey much more difficult and dangerous.

The crusades in the Iberian Peninsula, in contrast, achieved their aim in that Muslim rulers were replaced by Christian rulers. Initially, the conquered Muslims were allowed to keep their own law and practice their religion. Much beautiful Islamic architecture survives in the Iberian Peninsula to this day. However, after the fall of Granada in 1492, the degree of coexistence between different religious groups in the peninsula came to an end. Not only the Muslims but also the Jews and dissident Christian groups were forced into Catholicism.

The impact of the crusades in northeastern Europe was more complex. Here, crusading against pagans in Prussia and the Baltic States took place alongside German colonization of these areas. The Teutonic Order's conquests in Prussia, Lithuania, Latvia, Estonia, and what is now Russian territory gave twentieth-century German rulers a pretext for claiming territory in these areas, contributing toward two world wars in the twentieth century. It is not surprising that many eastern European historians have tended to regard the crusades in this area as simply disguised German imperialism. However, in the Middle Ages, Germany was too divided and the western emperor was too weak to initiate the crusades purely with the aim of conquering eastern Europe. The crusades were more the result of the German nobility's desire to win honor and glory in holy war against the enemies of Christendom. Clearly the peoples of this area—Catholic, Russian Orthodox, and pagan—suffered severely during the crusading period. From the point of view of western Christendom, the crusades did succeed in ensuring that these areas were oriented toward the West. If the Teutonic Order and the German crusaders had not moved into this area, the Russian princes would have moved in from the east. The crusades in this area limited and slowed down Russian expansion westward, so that whereas the princes of Novgorod were expanding their influence northward into Finland in the early thirteenth century, the grand duke of Moscow did not move westward into Livonia until the late fifteenth century. The Teutonic Order's presence in the Baltic forged strong historic links between the West and the Baltic States of Latvia, Estonia, and Lithuania, which are now being exploited to these states' advantage as they develop as independent nations. In contrast, the Greeks' traditions about the destruction that the Ottoman Turks inflicted on them during the later Middle Ages and early modern period have encouraged Greeks to oppose the admission of Turkey into the European Union.

It is debatable how far the crusades directly resulted in the spread of Christianity. The original purpose of the crusade was to defend Christendom, not to convert; in the Middle East and the Iberian Peninsula, the crusade was also intended to recover former Christian territory. However, crusaders hoped that Christian military success would encourage non-Christians to convert to Christianity.[1] Crusade and mission operated alongside each other in Prussia and the Baltic States. The crusades to the Holy Land gave Latin Christian missionaries an opportunity to come into the area and to preach. In the Iberian Peninsula, the crusade did not result in mass conversions of Muslims or Jews to Christianity until after the fall of Granada in 1492, when Isabella and Ferdinand instituted a program of forced conversion. The crusades against heretics did have some success. The Albigensian Crusades destroyed the noble families who supported the Cathar heresy in southern France in the early thirteenth century, yet the crusades against the Hussites in Bohemia in the 1420s made little impact on the Hussite heresy.

CULTURAL IMPACT

Catholic Christians did learn from the Muslims as a result of the crusades. In the eleventh and twelfth centuries, the crusades in the Iberian Peninsula brought ancient Greek scholarship to the notice of western European scholars through the recovery of the extensive library at Toledo in 1085. Arab learning based on this Greek scholarship came into western Europe through Spain and through southern Italy. The Palestinian Franks also took up Arab scientific learning.[2] The Franks

atouz les testes copet: se lost des xpiens passout iusques a tunes. et se il m aloit cut: il les deliueroit touz.

Comment mesire iehan diacre bouteil lier de france qui faisoit le guer daus tins sarrazins qui requiert le baptisme.

Figure 4. Crusade leaders and Muslims meet outside Acre, 1250–54, during the first crusade of King Louis IX of France, from a fourteenth-century French manuscript. British Library Picture Library.

also learned from the Muslims at an everyday level; the twelfth-century Syrian nobleman Usamā ibn Munqidh depicted them adopting the local customs of bathing regularly and eating Muslim food.[3]

Arab literature made some impact in the West. There is no doubt that *The Seven Sages of Rome* cycle, a series of fictional stories written in French in the second half of the thirteenth century, was heavily influenced by oriental tradition. Literary scholars have argued that other great works of western literature, such as Boccaccio's *Decameron* and Dante's *Commedia*, were influenced by Arab literature. The question is whether this influence occurred because of the crusades or through normal trade. Both Boccaccio and Dante were writing in the merchant cities of northern Italy, where merchants had regular trading contact with Muslims. *The Seven Sages of Rome* cycle is set in Italy and in the Byzantine Empire, and it is likely that these stories reached France via trading connections between Constantinople and Rome.[4]

Some European literature was inspired in whole or in part by the wars between Christians and Muslims. The *Chanson de Roland* (Song of Roland), arguably the most famous and influential piece of medieval European fictional literature, was based on the battle of Roncesvalles in northern Spain in 778. The original battle was between the forces of the emperor Charlemagne and the Christian Basques, but in the *chanson*, it becomes a battle between Christians and Muslims. Although the Muslims are depicted as valiant warriors, the Christians defeat them and the Muslims are either killed or converted to Christianity. The *Chanson de Roland* was translated into many European languages, and the hero Roland and his companions became the focus of a whole cycle of epic stories about Charlemagne's wars. In the late fourteenth and fifteenth centuries, under his Italian name of Orlando, Roland became the hero of two great Italian romances—Matteo Maria Boiardo's *Orlando innamorato* and Ludovico Ariosto's *Orlando Furioso*.[5]

The crusades to the Holy Land were the basis of a whole French cycle of stories, known as the Crusade cycle. Various writers added to this and rewrote it between the early twelfth and the fifteenth centuries.[6] Other literature produced in the West also reflected the combats of the crusades.[7] In the sixteenth century the First Crusade was the basis of Torquato Tasso's famous romantic poem *La Gerusalemme liberata*, which inspired many imitations and adaptations.[8]

In contrast, the Muslims took very little from the medieval European Christians, except for adopting some of their military skills and practices—especially siege techniques, such as undermining an enemy's fortifications. It was not until the sixteenth century and later that the Muslims began to take any interest in other aspects of European Christian culture, such as art.[9]

ECONOMIC IMPACT

While scholars agree that the crusades had an economic impact on medieval Europe, they do not agree over the nature and extent of that impact. In recent years, many scholars have argued that one of the main contributions of the crusades to European history was in encouraging the development of systems of taxation assessment and collection in order to pay for crusades. Because of the demands of crusading, European governments were forced to develop and improve their systems of administration more quickly than they might otherwise have done, thereby hastening the development of the modern state. In addition, systems of lending money (what we would now call "banking") and transportation had to be developed to enable the crusaders to equip themselves and travel to the crusading front. In this respect, the crusades had a major impact on the lives of Europeans.[10]

However, it could be argued that the kings who took part in the crusades already had the necessary governmental machinery in place. The only reason King Richard I of England could have organized his crusade in 1189 and departed so quickly from England was because England already had one of the most centralized governmental systems in western Europe. King Louis IX of France's impressive organization of his crusade relied on the administrative reorganization carried through by his grandfather King Philip II. By this argument, crusading was not a cause of governmental development, although it may have been a catalyst; it was a *result* of governmental development.[11]

The crusades certainly boosted the demand for certain products in the West, such as armor, horses, and certain foodstuffs. This would have encouraged production, thereby providing a boost to the economy. On the other hand, crusading also disrupted trade because the areas of fighting were on important trade routes.[12] Crusades took large numbers of able-bodied workers away from their work (and many of them did not return) and removed central governmental figures from the country for long periods of time, allowing law and order to break down.

The merchant cities of Italy, Genoa, Venice, and Pisa benefited from the trading rights that they were given in the Latin East. Yet the wars with Egypt and Syria also damaged their trade. The crusades did not encourage trade between Christians and Muslims. In fact, the papacy often threatened merchants who traded with Muslims with excommunication for trading with the enemy, although these trade embargoes had little effect; trade continued regardless of the crusades. In short, the economic impact of the crusades was both positive and negative.

IMPACT ON ATTITUDES

The crusades did not create negative western Christian ideas about Muslims. The Christians already regarded the Muslims as a terrible threat to Christianity long before the crusades began. Arguably, by bringing more western Christians into contact with Muslims, the crusades actually improved western Christian ideas about Muslims. Muslim men came to be viewed as romantic, dashing, chivalric warriors, while Muslim women were either beautiful, intelligent, resourceful, and loyal, or wise, resourceful, and cunning. In contrast, the Muslims admired the Christian warriors' courage but regarded them as rash and uncultured, and uncaring about the honor of their womenfolk. The Muslims thought that European Christian women were immoral and far too ready to be familiar with strange men.

In nineteenth- and twentieth-century Europe, the crusades to the Middle East came to be seen as a forerunner and a justification of European imperialist expansion into the Middle East. French and British conquests in Syria and Palestine during the First World War were depicted by some in the West as a successful ending to the medieval crusades. Others, following the same interpretation of the crusade movement but turning it on its head, argued that the crusades had been an example of unacceptable Western imperialist arrogance.[13]

In the late twentieth century, it became a commonplace of popular scholarship to say that the crusades had turned Muslims against Christians forever, ruining Islamic-Christian relations. In fact, until the end of the nineteenth century, Muslims took little interest in the crusades; there was no history of the crusades available in Arabic until 1865, and that was a translation of a French work. The first history of the crusades by a Muslim writer was published in 1899. This book showed that some in the Muslim world were aware of the European idea that the modern campaigns in the Middle East were a continuation of the crusades, but Muslims in general were not very interested in this interpretation of modern history.[14]

It was not until after the foundation of the modern state of Israel that the Arab world developed its modern view of the crusades as barbarous and unprovoked invasions that have continued under different guises until the present day. Ironically, the modern Islamic view of Saladin as a great champion of Islam is based on medieval and nineteenth-century European Christian respect for Saladin rather than Muslim tradition. In Muslim tradition, Saladin had always been regarded as an outsider, far less important than Nūr al-Dīn or Baibars.[15] In short, nations and individuals have interpreted the crusades to suit their own political agendas.[16]

FINALLY

Some scholars have argued that the discovery of the Americas was a direct result of the crusades. Christopher Columbus himself wrote that he had hoped to reach Jerusalem by sailing west rather than traveling east, as that route was closed by the Muslim conquests. When the hope of reaching Jerusalem via the western route proved to be impractical, the Americas were seen as a new opportunity sent by God to compensate the Christian faithful for the loss of the Holy Land. The military religious Order of Christ—originally set up in 1319 by King Denis of Portugal with the properties of the dissolved Order of the Temple to continue the war against the Muslims in the Iberian Peninsula—played an important role in mission work in the Portuguese exploration of the Americas.

The crusade indulgence was one of the activities of the Church that aroused Martin Luther's protests in his ninety-five theses (1517).[17] Thus, indirectly, the crusades helped to bring about the Reformation.

With the Reformation, western Christendom was divided, and the whole ethos of crusading as representing Christendom united against its enemies came to an end. However, some political commentators would argue that the modern Western conviction that it is the duty of the free West to impose civilization, capitalism, or democracy on the rest of the world is similar to the ideology of medieval crusading.

NOTES

1. On this subject, see Benjamin Z. Kedar, *Crusade and Mission: European Approaches towards the Muslims* (Princeton, NJ: Princeton University Press, 1984).

2. I. Draelants, A. Tihon, and B. van den Abeele, eds., *Occident et Proche-Orient: contacts scientifiques au temps des croisades: actes du colloque de Louvain-la-Neuve, 24 et 25 mars 1997* (Turnhout: Brepols, 2000).

3. Philip K. Hitti, *An Arab-Syrian Gentleman and Warrior in the Period of the Crusades: Memoirs of Usāmah ibn-Munqidh* (Princeton, NJ: Princeton University Press, 1987), pp. 165–66, 169–70.

4. *The Seven Sages of Rome, and the Book of Sindbad*, ed. Hans R. Runte, J. Keith Wikeley, Anthony J. Farrell, with the collaboration of the Society of the Seven Sages (New York and London: Garland, 1984); *Le Roman de Laurin*, ed. Lewis Thorpe, 2 vols. (Cambridge: Bowes & Bowes, 1950–1958), vol. 1, pp. 89–

117, vol. 2, pp. vii–ix; María Rosa Menocal, *The Arabic Role in Medieval Literary History: A Forgotten Heritage* (Philadelphia: University of Pennsylvania Press, 1987).

5. *Song of Roland*, trans. Glyn Burgess (Harmondsworth: Penguin, 1990); Ludovico Ariosto, *Orlando furioso: The Frenzy of Orlando: A Romantic Epic*, trans. Barbara Reynolds, 2 vols. (Harmondsworth: Penguin, 1975).

6. The "First Crusade Cycle" is published by Alabama University Press (1975–2003), ed. Jan A. Nelson, Emanuel J. Mickel, and others. For a study of the so-called "second cycle," see Robert F. Cook and Larry S. Crist, *Le Deuxième Cycle de la Croisade* (Geneva: Droz, 1972).

7. David Trotter, *Medieval French Literature and the Crusades, 1100–1300* (Geneva: Droz, 1987); Friedrich-Wilhelm Wentzlaff-Eggebert, *Kreuzzugsdichtung des Mittelalters: Studien zu ihrer geschichtlichn und dicherischen Wirklichkeit* (Berlin: de Gruyter, 1960); Helen Nicholson, *Love, War and the Grail: Templars, Hospitallers and Teutonic Knights in Medieval Epic and Romance, 1150–1500* (Leiden: Brill, 2001).

8. *Torquato Tasso's "Jerusalem Delivered,"* trans. Joseph Tusiani (Rutherford: Fairleigh Dickinson University Press, 1970); Elizabeth Siberry, "Tales of the Opera: The Crusades," *Medieval History* 3 (1993): 21–25.

9. Bernard Lewis, *The Muslim Discovery of Europe* (New York: W. W. Norton, 1982), pp. 221–22, 223–27, 239–43; Oleg Grabar, "The Crusades and the Development of Islamic Art," in Laiou and Mottahedeh, eds., *The Crusades from the Perspective of Byzantium and the Muslim World*, pp. 235–45.

10. Malcolm Barber, *The Two Cities, Medieval Europe 1050–1320* (London: Routledge, 1992), p. 139. See also Giles Constable, "The Financing of the Crusades in the Twelfth Century," in Benjamin Z. Kedar, Hans Eberhard Mayer, and R. C. Smail, eds., *Outremer: Studies in the History of the Crusading Kingdom of Jerusalem Presented to Joshua Prawer* (Jerusalem: Yad Izhak Ben-Zvi Institute, 1982), pp. 64–88.

11. Simon Lloyd, "The Crusading Movement, 1096–1274," in Jonathan Riley-Smith, ed., *The Oxford Illustrated History of the Crusades* (Oxford and New York: Oxford University Press, 1995), pp. 34–65, here p. 56.

12. Ibid., p. 65.

13. Elizabeth Siberry, "Images of the Crusades in the Nineteenth and Twentieth Centuries," in Riley-Smith, ed., *Oxford Illustrated History of the Crusades*, pp. 365–85; Jonathan Riley-Smith, "Islam and the Crusades in History and Imagination, 1 November 1898–11 September 2001," *Crusades* 2 (2003): 151–67.

14. Riley-Smith, "Islam and the Crusades," 160–61; Hillenbrand, *The Crusades: Islamic Perspectives*, pp. 589–90.

15. Riley-Smith, "Islam and the Crusades," 161–64; Hillenbrand, *The Crusades: Islamic Perspectives*, pp. 590–616.

16. For other modern uses of the image of crusading, see Daniel Gutwein and Sophia Menache, "Just War, Crusade and *Jihad*: Conflicting Propaganda Strategies during the Gulf Crisis (1990–1991)," *Revue Belge de Philologie et d'Histoire* 80 (2002): 385–400; Tomaz Mastnak, *Crusading Peace: Christendom, the Muslim World, and Western Political Order* (Berkeley, CA: University of California Press, 2002), pp. 346–47.

17. Grimm, ed., *Luther's Works*, vol. 31, *Career of the Reformer: I*, pp. 27–33.

BIOGRAPHIES

Baibars al-Bunduqdāri (sultan of Egypt, 1260–77), *Prominent Muslim Sultan and General*

A Mamluk, one of Sultan al-Ṣāliḥ Ayyūb's elite Baḥrī Mamluks who seized power in Egypt in 1250. The Arab historian al-Maqrīzī credited him with striking the first blow in the murder of Sultan Tūrān-Shāh. He was the general, under the Mamluk sultan Qutuz, who defeated the Mongol army at 'Ain Jālūt in Galilee in 1260. Shortly after the battle, Sultan Qutuz was murdered by the Baḥrī Mamluks, whose former leader he had murdered in 1254. As present leader of the Baḥriyya, Baibars now became sultan of Egypt. He was not renowned for his piety, but he was an excellent general and ruler.

Baibars set out to destroy the remaining crusader states. In 1263 he attacked Nazareth and threatened Acre, the capital of the kingdom of Jerusalem since 1191. In 1265 he captured Caesarea, Haifa, and Arsuf and again threatened Acre (see Map 1, p. 11). In 1266 he attacked Cilician Armenia, to the north of the crusader states, and also captured Toron (now Tibnīn in Lebanon) and the castle of Safed in Galilee, thereby winning control of the north of the kingdom of Jerusalem. He had promised that if Safed surrendered, all the defenders would be allowed to go in peace; but in fact he arrested and executed them.

In 1268 he captured Jaffa and besieged Antioch. The city surrendered and the inhabitants were massacred. As Hugh III, king of Cyprus and Jerusalem, was unable to bring military aid to the nobles of the kingdom, they had to come to terms with Baibars. In 1269 Isabella of Ibelin, lady of Beirut, made a separate truce with him, and he took Beirut under his protection. In 1271 John of Montfort, lord of Tyre, made a separate truce to cover Tyre alone. In 1271 Baibars captured the castles of Chastel Blanc, or Safitha (Templar), Crac des Chevaliers (Hospitaller), and Montfort (Teutonic knights). When the Lord Edward (later King Edward I of England) arrived at Acre on crusade, he made a truce with Baibars for eleven years. Assured now that the Franks would not be a threat to him, Baibars campaigned against other dangerous neighbors: the Seljuk Turks in Asia Minor, the Mongols in the north and east, the Armenians in the northwest, and the Nubians in the south of his territories.

Baibars died in 1277. By the time of his death, the Franks held only a handful of coastal cities. Tripoli would fall in 1289 and the rest in 1291.

Boabdil (Abū ʿAbd Allāh Muḥammad XI, king of Granada, 1482–92), *Last Muslim King of Granada*

The son of Abū al-Ḥasan ʿAlī ("Muley Hacén"), king of Granada, by his first wife.[1] By the 1480s, the Muslim kingdom of Granada at the southern tip of the Iberian Peninsula was under severe military pressure from the Christian kingdom of Castile to the north. In July 1282, Boabdil and his brother Yusuf fled from Granada to the city of Guadix, where Boabdil was declared king. The people of the city of Granada accepted Boabdil as king and his father and uncle, Abū ʿAbd Allāh Muḥammad az-Zaghall ("el Zagal," the valiant) were forced to flee to Málaga. The kingdom of Granada was divided into two warring parts.

In spring 1483, Boabdil attacked southern Castile, but was defeated and captured by the forces of Queen Isabella and King Ferdinand of Castile-Aragon. To win his release, he agreed to the Pact of Córdoba, by which he would hand over the part of the kingdom of Granada held by his uncle in return for the aid of Castile-Aragon in winning the city of Granada. On his release, he continued to fight his father and uncle while the Castilians attacked them from the north.

El Zagal deposed Muley Hacén and made himself king of Granada. In 1485 Muley Hacén died and Boabdil made peace with his uncle. In 1487 the city of Málaga fell to the Castilians, who now controlled the whole of western Granada. Boabdil offered to surrender the city of Granada to Isabella and Ferdinand in return for being allowed to rule Guadix and other towns in eastern Granada as a vassal of Castile-Aragon.

Isabella and Ferdinand agreed, and El Zagal surrendered to them rather than accept his nephew's authority. It appeared that Isabella and Ferdinand now had effective control of what was left of Granada—but Boabdil then went back on his promise of alliance and decided to fight them.

Isabella and Ferdinand assembled their army to attack Boabdil. Part of the army was drawn from the nobility and the towns, but there were also contingents supplied by the military religious orders and volunteers who had taken the cross and come to fight for Christ. The army was financed by crusade taxes and crusade indulgences. The Castilian army advanced to the city of Granada and began to set up a siege. As it became clear that the Muslims of Granada would not be able to withstand the large Christian army, Boabdil began to negotiate for terms of surrender. It was agreed that the Muslims would be allowed to continue to practice their faith. They could keep their property, and they would be governed by their own laws. Boabdil himself would be given lordship over the Alpujarras region to the south of Granada. Boabdil accepted the terms, and in January 1492 he surrendered the city.

Isabella and Ferdinand did not want the Muslim leaders to remain in Granada, in case they started a revolt, so they encouraged them to leave. In 1493 Boabdil and about 6,000 Spanish Muslims left for North Africa, where Boabdil died in battle in 1527. Though Boabdil and his people could certainly not withstand the military might and religious enthusiasm of Castile-Aragon, Isabella and Ferdinand had also encouraged and exploited divisions within the ruling family of Granada and taken advantage of Boabdil's ambitions to win his cooperation.

Bohemond "of Taranto" (d. 1111), *Prominent Christian Leader in the First Crusade*

Son of Robert Guiscard (d. 1085) and his first wife Aubrée. Robert Guiscard was a minor noble from Normandy who conquered Sicily in the 1060s and 1070s with the assistance of his younger brother, Roger (d. 1101), and later attacked Byzantine territory. Bohemond assisted his father in his campaigns, including his attack on Dyrrachium (Durazzo, now Durrës in Albania) on the eastern coast of the Adriatic Sea in 1081–82. On his father's death, he inherited his father's conquests in that area, but the Byzantines soon reconquered them, leaving Bohemond landless. According to one contemporary account, Bohemond was besieging the Italian city of Amalfi when he heard about the First Crusade in 1096. He promptly cut his best cloak into crosses to distribute to his followers, and led his army east to join the other crusaders.

At Constantinople, Bohemond made a great impression on Anna, the young daughter of Emperor Alexios Comnenos, who later described him in her history of her father's reign as a terrifying barbarian, cunning and clever. Alexios required all the crusade leaders to swear an oath to return to him all the territories they conquered that had belonged to the Byzantine emperor before the recent Turkish invasions. Bohemond took this oath.

He played an important role among the leaders of the crusade as the crusade advanced across Asia Minor, and was instrumental in capturing Antioch. Having obtained control of the city, he refused to surrender it to Alexios, claiming that Alexios' failure to come to the assistance of the crusaders had nullified the oaths sworn to him. Bohemond did not join the other crusaders on their march to Jerusalem but remained in Antioch, extending his conquests with the help of his nephew and ally Tancred. In August 1100, Bohemond was captured by the Danishmend emir in eastern Asia Minor. Tancred took over in Antioch in his absence, and continued to conquer former Byzantine territory. Bohemond was finally ransomed and freed in 1103. He and other Frankish leaders took part in an attack on the city of Harran (south of Edessa) in 1104, but this failed disastrously.

Emperor Alexios took advantage of Bohemond's recent setbacks to attack his territory in Cilicia and Syria. Anna Comnena related that to escape Alexios' forces and reach the West to get aid, Bohemond faked his own death and escaped from Antioch hidden in a coffin, leaving his nephew Tancred to rule Antioch. Back in western Europe, he recruited troops to help him attack the Byzantines. An attack on Dyrrachium in 1107 was unsuccessful, and in 1108 he had to make peace with Alexios in the Treaty of Devol. Alexios allowed Bohemond to keep Antioch, but he had to surrender his other Byzantine conquests. However, as Tancred did not agree to this treaty, it was not put into effect.

Bohemond returned to Italy, where he died in 1111. Modern historians regard Bohemond as a skilled and unscrupulous military leader who wanted to gain land and power, rather than a religious man who joined the crusade to serve Christ.

Frederick II of Hohenstaufen, emperor (b. 1194, d. 1250), *Christian Crusading Leader*

Born on December 26, 1194, only child of Constance, queen of Sicily, and her husband the emperor Henry VI of Hohenstaufen, ruler of the western empire. From his parents, Frederick inherited the kingdom of Sicily, a claim to rule the western empire, and an interest in the Holy Land. As king of Sicily he had many Muslims among his subjects. Although he was notoriously friendly toward Muslims and employed them in his armies, he was a fervent persecutor of heretics.

Orphaned before he was five, Frederick became a ward of the pope, Innocent III (1198–1216). After a long period of war, Frederick formally came of age in December 1208 and took over the government of Sicily. In 1212 he traveled north to claim the crown of Germany. The Welf Otto of Brunswick had been crowned emperor in 1209, but had quickly alienated the pope and key members of the German nobility. In December 1212 Frederick was crowned king of Germany at Mainz, and at the Battle of Bouvines on July 27, 1214, Frederick's ally Philip II of France defeated Otto and his allies. Frederick was crowned king of Germany at the imperial city of Aachen. In 1220 he traveled to Rome, where he was crowned emperor by Pope Honorius III, and he promised to go on crusade. He was expected to join the Fifth Crusade, which was then in Egypt, but he did not. Instead, he concentrated on reforming government in Sicily—making royal power more effective, and trying to enforce imperial rights in northern Italy. His reforms indicate that he believed that a king is appointed by God to protect his people and has authority over the Church. In contrast, he devolved his power in Germany to the German nobles.

The western emperors had long had an interest in the Holy Land and had a tradition of crusading. In addition, since 1196, the western emperors had been overlords of the island of Cyprus, which had been conquered by the crusaders in 1191 and was an important supply base for crusades to the East. In 1225 Frederick married Isabel II, queen of Jerusalem. He planned to set sail on crusade to the East in 1227, but turned back because he became seriously ill. In the following year Isabel died in childbirth, leaving a baby son, Conrad, as king of Jerusalem. Frederick set sail again, but the pope at the time, Gregory IX, was so exasperated by Frederick's reforms in Italy—which threatened papal authority—and his delays in going on crusade that he excommunicated him. Frederick continued to the East, asserting his authority in Cyprus by arresting key nobles and taking the young king into custody, then proceeding to the kingdom of Jerusalem where he negotiated a peace treaty with the sultan of Egypt, al-Kāmil (1218–38). This treaty returned the city of Jerusalem, except for the Temple Mount, to Christian rule for ten years. He then traveled to Jerusalem and staged a crown-wearing ceremony in the Church of the Holy Sepulchre. As tradition stated that the last emperor to rule before Christ's return to earth would be crowned in Jerusalem, Frederick may have meant to claim that he was the last emperor.

While the people of the kingdom wanted to cooperate with Frederick, the fact that he was excommunicated made relations difficult. He quarreled with the patriarch of Jerusalem and the Templars, and left the kingdom under a cloud (see Document 7).

Back in Italy, war with the papacy and with the northern Italian towns followed. Although Frederick made peace with the pope in 1230, relations deteriorated again because the pope believed that Frederick was aiming at domination of Italy, and in 1239 he excommunicated Frederick. The succeeding pope, Innocent IV, deposed Frederick as emperor in 1245.

Frederick never returned to the Holy Land. Instead, he—and after 1242 his son, Conrad—ruled from a distance through representatives. This was not very successful. In 1243 some of the political leaders in the kingdom of Jerusalem abandoned Frederick's policy of alliance with Egypt and allied with the ruler of Damascus. They recovered Jerusalem but lost it for good in the following year. Frederick condemned the abandonment of his policies but did not return to the East. He died in 1250, still at war with the papacy.

Gediminas of Lithuania (r. 1315/16–1341/42), *Pagan Opponent and Ally of the Crusaders*

Gediminas was the son of Pukuveras, a member of the ruling dynasty of Lithuania, and younger brother of Grand-Duke Vytenis of Lithuania.[2] He took power on his brother's death in the winter of 1315–16. Gediminas called himself "king, by the grace of God," and in many respects his power was similar to that of the Christian kings of Europe—he levied taxes, called on his subjects to perform military service, and made treaties with foreign powers. He seems to have been the first Lithuanian ruler to make Vilnius his principal residence; it later became the capital city of Lithuania. He tried to encourage merchants of the Hanseatic league to travel to Lithuania, and he was anxious to encourage settlers, to increase agricultural production. He expanded the influence and the borders of Lithuania through conquest, through diplomacy, and by marrying off his children (he had seven sons and six daughters) to the ruling families of eastern Europe, who were either Catholic or Orthodox Christians.

Gediminas continued his predecessors' alliance with Livonia, to the north of his kingdom, and maintained his position in relation to the Muslim Mongols or Tatars to the south of his kingdom, with whom he sometimes came to blows and sometimes allied. From the point of view of Catholic Christendom, however, his most important negotiations were with Pope John XXII. In 1322 he wrote to the pope, offering to allow Catholic Christianity to be preached in his territories and even to convert himself. His aim was to obtain a peace treaty to end the appallingly destructive war with the Teutonic Order. He refused to accept baptism from the brothers of the order, as this would be tantamount to a surrender on their terms. The brothers, furious at his attempt to circumvent them by appealing directly to the pope, did all they could to hamper negotiations, even arresting and hanging his messengers and burning the letters Gediminas was sending to the pope. Pope John imposed a peace treaty and sent missionaries to Lithuania, but he could not afford to offend the order, as he needed its political support against the Emperor Louis IV. Gediminas, on the other hand, did not want to offend his Russian Orthodox allies by moving too close to the Catholic cause. He gave up his negotiations with the pope but made a new alliance with King Władysław IV, the Short (Łokietek), of Poland, who was also at war with the Teutonic Order. In 1325 Gediminas' daughter Aldona-Anna married the future King Casimir III of Poland, and Gediminas agreed to supply Władysław with mercenaries to fight the Teutonic Order. In 1328 the war between the order and Lithuania broke out again.

Gediminas never converted to Christianity. He maintained and extended Lithuanian power through his own military might and by alliances with Catholic and Orthodox princes. Yet some of those with whom his forces fought against the Teutonic Order disliked fighting alongside pagans, and it was clear that as long as the Lithuanians remained pagan, they would never have peace from the Teutonic Order.

Gediminas was succeeded in Lithuania by his sons Olgierd (Algirdas) and Kiejstut (Kestutis). His grandson Jagiełło, son of Algirdas, married Queen Jadwiga of Poland in 1386, inaugurating the great Jagiełłonian dynasty of eastern Europe.

Giraude (Guirauda) of Lavaur (d. 1211), A *Leading Heretic during the Albigensian Crusades*

Daughter of Sicard and Blanche de Laurac. When her father died around 1200, her mother became a Cathar perfect and set up a Cathar women's house at Laurac. One of the members was Giraude's sister Mabilla. The rest of Blanche's children were either Cathar sympathizers or believers. Giraude's brother Aimery of Montréal inherited the lordship of Laurac; her sisters married prominent nobles of the area. In this way Cathar supporters among the nobility formed a network across the Albigeois.

Giraude married the lord of Lavaur, a fortified town and castle near Toulouse. On her husband's death, she remained at Lavaur, but her brother Aimery of Montréal acted for her as lord of Lavaur. Peter of Les Vaux de Cernay, a monk who took part in the Albigensian Crusades, called Giraude "a heretic of the worst sort,"[3] but did not explain what she had done to earn the epithet. As lady of Lavaur, she had a reputation as a good hostess; the contemporary commentator William of Tudela praised her generosity in feeding all travelers who sought hospitality at Lavaur. Presumably many of those who benefited from her good works were Cathars: the town was the seat of a Cathar bishopric, and Cathars lived openly there.

Giraude became a victim of the crusade through the actions of her brother. Aimery had initially made his peace with Simon de Montfort and joined the crusade in 1209 when Carcassonne fell to the crusaders. He surrendered Montréal, but it was given back to him on the understanding of his good behavior. However, he was also negotiating with King Peter II of Aragon, bypassing his oath of allegiance to de Montfort, and in 1211 he fortified Lavaur and defied de Montfort. De Montfort marched with a large army of crusaders to attack the town. After a bitter siege, the crusaders captured town and castle, beheaded Aimery and his knights, and threw Giraude down a well. They threw stones in after her, stoning her to death. Many of the prisoners taken at Lavaur were burned as heretics.

Giraude's life had been typical of a noblewoman—first a wife, then a generous and pious widow living off her own means. It was her misfortune that the religion she had chosen was Catharism rather than Latin Christianity. The little information we have about her life indicates that her lifestyle was very much like that of other noblewomen in western Europe who were not heretics. It is noteworthy that she was not burned as a heretic, a degrading punishment reserved for ordinary people. As a noblewoman her honor and virtue were spared, and she was killed without her blood being spilled.

Hermann von Salza (d. 1239), *Master of a Military Order*

Hermann von Salza came from a Thuringian *ministerialis* family, the equivalent of the knights of England and France. One way for a young *ministerialis* to move up in society was to join a religious order. This may have been one reason why Hermann von Salza joined the new military-religious Teutonic Order.

In 1209 Hermann became master of the order. He won the confidence of Frederick II of Hohenstaufen—leading patron of the order—and appears to have often acted more as a trusted friend and courtier than a religious man. He played a very important role in Frederick's crusade to the Holy Land, 1228–29. Frederick praised his aid and support, while condemning the lack of assistance he had received from elsewhere. Hermann also negotiated with Pope Gregory IX on Frederick's behalf, persuading the pope to lift the excommunication on the emperor in 1230. He was Frederick's negotiator with the Lombard League of northern Italian cities in the 1230s, and he acted as negotiator between Frederick and the German nobility. As relations between pope and emperor deteriorated in the late 1230s, Hermann worked tirelessly to bring the two sides together, but he was unsuccessful; in 1239, Pope Gregory IX excommunicated Frederick a second time, and Hermann died, as if brokenhearted by his failure.

However, Hermann's most important action was not in Frederick's service but as master of his order. The Teutonic Order was founded in the late twelfth century, when the Catholic Christians in the Holy Land were losing territory, and so the order had difficulty in obtaining land from which to finance its operations. In 1211 King Andrew II of Hungary granted the order Burzenland, on his southeastern frontier, in what is now Transylvania. The order's possessions formed a buffer between Hungary and the pagan tribes living to the east. Under Hermann's leadership, the order began to bring in colonists, found towns, and populate the area; one of the towns was even called Hermannstadt, after the master. However, the Hungarian nobility regarded the growing German influence in Hungary with alarm, and in 1225 Andrew drove out the order.

At this time, Poland was a divided kingdom. One of its dukes, Conrad of Cujavia and Masovia, asked Hermann for the order's assistance. He complained of savage border raiding by pagan Prussian tribes, but he probably also wanted to expand his territories and increase his power. He offered the order land at Kulm (which was in Prussian territory, not Polish) in return for military aid. After the order's experiences in Hungary, Hermann hesitated. He obtained Frederick II's approval for the undertaking in the Golden Bull of Rimini (1226), and in 1234 Pope Gregory IX also approved it. Both leaders allowed the order to keep any territory it captured to form an independent state. It is not clear whether this is what Conrad had originally intended. In any case, the Teutonic Order began military operations in Prussia, defeated the Prussians, and set up an independent state. In 1237 the order also took over the military-religious order of the Swordbrothers in Livonia.

Under Hermann von Salza, the Teutonic Order developed from a small military-religious order to an influential order with contacts in the imperial and papal courts and an important military presence in northeastern Europe.

Innocent III (pope, 1198–1216), *a Pope Who Began Three Crusades*

Born Lothar of Segni and elected pope at the age of thirty-seven, he was a reformer who preferred diplomacy to force and yet launched three crusades: the fourth, the fifth, and the crusades against the Albigensian heretics. Within the papal court, he reformed papal administration. He believed that as pope he had the authority to make and unmake kings; he excommunicated the emperor Otto IV for failing to keep a promise not to invade Sicily; King Philip II of France for refusing to take back his second wife, Ingebourg of Denmark; and King John of England for refusing to accept the pope's choice of Stephen Langton as archbishop of Canterbury. Innocent wanted to reform Christendom, so he also corrected the faults of religious orders. He wanted to bring heretics back into the Christian Church, and negotiated with both the Humiliati (Humble people) and the Waldensian heretics in an attempt to reconcile them to the Church—but this was only partly successful. He approved Francis of Assisi's new religious movement in 1210, whereas popes before and after him would probably have rejected the wandering, poor preachers as heretical. In 1215 he held the Fourth Lateran Council, attended by many bishops and abbots from Latin Christendom, which attempted to reform the Church, setting down a statement of faith and guidelines for the education and lifestyle of priests.

As soon as he became pope, Innocent called a new crusade to the East, levying a tax on the clergy and authorizing crusade preaching. The crusade set off four years later in spring 1202, but was diverted to Constantinople. The initial plan was to install Alexios Angelos as emperor, but when Alexios did not pay his debts to the crusaders, the crusaders captured the city and set up a Latin (i.e., Catholic) emperor in Constantinople. Innocent tried to depict the crusade as a success, claiming that the crusade would strengthen the Christian cause in the eastern Mediterranean because Constantinople and the crusader states in the Holy Land would now work together rather than being rivals. But he knew that an expedition to the Holy Land was still needed.

Innocent then called a different sort of crusade, this time against the Cathar heretics in the area of southern France known as the Languedoc. He had begun by trying to win the Cathars back to Catholic Christendom through peaceful preaching by Cistercian monks, but this failed. In 1208 Peter of Castelnau—the papal legate (or representative) in southern France—was murdered, and Innocent believed that Count Raymond VI of Toulouse, in alliance with the Cathars, was responsible. He called a crusade against him. The Albigensian Crusades, as they were later called, were successful in that they destroyed the power of the nobles who sheltered the heretics, but they did not stamp out Catharism.

Innocent III continued to work toward another crusade to the East.

In his crusading bull *Quia maior* (1213) he encouraged noncombatants (such as women) to take the cross and then pay a sum of money instead of going on crusade. This money then went toward financing crusaders. He planned the Fifth Crusade, but died before it set out.

Jadwiga, queen of Poland (b. c. 1374, d. 1399), *Brought About the End of the Prussian Crusade*

Regarded as a saint and national heroine in Poland, Jadwiga was born Hedewig, daughter of Louis I of Anjou, "the Great" of Hungary and Poland, and Elizabeth of Bosnia. Her elder sister, Mary, married Sigismund of Luxembourg, the son of Emperor Charles IV, king of Bohemia, who would later deal so unsuccessfully with the Hussites. Jadwiga was betrothed at the age of five to William, son of Duke Leopold III of Austria.

On Louis' death in 1382, one of his daughters was to inherit Poland and the other Hungary. The Polish nobles elected Jadwiga as their queen, as Maria had already been crowned queen of Hungary. In 1384 Jadwiga traveled to Poland and was crowned. The Polish nobles were anxious that she should marry a man who could carry on war and diplomacy with the Catholic Christian Teutonic Order to the north and pagan Lithuania to the East. While Jadwiga sent for her betrothed husband William of Austria, now aged fourteen, the Lithuanian grand duke Jogailo, or Jagiełło, sent an embassy to Kraków, capital of Poland, to ask for Jadwiga's hand in marriage. In return he offered to convert to Catholic Christianity and to unite his country to Poland. Jagiełło was an adult of thirty-five, a warrior of great renown; Jadwiga was a child around ten years old.

Since the 1230s, the Teutonic Order had been campaigning in northeastern Europe to conquer Lithuanian territory and/or force the Lithuanians to accept Christianity. The Poles, who had initially invited the Teutonic Order to Prussia both to neutralize the threat to Polish frontiers from aggressive pagan raiders and to win territory, had discovered that the Teutonic Order was hardly a less dangerous enemy than the Lithuanians. Jagiełło's offer would solve this problem; Lithuania would become a permanent Christian ally, and together the two countries could defeat the Teutonic Order.

Jadwiga, her own family, and her betrothed's family wanted her to marry William; but the Polish nobles voted for the Lithuanian alliance. William apparently reached Jadwiga but was evicted by some Polish knights. Jadwiga was prevented from following him. Jadwiga then gave way and agreed to marry Jagiełło. The situation was scandalous, for if William and Jadwiga had consummated their marriage, Jadwiga could not legally marry Jagiełło. Jagiełło's enemies, in particular the Teutonic Order, claimed later that Jadwiga had married William, but both Jadwiga and William denied it. In February 1386, Jagiełło came to Poland, was baptized (taking the name Władysław), married Jadwiga, and was acknowledged as king of Poland.

The marriage did not end the war with the Teutonic order. The order declared the marriage invalid and the conversion a sham. Jagiełło's cousin Witold rebelled against him in 1389 and allied with the order, which invaded Lithuania and besieged Vilnius in 1390 and again in 1392. In that year Jagiełło made peace with his cousin, agreeing that Witold would rule Lithuania as grand duke, under Jagiełło's overlordship as king of Poland. The Teutonic Order could still play Lithuania and Poland against each other, and the war continued, even though all parties were now Catholic Christians.

Jadwiga died in childbirth in 1399. In 1410 Jagiełło, in alliance with Witold, defeated the Teutonic Order at Tannenberg/Grunwald, the beginning of the end of the Baltic crusade. He ruled Poland until his death in 1434.

James I, king of Aragon (b. 1207, d. 1276), *Christian Crusading Leader*

Only son of King Peter II of Aragon, one of the heroes of the battle of Las Navas de Tolosa (1212), at which a Christian Spanish coalition force defeated the forces of Muslim al-Andalus, commanded by the Almohad caliph al-Nāsir. James' mother was Maria of Montpellier. When he was two years old, his father arranged for him to marry the daughter of Count Simon de Montfort, leader of the Albigensian Crusades, and James was sent to be brought up in Count Simon's household. After James' father was killed by Montfort's troops at the Battle of Muret (1213), Pope Innocent III insisted that James be handed back to his own people. James was entrusted to the Templars at Monzón, and he was brought up by them until he was nine.

Without an adult king, Aragon was divided between rival factions, and it was not until 1227 that James was able to take full control of his kingdom. In 1229 he took a naval expedition to the Balearic Islands, which were then in Muslim hands. In his autobiography, James depicted this campaign as a war in God's name, to convert or to destroy the Muslims. He captured the Balearic Islands and brought them under the control of the Aragonese monarchy. In 1233 he invaded the Muslim kingdom of Valencia, again depicting the expedition as being in God's name and with God's approval (see Document 8). In 1238 he captured the capital city of the kingdom. When James conquered an area formerly under Muslim rule, he did not remove all the Muslims from the country but allowed them to remain, follow their laws, and practice their faith. One of the reasons for this was that James did not have enough Christian subjects to repopulate all the areas he conquered. The rulers of Castile were also expanding southward into Muslim-ruled territory, and in 1243 Ferdinand III of Castile conquered Murcia. The only remaining territory in Muslim hands was the mountain kingdom of Granada, which could not easily be attacked. In 1244 James and the infante Alfonso (the future Alfonso X, the Wise), representing Ferdinand, reached an agreement in the treaty of Almizra (now the Campo de Mirra in the province of Alicante) as to where their respective southern frontiers lay; after this, they halted expansion south. For the next few decades, James concentrated on consolidating his power at home and settling border disputes in the north of his kingdom.

According to James himself, it was the Mongols, seeking assistance from the West after their defeat at 'Ain Jālūt in 1260, who urged him in 1268 to go to the East on crusade. In 1269 James set sail, but turned back because of bad weather. However, some of James' illegitimate sons reached the East and took part in military campaigns against the Mamluks. James attended the Second Council of Lyons in 1274, a Church council convened by Pope Gregory X to plan a crusade. He advised the pope to send a small expedition to the East, to be followed by a larger one. If the pope led the crusade, James would lead a thousand knights; but he wanted the pope to give him the money raised in crusade taxes from the Aragonese clergy. According to James, the other delegates at the council did not think that his plans could be successful and so he departed, and nothing was done.

James died in 1276. He had restored his kingdom to order after the disasters caused by the Albigensian Crusades, and vastly expanded his domains. Today he is generally known as "the Conqueror."

John Hunyadi (d. 1456), *Prominent Christian Military Leader against the Ottomans*

Legend made him an illegitimate son of King Sigismund of Hungary (1387–1437), western emperor, but this is doubtful. He was governor (voivode) of Transylvania from 1440 to 1456, and regent of Hungary from 1446 to 1452. From 1441 he inflicted a series of crushing defeats on the Turks. His experience on the frontier had made him familiar with Turkish tactics: he knew that the Ottoman army was largely made up of men drafted from the land, who would go home at the end of summer when their period of service had ended, so he attacked the Turks after the army had split up. He also used Hussite battle tactics, which the Hungarians had learned from the Czechs during the Hussite Crusades. In 1442 he and Ladislas the Jagiełłonian of Poland (otherwise known as Władysław III), elected king of Hungary, planned an expedition against the Turks. In 1443 their army advanced south, where they defeated an Ottoman force and captured Sofia (see Map 6, p. 79). They withdrew only because of the harsh winter weather. In 1444 the pair launched a second expedition, assisted by naval forces from the West. The crusaders met the army of Sultan Murad II at Varna; their fleet did not come to their aid. After a bitter battle with heavy losses on both sides, the Christians fled. Ladislas the Jagiełłonian died on the field.

In 1445 Hunyadi organized a joint campaign against the Ottoman Turks on the River Danube with Waleran of Wavrin, a Burgundian commander with hired Venetian ships, but they were unable to bring the Turks to battle. In 1448, he suffered a defeat at Kosovo. From 1446 to 1453 he was regent of the kingdom, as King Ladislas Postumus, or László V (1444–57), was too young to rule in his own name. In 1450 he agreed with Emperor Frederick III that the emperor would look after the king's upbringing until the king was eighteen, while Hunyadi ruled Hungary. But this arrangement was opposed by some of the nobles of Ladislas' domains, especially Ulrich of Cilli, who insisted that Ladislas be entrusted to his care. Hunyadi resigned as regent in 1452, but his

Figure 5. The assault on Belgrade in 1456 by the forces of Sultan Mehmed II, from a sixteenth-century Turkish manuscript. Bridgeman Art Library.

disputes with Ulrich of Cilli prevented him from taking military aid to Constantinople when it was besieged by Mehmed II in the spring of 1453. By early 1456 it was clear that Mehmed II intended to attack Hungary. John of Capistrano, an elderly Franciscan friar, preached the crusade in Hungary and raised a large crusading army from eastern Europe. In early July, Mehmed began to besiege Belgrade. John Hunyadi, Capistrano, and his motley crusading army set off to relieve the city.

Hunyadi believed that the situation was hopeless and wanted to negotiate an honorable surrender, but Capistrano persuaded him to defend the city. The crusading army managed to break into Belgrade and, with the people of the city, drove back a Turkish assault. As Mehmed began to withdraw, the Christian army rushed out of the city and captured his artillery. Christians believed that this victory was a miracle.

Hunyadi did not live long after his greatest victory, dying of the plague in October 1456. After his death, his sons László and Matthias Corvinus were imprisoned by King Ladislas Postumus. László was executed, and Matthias remained in prison. When Ladislas Postumus died suddenly in late 1457, it was commonly said in Hungary that it was God's punishment for the execution of László Hunyadi. George of Poděbrady, who had been King Ladislas' representative in Bohemia, released Matthias from prison, and in 1458, Matthias was elected king of Hungary, ruling until his death in 1490.

John Žižka (b. 1360, d. 1424), *Heretical Military Leader*

John Žižka came from a squire family of Bohemia; he was not knighted until 1421 or 1422. He served King Wenceslas IV and was part of the army that Wenceslas sent to Poland in 1410 to help King Władysław Jagiełło against the Teutonic Order. After their victory at Tannenberg/Grunwald, the Poles went on to capture the order's castle of Radzyń, and Žižka was one of those in the garrison who defended it from the Teutonic Order.

Žižka emerged as a military leader early in the Hussite crisis. He was made captain of the New Town of Prague, to defend the city against the Catholics and King Sigismund. When the New Town made peace with Queen Sophia—Wenceslas' widow—Žižka was made captain of the town of Pilsen, a center of Hussitism. The people of Pilsen decided to make peace with Sigismund, so Žižka went to Tabor, where he became general. Most of his troops were peasants—their only weapons were flails, and their only transport, wagons. Žižka made them into a deadly army and began campaigns against Catholic fortresses and towns in southern Bohemia. In 1420 the people of Prague decided to defy Sigismund and sent an appeal for help to Tabor. Žižka came with several thousand fighting men and their families; guns, crossbows, wagons, lances, maces, and flails. Another military community at Mount Oreb also sent help. The Taborites under Žižka defended the New Town and threw back Sigismund's forces when they tried to storm it. Sigismund decided not to bombard Prague and withdrew.

As the "traditionalist" and "radical" Hussites in Prague quarreled, the Taborites and Žižka went back to the south, where they campaigned against Catholics. In June 1421, Žižka was hit in his one good eye by an arrow and became totally blind. He continued to act as general, and his greatest victories came after this disaster.

In late 1421, Sigismund led another crusade into Bohemia, where his forces committed dreadful atrocities. Žižka moved his army to Kutná Hora (see Map 5, p. 66), where Sigismund's general attacked him. Although Žižka could not see the enemy, he instructed his troops to move forward with their war wagons, shooting at the enemy with the guns that were mounted on the wagons. They drove the king's army back and escaped. Then Žižka redeployed his troops, attacked Sigismund's army, and routed it. Sigismund left Bohemia and did not come back until 1436.

In the winter of 1422–23 after the failed third crusade, Žižka split with Tabor and went to Mount Oreb, where in July 1423 he founded a new military brotherhood. This was effectively his own army, and he used it to campaign against the Catholics. When the conservative Hussites and royalist Catholics in Prague allied, Žižka waged war on them together. Again he showed his tactical skill, his troops escaping from the enemy under cover of darkness and making intelligent use of the terrain—for example, filling wagons with stones and rolling them down a hill to smash the enemy's ranks.

When the Hussites elected Prince Korybut of Lithuania as their king, Žižka promised Korybut his loyalty. In spring 1424 they set out on a united campaign against Moravia, where Žižka died of the plague. After this, the Orebites called themselves "the orphans" because they had lost their father. According to Aeneas Silvius Piccolomini (later Pope Pius

II), the Orebites made a battle drum out of Žižka's skin. A pro-Hussite chronicle says that they made a banner painted with his portrait so that he could still lead them into battle as before.

Margaret of Beverley (b. c. 1130s, d. c. 1210), An "Ordinary Person" Involved in the Third Crusade

According to the account of her life written down by her younger brother, Thomas, Margaret was conceived in England, but as her parents—Sibil and Hulno—then set out for Jerusalem on pilgrimage, she was born in the Holy Land. Back in England the family settled in Beverley in Yorkshire, where Thomas was born, eleven years her junior. Her father having died, Margaret helped to bring Thomas up; he was later in the household of Thomas Becket, archbishop of Canterbury (d. 1170).

As an adult, Margaret returned to the kingdom of Jerusalem, and was in Jerusalem when it came under siege from Saladin in September 1187 (see Document 4). Thomas depicts Margaret saying: "like a fierce virago, I tried to play the role of a man," improvising a helmet from a metal cooking pot: "a woman pretending to be a man . . . terrified, but I pretended not to be afraid." Thomas describes how she brought water to the men who were fighting on the city walls, and was hit by a fragment of a stone hurled by one of Saladin's siege machines; the wound healed, but she carried the scar. This is such an overused, traditional depiction of women's role in war that Thomas may have invented it.

When the city surrendered to the Muslims, she paid for her freedom and set off for Lachish (possibly Laodicea), where her party believed they would be safe; however, they were captured by Muslims and enslaved. None of the troubles she went through, Thomas claims, could shake her morale, even though she had to gather stones and chop wood; was beaten and threatened; worked all the long, hot days; and had hardly any rest. There was a well-educated and pious priest among the captives, who used to preach to them and encourage them in their faith. "There will be an end to suffering," he said; "we suffer harsh things, but they are due to our faults." At last a man from Tyre (now Sūr in Lebanon; still held by the Christians in 1187) paid their ransom. Margaret set off through the desert—hungry, alone, and terrified—heading for Antioch, for she had taken a vow of pilgrimage to visit the tomb of St. Margaret there.

While she was in the city, it came under siege from Saladin's army (July 1188), but the enemy was defeated. Margaret set off south, but on the road not far from Tripoli she was again arrested by Muslims and thought her end had come. Not knowing any Turkish, she spoke the name "Saint Mary," which the Turkish lord recognized, and he released her. Reaching Acre after the forces of the kings of England and France—Richard the Lionheart and Philip II—had arrived there, Margaret embarked for the West. She went on pilgrimage to Santiago and Rome, and finally found her brother in France at the monastery of Froidmont. After all her troubles, Thomas persuaded her to leave the secular life and enter a nunnery. With the support of Count Louis of Clermont and Blois, she was admitted to the nunnery of the Virgin in the diocese of Laon, and remained there for eighteen years until her death. Thomas does not tell us exactly when she died.

Margaret was not a crusader in that she never "took the cross"; she became involved in the Third Crusade both as a bystander who took part in the defense of Jerusalem and as a pilgrim. Thomas depicts his sister as being miraculously helped by the Virgin Mary in her travels; modern readers regard her as a pious woman whose faith supported her in her troubles.[4]

Mehmed II (b. c. 1432, d. 1481), *Ottoman Conqueror of Constantinople*

Also called Mahomet by western historians. Son of the Ottoman sultan Murad II, he initially came to power on his father's abdication in 1443. In the face of the threat from western naval forces, however, his father returned to power. In 1451 his father died and Mehmed succeeded him. Christendom expected a period of peace, but Mehmed decided to capture the Christian imperial city of Constantinople, former capital of the eastern Roman Empire. The city was by this period completely surrounded by Ottoman territory, but it provided a place of exile for his political enemies and encouraged western Christians to come east on crusade. He began the siege in April 1453, with a large army and huge cannonry, and before western Christians had had the opportunity to come to its aid, the city fell on May 29, 1453. Mehmed made it his capital, and allowed the Greek people to continue practicing their faith.

The fall of Constantinople caused consternation in the West, where it was feared that Mehmed would now advance on the rest of Christendom. Mehmed did continue the Ottoman advance into the Balkans, and in 1456 he attacked Belgrade with ships, a large army, and many large cannon. If Belgrade fell, he would then be able to advance up the Danube river into Hungary (see Map 6, p. 79). A crusading army marched to relieve Belgrade under John Hunyadi. The relief was successful, and Mehmed withdrew. But he continued to campaign in the Balkans, and by 1459 Serbia was part of the Ottoman Empire. He occupied the Morea, leaving just a few ports in Venetian hands, and in 1461 he conquered the Greek Empire of Trebizond (Trabson in Turkey) on the south coast of the Black Sea. Mehmed developed Ottoman sea power, which he used at Trebizond and against the Venetians.

Despite various attempts in the West to launch a crusade against him, there was no large-scale opposition to Mehmed's advances, although George Castriota Scanderbeg, an Albanian prince, held back the Turks' advance until his death in 1468, while Matthias Corvinus—king of Hungary from 1458 to 1490—and the Venetians offered some military resistance. Matthias Corvinus built fortresses along his southern frontier with the Turks, and the Venetians fought the Turks over the Greek islands and ports on which Venetian trade depended. They allied with Mehmed's Turkish enemies, and their fleet attacked his coastal positions and islands. Nevertheless, Mehmed continued to advance to the east and west. He conquered Albania in 1478. In 1479 Venice made peace, acknowledging the loss of the island of Negroponte (Euboea) and other territories to Mehmed.

In 1480 Mehmed launched a naval attack on the island of Rhodes, the headquarters of the military religious order of the Hospital. At the same time, another part of his fleet invaded southern Italy, and his armies continued to campaign on land. Otranto was captured, but Rhodes—under the command of Grand Master Pierre d'Aubusson—resisted, and Mehmed's troops had to withdraw (see Document 12). Mehmed died in May 1481, and Otranto was recaptured by a crusading force in September. Political crisis after Mehmed's death halted the Ottoman advance westward.

Mehmed followed a policy of holy war against Christendom. Despite various crusading efforts, Catholic Christendom was unable to withstand his superior military forces, although he suffered a few defeats, as at Belgrade in 1456 and Rhodes in 1480.

Saladin (b. 1138, d. 1193), *Ayyūbid Conqueror* *of Jerusalem*

The first Ayyūbid sultan; his full name was Al-Malik al-Nāṣir Ṣalāḥ al-Dīn Abu'l-Muẓaffer Yūsuf ibn Ayyūb—the final phrase meaning "Joseph son of Job" (Ayyūb). Born into a Kurdish officer family, his father was governor of Baalbek, now in Lebanon. He served in the household of Nūr al-Dīn, sultan of Damascus, from 1152, but first came to prominence in Egypt, where he served under his uncle Shirkuh in the 1160s. His uncle became vizier of Egypt in 1169, but when he died two months later, Saladin succeeded him. As vizier he built up a new army, fortified Cairo, and beat off an attack by the king of Jerusalem in alliance with the Byzantines. He also ended the Shi'ite Fatimid dynasty of caliphs in Cairo, and made Egypt subject to the Sunni caliph in Baghdad. On Nūr al-Dīn's death in 1174, Saladin took over Damascus and married Nūr al-Dīn's widow. He was now overlord of Damascus and Egypt, and his territories encircled the crusader states. In the late 1170s he invaded the kingdom of Jerusalem; in 1183 he ravaged the kingdom but eventually withdrew.

Saladin had many Muslim rivals, and spent many years campaigning against Aleppo and Mosul rather than attacking the crusader states. Strictly orthodox Muslim, he portrayed his wars against the Christians as holy wars, a cause that might unify his Muslim subjects behind him. Otherwise, his states were not unified, and he relied on his relatives and supporters both to govern his territories as princes and to supply military forces to his army.

By the mid-1180s, Saladin had subjugated his Muslim enemies. He made an alliance with the Byzantine Empire and trade treaties with the Italian city republics to attract trade to Egypt. He came to an agreement with Count Raymond III of Tripoli whereby his troops could pass through his territory unharmed. In the south of the kingdom of Jerusalem, the lord of Transjordan—Reynald of Châtillon—exacted tribute from caravans traveling from Damascus to Egypt, or to the Muslim holy city of Mecca. In early 1187, a caravan that refused to pay was attacked and looted, and Saladin treated this as a pretext to attack the kingdom of Jerusalem. Although Reynald was pursuing his "rights" as lord of the area, Saladin was powerful enough to deny him those rights.

In May 1187, Saladin's forces passed through the county of Tripoli to ravage the kingdom of Jerusalem, and withdrew after engaging and destroying a Christian army at the Spring of the Cresson (May 1). In late June he besieged the town of Tiberias in Galilee. A relief army consisting of the entire military forces of the kingdom of Jerusalem and led by King Guy was surrounded and destroyed at Hattin on July 4 (see Document 3). Saladin went on to capture nearly all the fortresses and cities of the kingdom of Jerusalem, including the great port of Acre. Only the port city of Tyre and a few castles in the north and south of the kingdom still held out by the end of 1187. Jerusalem itself surrendered to him on October 2, 1187 (see Document 4). Saladin had the mosques purified by washing them with rosewater, the Christian symbols removed, and the Islamic law proclaimed over this city that was also holy to the Muslims.

In the West, the Third Crusade was called by Pope Gregory VIII in response to Saladin's successes (see Document 5). King Guy of Jerusalem, whom Saladin had released from imprisonment on the condition that he go overseas, remained in the country, raised an army, and marched to besiege Acre. At first Saladin had the upper hand, but as increasingly large forces arrived from Europe, the Christians won control of the sea, while Saladin's forces became tired of war and rebellious. Acre finally fell to the crusaders in July 1191. Saladin harassed the crusader army as it marched south, but was unable to halt its progress. However, due to problems in ensuring their supply lines, the crusaders did not besiege Jerusalem. In September 1192 a truce was made; the crusaders visited Jerusalem on pilgrimage and returned to the West.

Saladin died in March 1193, and was succeeded by his sons and his brother al'Ādil. His dynasty, the Ayyūbids, controlled Egypt until 1250 and Aleppo and Damascus until 1260. In the Muslim world he was largely forgotten until the nineteenth century, but in western Christendom his name became a byword for chivalry and good rulership, and many legends grew up around him.

Shajar al-Durr (d. 1257), *Ruler of Egypt during a Crusade*

Originally a Turkish slave and from 1240 a concubine of al-Ṣāliḥ Ayyūb, Ayyūbid sultan of Egypt, she became the sultan's favorite and was promoted to being his wife. The couple had one son, Khalīl, who

terre sus les anciens de la toi. Et lors   il prodient le port de vamiere.

S lan de lincarnation   tusques au tour du mercquedi apres p
nostre seigneur. m. cc. et.   ce que il nauoient pas tenps conuena

Figure 6. King Louis IX attacks Damietta in 1249, from a fourteenth-century French manuscript. British Library Picture Library.

died young. Shajar, or Shajarat, al-Durr's period of power and fame came after her husband's death, when she played a role in bringing about the end of Ayyūbid power in Egypt and the rise of the Mamluks.[5]

In November 1249, while King Louis IX of France's first crusade was attacking Egypt, Sultan al-Ṣāliḥ Ayyūb fell ill and died. According to the Arab historian al-Maqrīzī, writing nearly two centuries later, Shajar al-Durr called together the emir Fakhr al-Dīn ibn Shaykh al Shuyūkh—commander of her late husband's armies—and Djamāl al-Dīn Moḥsin; explained that her husband was dead; and asked them to keep the death a secret for fear of demoralizing the Muslims and encouraging the invaders. The three worked together to keep the government going until the heir, al-Malik al-Muʻazzam Tūrān-Shāh Ghiyath al-Dīn, could arrive from Hiṣn Kaīfā (now Hasankeyf in southeastern Turkey). Shajar persuaded the emirs and government officials to swear to acknowledge Tūrān-Shāh as heir. The people suspected that the sultan was in fact dead and that Fakhr al-Dīn intended to seize the throne, but Shajar continued to act as if he were still alive and told everyone that he was ill and could not see anyone.

The crusaders, who had already captured the important port of Damietta, heard rumors of the sultan's death and advanced toward Cairo. Fakhr al-Dīn led the Muslim defense. After a series of battles, the crusaders were defeated at Manṣūra and forced to withdraw (February 8, 1250), but Fakhr al-Dīn himself was killed. Shajar al-Durr continued to conduct affairs of state in the name of her dead husband until Tūrān-Shāh arrived at Cairo and was proclaimed sultan. The crusaders, meanwhile, began to retreat, but were surrounded by Muslim troops and forced to surrender. Many were executed; the leaders, including King Louis himself, were held for ransom. Having dealt with this danger, Tūrān-Shāh demanded that Shajar al-Durr hand over the dead sultan's treasure to him. Shajar al-Durr denied having the treasure and appealed to the Baḥrī Mamluks for aid.

The Baḥriyya were a crack fighting force of Turkish Muslims who were originally slaves, but who had been trained by Sultan al-Ṣāliḥ Ayyūb to be his personal elite troops and rewarded with lands and rights. They resented Tūrān-Shāh's threats to Shajar al-Durr and feared that he would also threaten them. They therefore murdered Tūrān-Shāh and made Shajar al-Durr sultana. Ruling in her own name, Shajar negotiated with the captive King Louis IX and with his wife, Queen Margaret, who was defending Damietta, for the surrender of Damietta and the release of King Louis and his fellow crusaders on payment of a ransom. Louis and his army left Egypt.

However, when the news of the murder of Tūrān-Shāh reached Damascus, many of the emirs there refused to acknowledge Shajar al-Durr as ruler of Egypt and threatened invasion. In May 1250 the Baḥriyya appointed 'Izz al-Dīn Aybak al-Turkumānī as military commander to rule jointly with Shajar. Shajar al-Durr abdicated in July 1250. A few days later Aybak also abdicated, and the Baḥriyya created a new sultan—the child al-Ashraf Mūsā, great-grandson of Sultan al-Kāmil (d. 1238). As an Ayyūbid, he was a more "valid" sultan than the upstart Aybak. Aybak continued to rule in the name of al-Ashraf Mūsā. In 1254 Aybak deposed al-Ashraf Mūsā and became sultan once more, now as husband of Shajar al-Durr. Historians do not agree over whether Shajar al-Durr actually wielded power herself while Aybak was sultan.

Aybak then took another wife, daughter of the ruler of Mosul. In April 1257, Aybak was murdered; Shajar al-Durr was blamed for her husband's death and murdered in revenge. Aybak's Mamluks, the Mu'iziyya, raised Aybak's young son 'Alī as sultan, but then the Mu'iziyya leader, Qutuz, took over control as the first of a long line of Mamluk sultans.

Süleyman I "the Magnificent" (b. 1494, sultan 1520– 66), *Arguably the Greatest and Most Famous of the Ottoman Sultans*

The only son of Selim I, conqueror of the Mamluk Empire; under his leadership the Ottoman Empire reached the summit of its power and influence. Western Christians called him "the Magnificent."[6]

When Süleyman succeeded, some of his father's allies and officials tried to take the opportunity to break away from Ottoman influence, but they were quickly crushed. Süleyman's first major victory against the western Christians was the capture of the city of Belgrade in 1521. He went on to further victories in Hungary, and in 1529 marched into Austria and besieged Vienna, but failed to capture it. In 1533 he made a truce that divided Hungary between Ottoman and Habsburg overlordship. Moving to his eastern front, in 1536 Süleyman captured Baghdad and territory to the north of that city.

For much of the rest of his reign, he was occupied with these two regions. In 1548–49 and 1553–54 Süleyman campaigned in what is now Iran. While he captured some territory, he could not make substantial gains. The Hungarian frontier continued to be a source of dispute, and his last campaign was in Hungary in 1566, where he died on the battlefield.

Another major field of conflict was the Mediterranean, where Süleyman's fleet captured many Greek islands from the Christian powers. The first were the islands held by the Hospital of St. John, when he captured Rhodes at the end of 1522. Süleyman supported North African corsairs, or privateers, who attacked Christian shipping and coastlines. He employed a North African naval captain, Hayreddin Barbarossa, as his admiral, and made an alliance with King Francis I of France against Emperor Charles V. In 1543 his fleet spent the winter in the French port of Toulon after an unsuccessful attack on Nice. In 1550 Charles V's fleet captured various strongholds on the North African coast, prompting negotiations between Süleyman and King Henry II of France over another alliance against the emperor, but nothing came of this. In 1551 Süleyman's fleet recaptured Tripoli on the North African coast; the city had been guarded by the Hospital of St. John.

In 1556 Charles V abdicated. His son, King Philip II of Spain, made peace with France and continued naval operations along the North African coast. Deprived of his French ally, Süleyman still managed to hold his own. Philip's fleet captured the island of Djerba (off the Tunisian coast), but it was quickly recaptured by Süleyman's admiral, and Philip's fleet suffered severe losses (1560). In 1565 Süleyman sent a large fleet to attack the island of Malta, but despite a long and desperately fought siege, his forces failed to capture it from the Hospital of St. John.

In the 1530s, Süleyman also began naval operations in the Indian Ocean against the Portuguese trading posts that were being established there. The Portuguese controlled the entrance to the Persian Gulf, preventing Süleyman's merchant ships from what is now Iraq from reaching the Indian Ocean. He was unable to dislodge them, although he did capture some territory in Yemen.

As a Muslim sultan, Süleyman's wars against Christian powers were presented to his subjects as holy wars. However, much of his warfare was in the east of his empire against Muslims in Iran. These Shi'ite Muslims were depicted as rebels against the Ottomans' legitimate authority and as heretics. Fighting them was as much a holy war and a religious duty as fighting Christians.

Süleyman suffered various problems within his empire. In 1526–28, a series of revolts in Anatolia forced him to withdraw from his campaign in Hungary. Toward the end of his reign, he faced revolt from his sons. In 1553 he executed his son Mustafa, whom he suspected of plotting rebellion. In 1558 his son Bayezid revolted. Defeated in battle, Bayezid fled to what is now Iran, where he was imprisoned and later executed. Süleyman was succeeded in 1566 by his only surviving son, Selim II.

NOTES

1. What follows is based on J. H. Elliot, *Imperial Spain, 1469–1716* (Harmondsworth: Penguin, 1970), pp. 47–51.

2. Rowell, *Lithuania Ascending*, pp. xxxii–xxxviii, 52–59.

3. Peter of les Vaux-de-Cernay, *The History of the Albigensian Crusade: Peter of les Vaux-de-Cernay's Historia Albigensis*, trans. W. A. and M. D. Sibly (Woodbridge, Suffolk, and Rochester, NY: Boydell, 1998), p. 111 note 11, p. 73 note 37 and p. 117.

4. Thomas' life of Margaret is printed in Paul Gerhard Schmidt, " 'Peregrinatio periculosa'. Thomas von Froidmont über die Jerusalem-Fahrten seiner Schwester Margareta," in Ulrich Justus Stache, Wolfgang Maaz, and Fritz Wag-

ner, eds., *Kontinuität und Wandel: Lateinische Poesie von Naevius bis Baudelaire. Franco Munari zum 65. Geburtstag* (Hildesheim: Weidemann, 1986), pp. 461–85. For a translation, see Julia Bolton Holloway, "Margaret of Jerusalem/Beverley and Thomas of Beverley/Froidmont, Her Brother, Her Biographer," at http://www.umilta.net/jerusalem.html.

5. For a summary of studies of Shajar al-Durr, see David J. Duncan, "Scholarly Views of Shajarat al-Durr" (1998), at www.ucc.ie/chronicon/duncan.htm, accessed 11 June 2003. For al-Maqrīzī, see R.J.C. Broadhurst, *A History of the Ayyūbid Sultans of Egypt, Translated from the Arabic of al-Maqrīzī* (Boston: Twayne Publishers, 1980).

6. What follows is based on Colin Imber, *The Ottoman Empire, 1300–1650: The Structure of Power* (Basingstoke and New York: Palgrave Macmillan, 2002), pp. 48–61.

PRIMARY DOCUMENTS

DOCUMENT 1
Letter of Count Stephen of Blois to His Wife, Adela of Normandy, March 29, 1098

Count Stephen of Blois, an important lord of northern France, was one of the leaders of the First Crusade. This is his second letter home to his wife, Adela of Normandy, daughter of the famous Duke William who had conquered England in 1066. She was ruling Blois in his absence. The crusaders had arrived at Antioch in late October 1097 after a prolonged journey across Asia Minor. They set up a siege around the city and built fortifications (see Figure 7).

Stephen's writing style is somewhat breathless. He dictated this letter to a scribe, his chaplain Alexander, and then entrusted it to a messenger to be carried back to France. His final words suggest that even though he was committed to the crusade, he was homesick and wished that the enterprise were over.

His letter contains many useful details about the progress of the crusade. He shows that the crusaders had captured many cities and fortresses in Asia Minor, and that they had made a treaty with the Fatimid ruler of Egypt. He also shows that the crusaders believed that God was helping them in every battle and that the souls of crusaders who were killed went straight to Heaven.

The crusaders captured Antioch at the beginning of June 1098. Stephen left the crusading army shortly afterward, just before Kerbogha of Mosul arrived to besiege the city. He returned to the East in 1101 and died in Asia Minor in 1102.

Information added by the translator is in square brackets.

Stephen the count to Adela, his sweetest and most lovable wife, and his dearest sons and all his faithful people, both great and small, grace and blessing of all salvation.

You can be absolutely certain, my dearest, that the messenger whom I have sent your dear self left me outside Antioch healthy and well, highly thought-of and in every prosperity, by the grace of God. We have now held the camp of the Lord Jesus here continually for twenty-three weeks with the whole elect army of Christ, with His great strength. Know for certain, my beloved, that I now have double the gold and silver and many other riches that I had when I left you and that your dear self gave me, because all our princes, by common agreement of the whole army, have made me for the time being their lord, administrator in all their actions, and governor, although I did not want the position. You have already heard that after capturing the city of Nicaea we had a great conflict with the perfidious Turks, and with the Lord God's help we defeated them. After this we won for the Lord parts of the whole of Romania [the former Byzantine Empire in Asia Minor]. Later we went to Cappadocia, and in Cappadocia we knew that a certain prince of the Turks named Assa [Hassan] lived. We headed in that direction, we captured all his castles by force, and we pursued him into a certain very strong castle situated on a high crag. We gave Assa's land to one of our princes, and we left him there with many of Christ's knights so that he could wage war on the said Assa. Then we chased the wicked Turks who were always following us, through the middle of [Cilician] Armenia as far as the great river Euphrates, and they left all their baggage and baggage-animals on the bank of that river and fled through the river into Arabia [Iraq?]. The bolder knights among those Turks hurried ahead, galloping swiftly by day and night, into the Syrian region, so as to enter the royal city of Antioch before we arrived. When the whole army of God realized this, they rendered worthy thanks and praise to the all-powerful Lord, and, hurrying to the aforesaid principal city of Antioch with great joy, we besieged it.

We very often have many conflicts with the Turks there. Truly, we have fought seven times with the citizens of Antioch and with countless people who come to bring them aid. Because Christ is our commander we have met and attacked them with fiercer spirits, and in all of the seven aforementioned battles, with the help of the Lord God, we have conquered and we have killed a countless number of them. In those battles and in very many engagements in the city they have killed many from our Christian brotherhood, whose souls they placed in the joys of Paradise.

We certainly found Antioch to be an enormous city, much stronger and more difficult to capture than can be believed. More than 5,000 bold Turkish knights had flocked together into the city, as well as Saracens, Publicans, Arabs, Turcopoles, Syrians, Armenians and various other peoples, an infinite multitude of whom had assembled in that place. So through the grace of God we have borne many labors and countless evils in attacking these enemies of this same God and us. Many have already used up everything they have in this most holy suffering, and many of our Franks would have suffered physical death from hunger if God's clemency and our money had not supported them. For the sake of the Lord Christ we have suffered excessive cold and endless rain through the whole winter outside the city of Antioch. It is not true what some people said, that the heat of the sun in Syria is almost unbearable, for the winter is similar to what we have in the West.

When Caspian [Yaghisiyan], the emir of Antioch (that is, prince and lord), saw that he was heavily oppressed by us, he sent his son, named Sensaldo [Shams-ad-Daulah], to the prince who holds Jerusalem, and to Prince Rodoan of Calep [Ridwan of Aleppo], and to Docap [Duqaq], the prince of Damascus. He also sent to Bolianuth [Baghdad?] in Arabia [Iraq?] and to Hamelnuth [Alamut?] in Corathania [Khorazan]. These five emirs came at once with 12,000 choice Turkish knights to assist Antioch. We, meanwhile, knowing nothing about this, had placed many of our knights in cities and castles, for there are 165 cities and castles under our own personal lordship in Syria. However, a little while before they arrived at the city, we met them about three leagues away with 700 knights on a plain at the Iron Bridge [Jisr al-Hadid]. God fought against them for us, His faithful people: for that day through the strength of God we defeated them in battle and we killed a countless number of them, with God always fighting for us, and we carried more than 200 of their heads to the army, to bring joy to Christ's people. The emperor of Babylon [Egypt] sent his Saracen messengers with his letters to us in the army and, through them, agreed peace and affection with us.[1]

I am delighted to inform you, my dearest, what happened to us this Lent. Our princes who were encamped before a certain gate which is between our castle and the sea, had decided to build a castle, because Turks going out through that gate each day were killing our people who were going to the sea. (The city of Antioch is five leagues from the sea.) For this reason, they sent the distinguished Bohemond and Count Raymond of St. Gilles with a company of just sixty knights to the sea, so that they could escort sailors from there to help with this work. As they were returning to us with the sailors the Turks, who had gathered together an army, took our two princes by surprise and put them to dangerous flight. In that ill-considered pursuit (as we described it) we lost more than 500 of our foot soldiers to the praise of God, but we lost only two of our knights. That day we went out to meet our colleagues to receive them with joy, not knowing about their mishap. When we approached the aforementioned gate of the city, the troop of Antiochene

Figure 7. The crusaders' siege of Antioch in 1097–98, from a thirteenth-century manuscript of William of Tyre's *History* of the kingdom of Jerusalem. Bridgeman Art Library.

knights and foot soldiers were celebrating the victory that they had won, and rushed on us in the same way. When we saw them, we sent to the Christian camp with instructions that everyone should prepare for battle and follow us. While our people were still assembling, the dispersed princes, i.e., Bohemond and Raymond, arrived with the rest of their army and told us about the grave mishap that had befallen them. Our men, incensed with anger at the bad news, charged the sacrilegious Turks, ready to die for Christ out of grief for their brothers. The enemies of God and ourselves fled before us without delay, trying to enter their city, but by the grace of God matters went completely differently. When they tried to cross the bridge over the great river, built by Moscholus, we, chasing them in close combat, killed many of them before they reached the bridge, threw many into the river, who were all killed, and killed many on the bridge and a great many in front of the gate entrance. I tell you, my dearest, and you can believe that it is completely true, that in that same battle we killed thirty emirs, that is princes, and 300 other noble Turkish knights, as well as other Turks and pagans. The number of dead Turks and Saracens is calculated at 1,230, but we did not lose one single man ourselves.

While my chaplain Alexander was writing this letter in the greatest haste on the day after Easter, a division of our men ambushed the Turks and had a victorious fight with them, the Lord presiding, and killed sixty of their knights, and brought all their heads to the army.

These things, dearest, that I write about to you are only a few out of many that have happened. Because I cannot express to you all the things that are on my mind, dearest, I instruct you to do well and govern your lands excellently and deal with your children and your people honorably, as befits you, because you will certainly see me as soon as I can.

Goodbye.

Latin text: *Epistulae et chartae ad historiam primi belli sacri spectantes quae supersunt aevo aequales ac genvinae. Die Kreuzzugsbriefe aus den Jahren 1088–1100. Eine Quellensammlung zur Geschichte des ersten Kreuzzugs*, ed. Heinrich Hagenmeyer (Innsbruck: Wagner'schen Universitäts-Buchhandlung, 1901; reprinted, Hildesheim and New York: Georg Olms, 1973), pp. 149–52.

DOCUMENT 2
The Battle of Antioch, June 28, 1098

The crusaders of the First Crusade had succeeded in capturing all of Antioch except for the citadel of the city; but they were now under siege from the Muslim relief force, under the command of Kerbogha of Mosul. At this point, they must either starve to death or sally out to face the Muslim forces. Unknown to them, Kerbogha was having his own problems with disputes between the various forces he commanded. Historians generally agree that the following account is by a crusader eyewitness to the battle. They disagree, however, over whether the writer was a warrior or a cleric; the account is written in simple, straightforward Latin, indicating that the author was a well-educated warrior or a minor cleric.[2]

At last after three days of fasting and formal processions from one church to another, they [the crusaders] were confessed and absolved of their sins, and devoutly took the Body and Blood of Christ in communion, and gave alms so that masses could be celebrated. Then six battalions were established from those within the city. In the first battalion, i.e., first, at the head, was Hugh the Great [of Vermandois], with the French and the count [Robert] of Flanders. In the second was Duke Godfrey [of Bouillon] and his army. In the third was Robert [Curthose] the Norman with his knights. In the fourth was the bishop [Adhémar] of Le Puy, carrying with him the Saviour's lance,[3] with his people, and with the army of Raymond, count of St. Gilles, who stayed behind to keep watch on the citadel for fear of the Turks, in case they came down to attack the city. In the fifth battalion was Tancred, the marquis' son, with his people. In the sixth was the wise man Bohemond, with his body of knights. Our bishops and priests and clerics and monks, clad in their holy vestments, came out with us with crosses, praying and beseeching the Lord to keep us safe and guard us and rescue us from all evil. Others stood on the wall over the gate, holding holy crosses in their hands, making the sign of the cross over us and blessing us. So we, drawn up in order and protected by the sign of the cross, went out through the gate which is opposite the mosque.

When Kerbogha saw the Franks' battalions, drawn up so beautifully, coming out one after the other, he said: "Let them come out, so that we will have them better in our power." But when they were out of the city and Kerbogha saw the huge Frankish host, he was extremely afraid. At once he instructed his emir who was responsible for everything that if he saw a fire lit at the head of the army he should at once have the order given for the whole army to retire, knowing that the Turks had lost the battle.

Kerbogha then began to draw back little by little, toward the mountain, and little by little our people followed him. Then the Turks divided: one part went toward the sea, and the other stayed where it was, thinking to trap our men between them. Seeing this, our men did a similar thing: a seventh battalion was drawn up, from the battalion of Duke Godfrey and the count [Robert Curthose] of Normandy, and at its head was Count Rainald [III of Toul]. This was sent to meet the Turks who came from the direction of the sea. The Turks fought with them and killed many of ours with arrows. Other squadrons were drawn up from the river as far as to the mountain, which was two miles away. The squadrons began to come out from each side and they surrounded our men on all sides, throwing javelins, shooting arrows and wounding.

And then a countless host came out from the mountains, with white horses, and all their standards were white. When our men saw this army they were completely ignorant of what it was and who they were; until they realized that they were from Christ's helpers, and their leaders were the saints George, Mercurius and Demetrius.[4] These are words that should be believed, because many of our people saw this.

The Turks who were standing on the side by the sea, seeing that they could not bear any more, set fire to the grass, so that those who were in the tents would see and flee. They, recognizing the signal, grabbed everything worth taking and fled. Our men fought little by little toward where their greatest force was, that is, the tents. Duke Godfrey and the count of Flanders and Hugh the Great rode next to the water, where the Turks' force was. They were first to attack, all together, fortified with the sign of the cross. Seeing this, the other battalions attacked them in a similar way. The Persians and Turks shouted out a challenge. Then we, invoking the true and living God, rode against them; and we began the battle in the name of Jesus Christ and the Holy Sepulchre, and with God's help we defeated them.

The terrified Turks took to flight, and our men pursued them past the tents, for the knights of Christ loved to pursue them more than to look for booty. They pursued them as far as the Orontes Bridge, and from there as far as Tancred's castle. They [the Turks] left behind their pavilions, and gold and silver and many decorations, sheep and oxen, horses and mules, camels and donkeys, grain and wine, flour and many other things which were essential to us.

The Armenians and Syrians who lived in those parts, hearing that we had overcome the Turks, rushed toward the mountain to meet them, and killed every one that they could seize. We, however, returned to the city with great joy, praising and blessing God, who had given victory to His people.

Latin text: "Gesta Francorum," in *Recueil des Historiens de Croisade, Historiens Occidentaux*, vol. 3, part 1, ed. l'Académie des Inscriptions et Belles-Lettres (Paris: Imprimerie Impériale, 1866; reprint, Farnborough: Gregg International, 1967, and Ann Arbor, MI: UMI, 2000), pp. 150–51.

DOCUMENT 3
Brother Thierry of the Order of the Temple Writes to All the Templars about the Capture of the Kingdom of Jerusalem by Saladin, July 1187

This is a typical appeal for aid, sent by a leading member of the Order of the Temple to the brothers of the order in western Europe. Brother Thierry (Latin: Terricus) calls himself "grand commander of the very poor house of the Temple." He also sent copies of this letter to Pope Urban III, Count Philip of Flanders, and to all Christians. As grand commander, Thierry would have been the leading official in the order after the capture of the master at Hattin on July 4, 1187, and the death of the marshal at the Spring of the Cresson on May 1 in the same year. As he states in the letter, almost all of the brothers at the convent, or central house of the order, had been killed in these two battles. This letter is unique as a Templar account of the battle of Hattin. Note that unlike later Christian sources, Thierry does not accuse any of the Christians of treachery, and that he states that he escaped from the battlefield with Count Raymond of Tripoli and his allies—even though some later accounts of the battle stated that the count and the Templars were deadly enemies. It appears, then, that these stories of bad relations were exaggerated.

Thierry sent two letters to the West appealing for aid: this one, which was probably written late in July 1187, and a second, written early in 1188, to King Henry II of England.[5] The letter to King Henry is deliberately upbeat, stressing that despite the disasters in the East, the Christians are holding on and awaiting help from the West. The first letter is far more pessimistic and is a heartfelt cry for assistance. It is written in the normal ornate style of Latin ecclesiastical correspondence of the late twelfth century.

Brother Thierry, called grand commander of the very poor house of the Temple, and every very poor brother and the almost completely annihilated convent, to all the commanders and brothers of the Temple whom this letter reaches, greeting; and lament in Him at whose beauty the sun and moon marvel.

Neither letter nor tearful voice can describe to you, alas! the many great calamities that God's anger has allowed to scourge us at the present time, because of what our sins deserve. For the Turks assembled an immense multitude of their peoples and began a bitter attack on our Christian boundaries. Our people's battalions assembled together to engage them in battle in the week after the feast of the Blessed Peter and Paul [June 29] and ventured to set out for Tiberias, which they had violently captured—only the castle still held out. They drove us into the worst crags and attacked us so bitterly [July 4: battle of Hattin] that the Holy Cross [the sacred talisman of the kingdom] and our king [Guy of Lusignan] were captured, and all our multitude were killed, and—as we truly believe—230 of our brothers were beheaded, apart from the sixty who were killed on May 1 [at the Spring of the Cresson]. The lord count [Raymond III] of Tripoli and lord Reginald of Sidon and lord Balian [of Ibelin] and I were scarcely able to escape from that miserable field. Then the pagans, raging for Christians' blood, wasted no time in coming against the city of Acre with all their multitude. Having violently captured it [July 9], they invaded and captured almost the whole land. Only Jerusalem, Ascalon and Beirut are left to us and Christendom, and unless God's help and yours are forthcoming we can in no way hold on to those cities, because almost all the citizens have been killed. At the present time they [the Muslims] are bitterly besieging the city of Tyre, and do not stop their assault by day or by night; and so great is their force that they cover the whole face of the land from Tyre to Jerusalem and as far as Gaza, like ants. Therefore, as fast as you can, be so good as to help us and the Christians of the East who are at present completely desperate, so that through the eminence of the Lord and your brotherhood, with your support to strengthen us, we may be able to save the cities that are left.

Farewell.

Source: Roger of Howden, *Gesta regis Henrici Secundi: The Chronicle of the Reigns of Henry II and Richard I*, ed. William Stubbs, 2 vols., RS 49 (London, 1867), vol. 2, pp. 13–14.

DOCUMENT 4
Saladin's Secretary 'Imād al Dīn Describes the Assault on Jerusalem, September 20, 1187–October 2, 1187

> *Saladin's secretary, 'Imād al Dīn, was aware that his lord had many enemies. In his history of Saladin's conquests, he attempted to show that Saladin's critics were in the wrong by emphasizing Saladin's virtues and piety. He used a very ornate style, piling praise on praise and adjective on adjective to create an imposing picture in words. Note that the Muslim troops are described as fighting with religious zeal, and the Christians are called infidels (unbelievers)—a direct reversal of the Christian sources. This translation is based on Henri Massé's French translation of the Arabic text.*

At last the sultan [Saladin] departed from Ascalon, heading toward Jerusalem, distinguished by his determination, accompanied by victory, with grandeur in his train. His desire was mastered and submitted itself to him; the garden of his wealth became fertile; his hope became full and perfumed throughout; his good actions were scattered widely; his perfume was sweet; his strength showed itself; his power conquered. The brilliance of his army threw its light across the area; filling the world, it scattered its exploits; the dust raised by his army made one long for dawn; one would have said that this dust changed morning light into shadowy night. So the land complained of the injustice of the armies while the sky absorbed the masses of dust. And the sultan went on, rejoicing at his prosperous situation. The history of the great conquests that he had won with lances was narrated; the list of his successes were unfolded, as his successes matched his hopes; the lands where his victories were grown and his horizons, the harvests, and the demonstrations were sweet and lofty. Islam demanded Jerusalem as a wife, offering her as a dowry the lives of the combatants, bringing her well-being so as to take misfortune away from her. . . . [6]

. . . [The Franks'] spies came to them with the fervor of evil. They informed them of the approach of the armies of an-Nāṣr with the victorious militias, with standards unfurled. . . . [7]

. . . On Friday 20 rajab, the sultan moved his troops to the northern side [of the city of Jerusalem] and camped there, barring the roads to the Franks, multiplying their dangers, installing machines of war, making calamities fall like rain falls from the clouds. He made the Ṣakhra [the Dome of the Rock] resound with the blows of boulders [hurled from his siege machines] and drew out, behind the ramparts, the perverse multitude [of the Christians]. Their chiefs no longer emerged from the enclosure without meeting misfortune and a terrible day's work, without running into loss.

The Templars made tumult; the barons threw themselves into the gulf of perdition; it was ruin for the Hospitallers; the Brothers did not escape death; they had no shelter against the stones that whirled and the weapons that hurled. The hearts of all the men in the [sultan's] troop were enflamed by the fire of zeal, although their faces were uncovered to receive kisses from iron weapons, their hearts shook with ardor for combat, their hands were clenched on the hilts of shining sabers, their souls were given over to anxiety at the delay in achieving their desires. The foundations of the walls and the indentations of their crenellations were destroyed and demolished by the stones that issued from the siege machines. One would have said that the mangonels became mad when they were operated, they were like gallants without equal; they seemed like mountains drawn along by ropes. One would have said that they were leaping grasshoppers powered by men, mothers of misfortune and death, pregnant women giving birth to calamities. There was no protection against their stones, no security near them, even for those on their guard. Danger accompanied their projectiles' advance; their passage created only bitterness for humans. If the stars could fall from the height of the heavens! if rocks could leap out of their places! if firebrands could scatter like their sparks!—they would be nothing like the ravages caused by these projectile-bags, the marks of the wounds they left, the results of their attacks, the precision of their sudden blows, the traction of their ropes. Without ceasing, these females uprooted everything with their slings, struck with their whole frame, pulled with gusto on their ropes, hit, demolished, overthrew, split, drew on their reserve of stones, prepared the evil they were going to do, disturbed the stones arranged in the rampart with boulders hurled one after the other, destroyed the cohesion of the edifices they broke up, exposed and broke up the bases of the walls by reaching their foundations, unfastened the keystones of the vaults which felt the effect of their ropes, dried up cisterns and drank at their hollows.

In brief, they left the ramparts in ruins and repulsed the enemy from them. The enemy found themselves defeated, their organization destroyed. The ditch was crossed; the troops were thrown forward; victory emerged for Islam, demise for the infidels. The breach was seized, the difficulty smoothed away, the object of effort obtained, the plan realized, the desire fulfilled, the rebels wounded, their front broached, the business ended. Our ardor had increased and our cause was in good order. The gentiles [Christians] feared violence; they exchanged health for sickness. The city surrendered, the belt of its ditches was broken.

Source: 'Imād al-Dīn al-Isfahāni (519–597/1125–1201), *Conquête de la Syrie et de la Palestine par Saladin (al-Fath al-qussî fî l-fath al-qudsî)*, traduction française par Henri Massé (Paris: Paul Geuthner, 1972), pp. 44–46.

DOCUMENT 5
Audita tremendi: Pope Gregory VIII Calls the Third Crusade

In response to the news of the battle of Hattin—the loss of the relic of the Holy Cross and the capture of King Guy of Jerusalem (see Document 3)—Pope Gregory VIII issued a circular letter to all Christians calling on them to go to the aid of the Christian territories in the East. This "crusading bull" follows a standard pattern: he sets out the terrible events in the East that have prompted his appeal, he explains what must be done, and he sets out the privileges that crusaders will receive. Note that the pope calls himself a bishop, as he is properly bishop of Rome. He also calls himself "servant of the servants of God," the modest title used by popes that underlined the fact that the pope's role is to help other Christians, not to rule them. Yet he also refers to himself as an apostle, because he is the successor of the apostle Simon Peter.

Gregory the bishop, servant of the servants of God, to all the faithful people of Christ whom this letter reaches, greetings and apostolic blessing. We have heard and tremble at the severity of the judgment that the Divine hand has executed over the land of Jerusalem. We and our brothers [the cardinals] are completely distraught with horror and struck with such great sorrow that we cannot easily see how to act, or what we ought to do, except as the psalmist bewailed and said: "God, the heathen have come into Your inheritance, etc." [Psalms 79:1]. Because of some disagreement that came about in that country through human malice from diabolical instigation, Saladin entered that area with a great many armed men. He encountered the king and bishops, Templars and Hospitallers, barons and knights with the people of the country, and the Lord's Cross—which used to be a reliable protection to them and a desirable defense against the pagans, because of the Christians' memory of and faith in the suffering of Christ, Who was suspended on it and redeemed the human race on it. There was a military engagement between them, and our side was overcome, the Lord's Cross was captured, the bishops were cut to pieces, the king was captured, and almost everyone was either killed by the sword or seized by hostile hands, so that very few escaped by fleeing. The Templars and Hospitallers themselves were beheaded before his eyes.

We do not believe that it is necessary to explain in our letter how, having overcome the army, he subsequently invaded and seized everything, so that only a few places are said to remain which have not fallen into their power. Although we may say with the prophet, "Who will turn my head into water and my eyes into a spring of tears, so that I may weep night and day for my people who have been killed?" [Jer. 9:1], we should not be so downcast, in case we fall into defiance [of God] and believe that God is so angry with His people that He permits Himself to become angry about the multitude of common sins, and that his anger is not quickly relieved through His mercy, placated by penance, and through lamentation and weeping leads His people to exultation.

Every discerning person can estimate not only how much a person is not of the Christian faith if, in the face of such mournful news, they do not mourn in their body and in their heart—for our faith teaches us to weep with those who weep—but also how far they have forgotten our common humanity, since that enormous danger and barbaric ferocity, thirsting for Christian blood, puts all its strength into profaning holy things and seeks to remove God's name from the land. So we will say nothing about this.

First the prophets worked first with every determination, and afterward the apostles and their followers worked to ensure that Divine worship would exist in that country, and flow out from it to every region of the world. The greatest and unutterable thing is that God, through Whom everything is made, wished to become flesh through His unutterable wisdom and incomprehensible mercy, and wished through the weakness of body, hunger, thirst, cross, and death and resurrection, to work out our salvation there. In accordance with what is said in scripture, "working salvation in the midst of the earth" [Psalms 74:12], through Himself He deigned to work for this. Tongue cannot tell, nor perception understand, how much we and the whole Christian people should mourn that that country is now suffering in the same way that it is recorded to have suffered under ancient people. We ought not to believe that this has happened because of the injustice of a killing Judge, but rather because of the wickedness of a delinquent people, because we read that when the people turned to the Lord, one could put a thousand to flight, and two could put ten thousand to flight, and when the people were resting, the army of Sennacherib was destroyed by angelic hand. But that country devoured its inhabitants, and it cannot long have a quiet state, nor keep those who transgress the divine law. Instead, it gives doctrine and example to those who keep their mind fixed on the heavenly Jerusalem, because they cannot reach it except by the exercise of good work and through many temptations. However, they should have been afraid a long time ago when Edessa and other lands passed into the pagans' power [1144], and it would have been good foresight if the people who remained in the country had turned to repentance, and appeased God—Whom their prevarication had offended—with their conversion. For His anger did not come suddenly. He put off His revenge and gave them time for repentance, but at last, because in mercy He cannot forget judgment, He exercises His vengeance to punish the transgressor, and to guarantee those who are to be saved.

In the face of such a great disaster crushing that country, we must be aware not only that the inhabitants have sinned but also that we have sinned, as have all the Christian people, since from all sides we hear of quarrels and scandals between kings and princes, cities and cities. We must mourn with the prophet and say: "There is no truth or knowledge of God in the country. They are inundated with lying, homicide and adultery, and blood seizes blood" [Hos. 4:1]. So we fear that what is left of that country will be completely destroyed, and their power will rage violently against other regions.

Everyone must think about this and act on it, so that by correcting our sins through voluntary punishment, we may turn through penance and works of piety to Our Lord God. First we should amend the evil things that we do, and then we may turn our attention to the ferocity and malice of the enemy. Just as they do not fear to go against God, we should in no way hesitate to act for God. Think, my sons, how you came into this world, and how you will leave it, how everything is transient and that you yourself are equally transient. Take advantage of a time of penitence and good works, as far as it relates to you, with acts of grace, and give your property, give yourselves too, not to be destroyed but converted to Him from Whom you received yourself and everything that you have; because you do not come from yourself nor do you have anything of yourself, as you cannot make a single gnat on the earth. I do not say that you should give up the barns that you have, but you should send them on ahead of you to heaven, and give them to Him with Whom rust does not destroy things nor does the moth, nor do thieves break in and steal. So you will be working for the redemption of the country in which for our salvation Truth was born on Earth and for our sake did not disdain to bear the gallows of the cross. Do not give your attention to this lucre or worldly glory, but to the will of God Who taught us by His own example to lay down our lives for our brothers, and commit your wealth to Him, because—whether you like it or not— you do not know what heirs you will be left at last.

It is certainly not new for this country to be struck by God's judgment, but neither is it unusual for mercy to follow a scourging and punishment. The Lord could preserve it by His will alone, but we cannot ask Him why He did not do so; for perhaps He wishes to find out and bring to the notice of others whether anyone has understanding or is seeking God who will cheerfully embrace a time of repentance when it is offered, and by laying down their life for their brothers will perfect it and complete the work of many years in a short time. Look at how the Maccabees, inflamed with zeal for the Lord's law, experienced every extreme danger to liberate their brothers, and taught others not only to lay down their property but also their own persons for the salvation of their brothers, encouraging each other and saying: "Arm yourselves, and be powerful, my sons; since it is better to die in battle than to see things that are evil to our people and the saints" [1 Macc. 3:58]. They acted under one established law, whereas you, through the Incarnation of our Lord Jesus Christ, led by the light of truth, and instructed by the many examples of the saints, may act without any trepidation. And those to whom good things have been promised and laid up in store, "which neither eye has seen nor ear heard, nor conceived in the human heart" [1 Cor. 2:9] and to whom the apostle said that "the suffering of the present time is not worth comparing to the future glory that will be revealed to us" [Rom. 8:18], should not fear to give away earthly things which are few and last only a short time.

To those who with contrite heart and humble spirit take up the work of this journey and depart in penance of their sins and in right faith, we promise full indulgence for their crimes and eternal life. Whether they survive or die, they should realize that through our authority by the mercy of the Almighty and the apostles Peter and Paul they will have release from penance imposed for all their sins for which they have given proper confession. Also the property of those who receive the cross, with their families, will stand under the protection of the holy Church and of the archbishops and bishops and other prelates of God, and no legal case may proceed about things that they possessed in peace when they took the cross until there is certain knowledge of their death or their return; but in the meantime their property should remain complete and peaceful. They cannot be forced to pay any interest if they owe a debt to anyone; nor should they wear valuable clothes, or travel with dogs or [hunting] birds, or with other things that seem for show rather than necessary use; but they should travel with modest equipment and clothing, which seem to reflect penitence rather than inane glory.

Source: Roger of Howden, *Gesta regis Henrici Secundi: The Chronicle of the Reigns of Henry II and Richard I*, ed. William Stubbs, 2 vols., RS 49 (London, 1867), vol. 2, pp. 15–19.

DOCUMENT 6
The Albigensian Crusades: The Massacre at Béziers, July 22, 1209, according to Caesarius of Heisterbach

This is not a contemporary account, but was written after 1219 and before 1223, at least ten years after the massacre occurred. It is included here because it was the earliest account of the massacre to state that the papal legate Arnold Aimery told the crusaders to kill all the besiegers because "God will know His own." Earlier versions of the siege state that the massacre was not ordered by the crusade leaders. However, it has been argued that the leaders were delighted by the massacre.[8]

Caesarius of Heisterbach was a Cistercian monk who was one of the preachers of the Fifth Crusade. Although his book of "dialogues" shows him to have been a humane and kindly man in general, this passage shows that he detested and feared heresy. His book is written in the form of a conversation between an experienced monk and a novice who is learning about Christianity.

On the Albigensian Heresy

Monk: At the time of Pope Innocent, predecessor of the Honorius [III, 1216–27] who now holds the papacy, and while the dispute was still in progress between Philip [of Swabia] and Otto [of Brunswick], rival kings of the Romans [emperors-elect], through diabolical ill will it came about that the Albigensian heretics began to spring up—or, to speak more accurately, to reach their full development. For they were so strong that it seemed as if all the wheat of faith among that people had been turned into the thistles of error [see Matt. 13:24–30]. Abbots of our Order were sent with certain bishops to eradicate the weeds with the hoe of catholic preaching. But the enemy of humanity, who had sewn the weeds, opposed them so that they saw little improvement.

Novice: What was their error?

Monk: The leaders of their heresy had taken some points from the Manichaean religion, some from the errors that Origen is said to have written in his book *Periarchon*, and added great many things that they dreamt up for themselves. With Mani they believe in two principles, a good god and an evil god, that is, the devil, whom they say created every body, while the good god created all souls.

Novice: Moses confirms that God created both bodies and souls, when he says: "God formed a human," that is, a body, "from the mud of the ground, and he breathed into its face the breath of life," that is, a soul [Gen. 2:7].

Monk: If they accepted Moses and the Prophets, they would not be heretics. They deny that human bodies will rise again on the Last Day; they laugh at anything that the living may do to benefit the dead; they say that to go to church or to pray in a church gives no benefit. In these respects they are worse than Jews and pagans, because Jews and pagans believe in these things. They have thrown out baptism; they blaspheme the sacrament of the Body and Blood of Christ.

Novice: Why do they put up with so many persecutions from the faithful, if they do not expect any reward for this in the future?

Monk: They say that they expect their spirit to be glorified. A monk in the service of one of the above-mentioned abbots saw a certain knight sitting on his horse talking to his ploughman, and thinking that he was a heretic—as he was—hurried up to him and said: "Tell me, good man, whose is this field?" When he replied: "It is mine," he continued: "And what do you do with its crop?" "I and my household live on it," he said, "and I give some of it to the poor." When the monk asked, "What good do you hope to gain from your charity?" the knight replied in these words: "That my spirit may go on gloriously after my death." The monk asked: "Go on where?" The knight said: "According to its merits. If it lived a good life, and has deserved this in God's eyes, when it leaves my body it will enter the body of some future prince, or king, or some other illustrious person, in which it will live a delightful life; but if it has lived a bad life, it will enter the body of an unfortunate and poor person, in which it will suffer." The fool believed, just as the other Albigensians do, that the soul travels through various bodies according to what it deserves, even the bodies of animals and reptiles.

Novice: What a horrible heresy!

Monk: At last the error of the Albigensians became so powerful that in a short time it infected up to a thousand cities, and if it had not been curbed by the sword of the faithful, I think that it would have corrupted the whole of Europe. In the year of Our Lord 1210 the cross [of the crusade] was preached in the whole of Germany and France against the Albigensians, and in the following year Duke Leopold of Austria, Engelbert, then provost and later archbishop of Cologne, and his brother Count Adolf of Altenberg, Count William of Jülich, and many others of different condition and status set out to attack them. The same was done in France, Normandy and Poitou. The preacher and head of all these things was the Cistercian abbot Arnold, later archbishop of Narbonne.

They came to a great city, which is called Béziers, in which there was said to be more than 100,000 people, and besieged it. Before their very eyes the heretics pissed on a volume of the gospels and threw it at them from the wall, and shot arrows after it, shouting: "There's your law, wretches!" But Christ, the producer of the Gospels, did not leave this insult against him unavenged. For some men-at-arms were inflamed with zeal for the faith. Like lions, and following the example of those of whom we read about in the Books of the Maccabees, they placed ladders against the walls and intrepidly climbed up. By divine power, the heretics were terrified and ran away. The men-at-arms opened the gates to those who followed, and captured the city.

Realizing from what they said that catholics and heretics were mixed together, they said to the Abbot: "What shall we do, sir? We can't tell the difference between the good and the bad." The Abbot and the rest, fearing that the heretics would pretend to be catholics because they were afraid of death, and that after the army had left they would return again to their faithlessness, is said to have replied: "Kill them. For the Lord will know who are His." And so countless people were killed in that city.

In the same way, with divine assistance they captured a huge city, called "Beauval" from its location,[9] which is situated close to Toulouse. When they examined its population, although everyone [else] promised that they wished to return to the [Christian] faith, 450 stubbornly refused, because the devil had made them obdurate. Four hundred of them were burned in a fire, the rest hanged. The same was done in the other cities and castles, the wretches voluntarily going to their deaths. The people of Toulouse were besieged and they promised every compensation, but—as appeared later—this was a fraud. For after the treacherous count of St. Gilles, prince and leader of the heretics, gave up all his possessions at the [Fourth] Lateran Council [1215]—i.e., his fiefs and allods [freehold property], cities and castles, most of which had been taken by Count Simon de Montfort, a catholic man, by the right of war—he took himself to Toulouse, and until this very day he has never stopped troubling and attacking the faithful from there.

Source: *Caesarii Heisterbacensis monachi ordinis Cisterciensis Dialogus miraculorum*, ed. Joseph Strange, vol. 1 (Cologne, Bonn and Brussels: H. Lempertz, 1851), dist. 5, ch. 21, pp. 300–303.

DOCUMENT 7
The Crusade of Emperor Frederick II of Hohenstaufen, 1228–29

The crusade of Emperor Frederick II could have been regarded as a great success; through an alliance with the sultan of Cairo, al-Kāmil (1218–38), he recovered the city of Jerusalem for Christendom—although not the Temple Mount, and without any rights to refortify the city. However, al-Kāmil only controlled part of Palestine, and did not actually have legal rights over Jerusalem. Legally, the area covered by the treaty belonged to al-Nāṣir Dā'ūd, prince of Damascus. As the treaty did not allow Jerusalem to be refortified, as soon as Frederick left the kingdom, al-Nāṣir would probably attack it.

What was more, some of the Christian sites in Jerusalem were left in Muslim hands, such as the Augustinian religious house attached to the Lord's Temple (actually the Dome of the Rock) and Solomon's Temple— the former headquarters of the military religious Order of the Temple (actually the Aqsa mosque). Matters were made even more complex by the fact that Pope Gregory IX had excommunicated Frederick II as he set out on his crusade, so that no Christian should associate with him (see biography of Frederick, pp. 105–6).

At the same time, it was clear that Frederick wanted to rule the kingdom of Jerusalem himself—after all, he had married the heiress to

the kingdom, Isabel II of Jerusalem. But she had already died in childbirth
before Frederick came out to the East, so Frederick was not king—only
regent for his baby son, Conrad. Frederick also claimed that as the western emperors were overlords of Cyprus, he should be regent of Cyprus
while little King Henry of Cyprus was underage (he was eleven in 1228).
But, according to Cypriot law, Henry's mother, Alice, was regent, and
the local nobility did not want Frederick as regent. All in all the political
situation in the East during the crusade was extremely messy, as this
letter from the patriarch of Jerusalem makes clear. The patriarch of Jerusalem was the leader of the Latin Church in the kingdom of Jerusalem.
The references to "pilgrims" probably mean armed crusaders.

Gerald, patriarch of Jerusalem, to all Christ's faithful, greeting in the
Lord. How marvelous—no, how miserable—the emperor's progress on
this side of the sea has been from the start, with grave damage to Jesus
Christ's affairs and contempt for the Christian faith! You may understand that there was no sanity in anything he did from the soles of his
feet to the top of his head. He arrived as an excommunicate, bringing
hardly 240 knights with him, and without money, hoping to support
himself by plundering the land of Syria. First he came to Cyprus and
arrested the nobleman John of Ibelin and his sons, whom he had summoned to discuss the business of the Holy Land—a discourteous deed,
for he had invited them to dine with him. Afterward he summoned the
king [Henry], and held him as if he were a prisoner. So he occupied the
whole kingdom through violence and treachery.

Having done this, he crossed to Syria. And although at the start he
promised to do great things and boasted about this to the naïve, it was
all words, because he immediately sent messengers to the sultan of Babylon [Cairo: i.e., to al-Kāmil] asking for peace. For this reason he was
despised by the sultan and his pagans, especially when they realized that
he had not brought a large enough armed force with him to do them
any damage. Meanwhile, on the excuse of fortifying Joppa [Tel Aviv/
Jaffa] he headed that way with the Christian army, so as to get nearer
to the sultan, so that he could negotiate with him more easily for peace
or a truce. What more shall I say? After long drawn-out negotiations
and without asking advice from anyone in the country he suddenly an-
nounced one day that he had made peace with the sultan. No one saw
the peace treaty when the emperor swore to preserve its terms. However,

you can clearly see the malice and fraudulent dealing in some of the clauses of that truce from the copy of it we have sent you. The emperor wished to have this word in order to magnify his authority, and he obtained that word from the sultan. Among other things it said that the holy city was to be restored to him.

The Christian army went there on the eve of the Sunday on which "Oculi Mei" is sung [March 17, 1229]. On the following Sunday, a disordered and confused day, even though he was under excommunication he placed the diadem [crown] on his own head, in blatant infringement of imperial honor and prestige.[10] The Saracens hold the Lord's Temple and Solomon's Temple in their hands and proclaim Muḥammad's law publicly as before, causing great confusion and grief for the pilgrims. The same emperor, although he had already promised many times that he would fortify the city, the following Monday left the city at the crack of dawn without a word of farewell to anyone. The brothers of the Temple and Hospital who were present solemnly insisted that if he wished to fortify the city as he had promised they would give him all the counsel and aid that they could to help him do it. But he, who had no concern to mend matters, seeing that the treaty could have no strength and the city could not be held or fortified now that it had been returned [to the Christians], was content with just the word [rather than the deed] of restitution. That same day he hurried back to Joppa with his household. When the pilgrims who had entered the city with him saw this they did not want to remain after he had left.

The next Sunday, i.e., when "Laetare Jerusalem" is sung [March 25] he came to Acre. Drawing the people in the city to him he conceded a privilege of liberty [civil rights] to them, as a means of begging their favor for himself. As for why he did this, God knows and his following actions showed.

As the time to set sail was drawing near and all the pilgrims together, great and small, had visited the Sepulchre and completed their pilgrimage, they prepared to go back home. As we do not have a truce with the sultan of Damascus, and seeing that the country was now destitute and the pilgrims had abandoned it, we called an emergency council and decided that we would hire knights out of the alms of the king of France of blessed memory[11] for the common good. When the emperor heard this he informed us that he was amazed, since he had made a truce with the sultan of Egypt. We replied that the iron was still in the wound[12] because no truce or peace had been made with the sultan of Damascus, the nephew of the said sultan, who was opposed to him; adding that Damascus could do us a great deal of damage against the sultan of Egypt's will. The emperor replied that, since he was king of Jerusalem, knights should not be hired to fight in the kingdom without his advice and permission. We replied that we were very sorry to hear this because we could not wait for his advice on this and similar things without danger to our souls, since he was an excommunicate. The emperor made no reply to this.

On the following day he sent out a public proclamation that the pilgrims who were living in the city should assemble outside the city on the sand; and the prelates and religious were also summoned through special messengers. He personally stood in their midst and first began to complain bitterly about us, piling up false accusations. Then he turned his speech to that venerable man the master of the Temple [Peter of Montaigu], and tried to tarnish his reputation considerably with various false statements. In this way he intended to twist his own fault, which was already obvious, on to others. He added finally that now we were going to hire mercenaries to his prejudice and damage, and for this reason he was forbidding all the pilgrim knights of any nation, as they loved him, to remain in the country from that day forth. He ordered Count Thomas [of Acerra], whom he had assigned to remain as his representative in the country, to punish any pilgrims he found in the country, so that the punishment of the one would terrify the many. When he had said all this he departed without allowing any defense or reply to those slanders that he had so ignominiously spread, and immediately decided to station his crossbowmen at the city gates, ordering them not to allow the brothers of the Temple to go out or in. He ordered the churches and other tall buildings in the city to be equipped with crossbows, and especially those places which gave access to us and the house of the Temple. You should know that he had never been so harsh or harmful toward the Saracens, or so resolutely against them.

Weighing up his obvious malice, we decided to call together the prelates and pilgrims and excommunicated all those who gave advice or aid to the emperor against the Church, the brothers of the Temple and other religious or pilgrims of the country. The emperor swelled with anger at this and had every entrance carefully guarded, forbidding anyone carrying food to come near us or those who were with us. He placed crossbowmen and archers everywhere, and with them seriously attacked us and the brothers of the Temple and pilgrims. And in order to complete his scheming malice, he had the Friars Preacher and some Minors [Dominican and Franciscan friars] who assembled on Palm Sunday [April 8] in set places to preach the Lord's word, torn out of their pulpits by his men-at-arms and thrown to the ground, dragged out and beaten through the town like criminals.

Then, when he saw that he could not get what he wanted through siege, he began to treat for peace. We replied to this that we did not wish to negotiate for peace until the guards, crossbowmen and other armed men had been removed and the property which had been taken from us restored, so that all was in the same state and as free as the day he entered the city. He at once ordered that what we requested be done, but it was not put into effect and so we placed the city under interdict [banned all Church services in the city]. The emperor, seeing that his malice could not make any progress, did not wish to drag out his stay in the country any longer. Yet, as if he wanted to destroy everything, he had the crossbows and weapons which had been kept for a long time for the defense of the country placed secretly into ships at Acre; and he sent many things to the sultan of Egypt, as if to his dear friend. He also sent some of his knights to Cyprus, and had no little money extorted from the inhabitants. What seemed even more amazing to us was that he had the galleys which he could not take with him destroyed. When we heard this we decided that he should be rebuked for it. But he, despising the rebuke and correction, on the feast of the Apostles Philip and James [May 1] went secretly on board a galley, using a secret road and harbor, and hurried toward Cyprus. He bade farewell to no one, leaving Joppa abandoned, and may he never return!

Already the representatives of the said sultan have barred the way outside the walls of the city to poor Christians and Syrians, so that many have failed on the pilgrim road. The emperor committed these things in the Holy Land and to the detriment of his soul, and many others that the world knows and which we leave to others to tell. May the merciful Lord deign to control them when He pleases. Farewell.

Source: Matthew Paris, *Chronica majora*, ed. Henry Richards Luard, Rolls Series 57, 7 vols. (London: Longman, 1872–83), vol. 3, pp. 179–84.

DOCUMENT 8
King James I of Aragon Plans an Attack on the Muslim Kingdom of Valencia: 1233

King James I of Aragon (1213–76) conquered first the Balearic Is-
lands and then the kingdom of Valencia from their Muslim rulers. In this
extract from his autobiography, he describes how he first decided to invade
the kingdom of Valencia. The invasion began in 1233 and the city of
Valencia itself fell to James in 1238. Note how the speakers repeatedly
refer to God supporting the king and the projected expedition being God's
will. James writes in his own language, and the style is colloquial.

I was in my kingdom of Aragon, relaxing and amusing myself. I was at
Alcañiz, and with me were the master of the Hospital [in Aragon] and
Lord Blasco d'Alagón. They were both with me on a terrace. As we
were relaxing and talking, the master of the Hospital, whose name was
Sir Hugh de Forcalquier, began to speak. "My lord," he said, "since God
guided you so well in your capture of Majorca and the islands, why don't
you and we undertake something on this side of the sea, in the kingdom
of Valencia, which for so long has defied your lineage and for so long
they have tried to capture part of it and have not been able to. God
help me, it would be a good idea to think about this, since we are here
with you: for Lord Blasco knows more about it than any man in the
world, and he can tell us where in that country he thinks you should
attack from to capture it."

Lord Blasco d'Alagón replied: "I will certainly tell the king all that I
know, and what would be best; and since you wish me to speak, Master,
I will." So I requested him to say where he thought we could first enter
the kingdom of Valencia.

Lord Blasco turned to me, and said: "My lord, the Master of the
Hospital is speaking the truth. Since God has allowed you to make
conquests overseas, you should now conquer what is at the gates of your
own kingdom. It is the best country and the most beautiful country in
the world; for I was in it, my lord, for a good two years and more when
you threw me out of your country. I have not seen under God so delightful a location as the city of Valencia and the whole of the kingdom.

The kingdom is a good seven days' journey in length. If God wishes you to conquer it, and you wish to, you will conquer the most delightful place with the strongest castles in the whole world.

"I will tell you what I think about this. If I advised you to go and besiege a strong castle, I would be giving you bad advice, because there are a good forty or fifty that you and all your forces could never take while their supplies last. So I will advise you, according to my own knowledge and understanding, to go to Borriana, for the reason that Borriana is in a flat place and is close to your own land, and you can reach it by sea and by land better than you could if it were inland. And, trusting in God, you should be able to capture it within a month, and you will find a great deal of food there. That is the best place I know for you to begin the conquest of the kingdom of Valencia."

The Master of the Hospital said: "My lord, Lord Blasco has told you the truth: there is no better place in the world for you to capture. Everyone who has been in the kingdom of Valencia says so, and so does popular opinion."

I said: "I have heard your and Lord Blasco's advice, and I believe that it is good and loyal, and, since you are in agreement, in God's name may it be that you have advised me for the best. I will tell you something that indicates that God wants this. I was at Majorca at Cap de Pera when Minorca surrendered; and I had with me Lord Sanç d'Horta, and his brother Lord García d'Horta, and Pero Llopis de Pomar, who had been to the *alcaid* of Xàtiva as my messenger, and we were praising the country of Majorca a great deal. But while we were praising it, Lord Sanç d'Horta said: 'My lord, you can praise Majorca and the kingdom of Majorca all day, but go and conquer Valencia and all that kingdom, for this is nothing next to that. You will find at Valencia that five or six thousand crossbowmen and countless others will attack you so that you cannot engage the army of the town, such is the strength of the crossbowmen and the forces that are there. And if you take that town, you will certainly be able to say that you are the best king in the world, because you have done so much.' "

Source: Jaume I, *Crònica o llibre dels feits*, ed. Ferran Soldevila (Barcelona: Edicions 62, 1982), chs. 127–29, pp. 157–59.[13]

DOCUMENT 9
The Prussian Crusade, 1260–61

According to the letter of dedication at the beginning of his chronicle,
Peter von Dusburg was a priest and brother of the Teutonic Order. His
chronicle begins with the foundation of the order in 1190 and ends in
1330. Here he describes how the Prussian lords, having made a peace
treaty with the Teutonic Order and converted to Christianity, abandoned
the treaty and began the war again. This was the second time that this
had happened. The order called these revolts "apostasies"—that is, aban-
doning the Christian religion. In fact the real cause of the revolt would
have been that the Prussians wanted more rights and independence than
the order allowed.

Book III, Chapter 89: The Second Apostasy of the Prussians, which Lasted 15 Years

In that same year [1260], on the eve of the feast of the blessed apostle
and evangelist Matthew [September 20], the Prussians, seeing that the
war had left the brothers [of the Teutonic Order] short of brothers,
squires, horses, arms and other things that are necessary for battle, added
evil to evils and sorrow to sorrow by apostasizing from the faith and the
faithful for a second time and returning to their original errors. They
elected as captains and leaders of their army a certain man from Samland
called Glande, one Henry Monte from the Natanger people, one Glap-
pus from Warmia [Ermland], Auttume from the Pogesanier people and
Diwanus from the Barth people.[14]

Chapter 90: Much Shedding of Christian Blood

These captains and leaders of the army decided on a certain day when
they should all come together under arms and kill anyone who professed
the Christian faith, until they had all been wiped out. And they carried
this out, because all the Christians whom they found outside the fortifications in the land of Prussia they either pitifully cut to pieces or led
away as prisoners to perpetual slavery. They burned the churches, chap-
els and oratories of God, treating the Church sacraments irreverently,
taking the holy vestments and vessels for forbidden uses and pitifully

cutting to pieces the priests and other ministers of the Church. They seized a certain man from Samland, a priest-brother of the Teutonic Order, who had been sent to baptize them, and pressed his neck between two boards, until he collapsed and expired. They claimed that this kind of martyrdom was suited to holy men, whose blood they did not dare spill.

Chapter 91: A Conflict in Pokarben, where Many Christians were Killed

In the Year of Our Lord 1261, flying rumors of this persecution shook princes and barons throughout Germany. The lord of Reyder and many nobles from other parts of Germany, sympathetic to the faith and the faithful and regretting that a new plantation of the Church in Prussian parts, set up through the shedding of the blood of many of the faithful, should perish so miserably, came to the said country to help. With them, the brothers and their squires entered the land of the Natanger and devastated it with fire and pillage, capturing and killing many. Then they returned to the place where the castle of Brandenburg is now situated, and marked out their camp.

The brothers and pilgrims [i.e., crusaders] decided that one part of the army should return into the said country to ravage it again, while the other remained in the said place. The Natanger people considered this, and because they were few in number and did not dare to plunder their land, they assembled and attacked the part of the army that had stayed behind at Pokarben. The pilgrims and brothers opposed them manfully, and especially a knight from Westphalia named Stenckel von Bentheim, who had heard a certain sermon by a bishop that said that the soul of a faithful Christian killed in Prussia should fly up into heaven without any purgatory. He pressed on his warhorse, applying his spurs, and with lance directed in knightly manner he passed through the enemy's ranks, slaying the impious to the right and the left, and they fell back from him hither and thither. But, as he returned, while he was coming through the midst of them, he was killed and a bitter battle broke out between them, with many on both sides fatally wounded and killed. At last, as God pleased, it was done. The lord of Reyder himself was killed, with a great part of his army and the brothers who were with him. Some were captured, and the rest turned and fled.

While these things were happening, the brothers with the other part of the army were approaching the place of the contest and saw that the Christian army was routed and could not be rescued because the enemy's numbers were too great. So they returned to their base by another route.

After this slaughter, the Natanger people, wishing to offer a victim to their gods, threw lots over their German captives and it fell twice on a certain noble and wealthy burgher of Magdeburg called Hirtzhals. Placed in these straits, he asked Henry Monte [the leader of the Natanger people] to remember the benefits that he had often shown him in the city of Magdeburg, and free him from this misery. Hearing this, Henry was sorry for him and freed him twice. But when the third lot fell on him again, he did not wish to be redeemed, but instead voluntarily offered himself in good confession as a sacrifice to God. He was tied on his horse and burned. Note this, that the same Henry and many others affirmed later on their oaths that when that same burgher who was burned on his horse gave up his spirit, they saw a pure white dove fly out of his mouth.

Chapter 92: A Foresight of this Battle

There was in the German region a certain woman of holy life living as a recluse. Hearing a crowd of demons passing by her cell making a great crashing and clattering, she adjured them and asked them where they were going. "To Prussia," they said. "There will be a great battle there tomorrow." "When you come back," she said, "tell me what happened." When they came back they said that the Christians had lost the victory and that every soul whose body had been killed there was saved except for three who had not come to the battle out of religious devotion but for military exercise.

Source: Peter von Dusburg, *Chronik des Preussenlandes: Petri de Dusburg Chronica terre Prussie*, text of Max Toeppen, ed. Klaus Scholz and Dieter Wojtecki (Darmstadt: Wissenschaftliche Buchgesellschaft, 1984), bk. 3, chs. 89–92, pp. 210–14.

DOCUMENT 10
The Douglas Goes on Crusade, 1329

Jean le Bel, contemporary of these events, tells how in 1329 King Robert Bruce of Scotland, on his deathbed, requested his friend and noble knight James Douglas to take his heart to the Holy Land after his death. The story is supported by the English government records, which record that on September 1, 1329, King Edward III of England granted letters of safe conduct to James Douglas, who was going on crusade to the East with the heart of King Robert Bruce of Scotland, recently deceased. Edward also wrote to King Alfonso XI of Castile, recommending Douglas to him and asking him to allow him to pass through his lands in peace. Jean exaggerates Douglas' rash courage, which he regarded as typically Scottish. His account illustrates the importance of crusading to the nobility of western Europe in the fourteenth century. Jean calls Douglas "William." In fact, his successors were named William; the famous crusader was James.

While this truce [with the English] was still in force, it came about that King Robert [Bruce] of Scotland, who had been so doughty, became old and feeble, and infected with a great disease, so that people said that he was going to die. When he saw that he was certainly going to die, he sent for all the barons of his kingdom in whom he trusted the most, and told them that he must die, as they could see. He begged them affectionately and entrusted them with the task, on their good word, of loyally guarding his kingdom for David, his son. When David should come of age, they should obey him and crown him king and marry him to someone who was of suitable rank for him. And after that, he called the noble knight Sir William [James] Douglas, and said to him before all the others: "Sir William" [James] "knight and friend, you know that I have had much to do in my time and I have suffered a great deal to uphold the rights of this kingdom. And because I have had so much to do, I made a vow that I have not been able to carry out, which troubles me: I vowed that, if I was able to win my war and could govern this kingdom in peace, I would go to wage war on the enemies of Our Lord and those who are against the Christian faith overseas, as far as I could. My heart has always yearned for this, but Our Lord has not agreed to it. He has given me so much to do in my time and at the last He has so overtaken me with feebleness and serious disease that I must die as you see me. Since my body cannot go nor carry out what my heart has so desired, I want to send my heart in place of my body, to carry out my vow on behalf of myself and my wish. Because I do not know anyone in my kingdom more doughty than you, nor better placed to carry out this vow in my place, I wish and I beg you, my knight and my special friend, as much and as affectionately as I may, to carry out this journey for love of me and to acquit my soul in the eyes of Our Lord. . . ."

. . . Chapter 16: How Sir William [James] Douglas Left Scotland to Make His Journey

When spring came and with it the good season for traveling for those who wish to cross the high seas, and the noble knight Sir William [James] Douglas had made the preparations that were necessary for him to carry out his instructions, he embarked on the sea from Scotland and went to Flanders. He went straight to Sluis to hear news of whether anyone on this side of the sea were getting ready to go to the holy land of Jerusalem, so that he could have better company. He stayed at Sluis a good twelve days before departing, but during the whole of the twelve days he refused to put a foot ashore, preferring to remain on his ship, and he always held his court honorably, with trumpets and drums, as if he were the king of Scotland. He had a knight banneret in his company with six others from among the most doughty warriors of the country, and a good twenty squires, young and fine-looking, the most suitable that he could select from his country, and no other attendants. He had a great many silver dishes, pots, basins, plates, drinking cups, bottles, basins, barrels and other such things. All those who wished to go there were entertained with two sorts of wine and two sorts of spice, provided that they were people of estate.

At last, when he had stayed there long enough, he heard that the king of Spain [Castile: Alfonso XI] was waging war on the king of Granada [Muḥammad IV], who was Saracen.[15] So he decided that he would go in that direction, so as to make the best of the opportunities of his journey, and when he had carried out his business he could continue on his way to carry out what he had been commanded to do. So he left

Sluis and went toward Spain, and first arrived at the port of Valencia the Great, and then he went to the king of Spain, who was with his army fighting the king of Granada, and they were quite close to each other on the frontiers of their kingdoms.

One day, after Sir William [James] Douglas had arrived, it happened that the king of Spain went out into the fields to approach his enemies. On the other side, the king of Granada went out, so that each king saw the other with all his banners, and they began to draw up their battle lines, one against the other. The said Sir W. withdrew to one of the flanks, the better to carry out his business and show off his efforts. When he saw all the battle lines drawn up and saw the king's line move a little, he thought that it was going to engage the enemy. He, who preferred to be among the first rather than the last, spurred his horse with his whole company and went toward the king of Granada's division, believing that the king and all his battle lines were following him. But he was gravely mistaken, because they never moved that day; instead, the said Sir William [James] and all his company were surrounded by the enemy and not one of them escaped. They were all killed, which was a great pity and a great loss for the Spanish.

Source: *Chronique de Jean le Bel*, ed. Jules Viard and Eugène Déprez (Paris: Renouard, 1904; reprinted, Paris: Honoré Champion, 1977), vol. 1, pp. 83–84, 86–88.

DOCUMENT 11
The Second Crusade against the Hussites, September 1421

> *The second crusade against the Hussites attacked from the northwest of Bohemia and besieged the city of Žatec. After three weeks, Žižka approached with an army to relieve the city. At news of his coming, the crusaders fled. The Hussites pursued them and killed many of them. This account, by a Czech writer, includes a description of the crusade indulgence offered to the crusaders. The author emphasizes the cruelty of the crusaders and states that they treated the Czechs savagely in order to prove their Christian piety. At the same time, the writer believes that the Czechs defeated the crusaders through God's help. Captured Czechs were burned as heretics. The "Praguers" were Hussites from Prague; the "Germans" were the crusaders.*

*A few additions have been made to this translation to make events
clear to readers of this book; these are in curly brackets.*

On the day after the nativity of the Blessed Virgin, the cities of Cho-
mútov and Kadaň were occupied [{by the crusaders}, having already been
evacuated] by the Praguers. Thus it happened that the captains in charge
of the army of the Misnians and Germans already in the area making
conquests, partly destroyed the city walls without even waiting for the
Praguers to appear. They did this to their own damage and to the shame
of the Praguers and also burned some houses and then proceeded on to
Žatec. After the previously mentioned Germans of Meißen had, together
with some Czechs sympathetic to them, conquered the towns of Cho-
mútov and Kadaň, they laid siege to the fortress of the town of Bílina
which belonged to the lord of Koldov. They destroyed the surrounding
fortresses and villages and did not spare either peasants or women at all
but inhumanely slaughtered many pregnant women. When the Praguers
heard of these wicked acts, the thirteenth of September, that is to say
on the Saturday before the raising of the cross, two communal divisions
of soldiers left Prague on foot together with a large number of peasants
in order to drive those Germans from the field. When the Germans
heard of the approach of the Praguers, they abandoned the siege of the
fortress of Bílina. Likewise, Sigismund of Děčín [and Vartenberk], together with his allies, abandoned the siege of the new fortress called
"Chalice" at Litoměřice before the citizens of Prague arrived.[16]

At this same time a large number of Germans, together with the
prince-electors of the empire, had invaded Bohemia through Cheb en
route to Žatec. They expelled those of Prague waiting in Slaný and sent
them off to the allied barons. Word came to Žižka and to the other
Táborites that they should advance to Slaný with the largest possible
army in order to move against the Germans and expel them. This was
on account of the fact that it was rumoured that the prince-electors of
the empire, along with the ecclesiastical and secular lords and the Ba-
varian and Rhineland electors, dukes, counts, barons and knights, together with an even larger number of armed people, on the initiation
of the papal crusade, had crept clandestinely into the kingdom of Bohemia. When they reached the Czech borders, the bishops dismounted
and in front of them all expressed humility, false though it was, in order
that God might grant good success in terms of defeating the Bohemian

heretics, then they walked across [the border]. Among the bishops of great esteem included the following: Johannes, archbishop of Mainz, the archbishop of Cologne, the archbishop of Trier, Duke Ludwig, the son of Klem, the count of Nassau, together with many others whose names we do not know.

When they had laid siege to Žatec, they made six attempts on the Friday before [the day of] St. Matthias to storm the town. However, they were badly beaten and with considerable damage were repulsed by the help of God's grace. It was reported by those living in the town that about sixty of them had been killed, although many wounded had been carried off by the enemy. At least sixty prisoners had been taken into the town. At this time an enormous crowd, of more than 6,500, had congregated at the town on behalf of the German tyranny. There were more than 5,000 warriors on foot and 400 cavalry. Many people had come from all over Christendom to join the German army, people with different languages from far away. They had come to join in the great remission of all guilt and sin which had been offered and extended by the pope. Even these people who saw the [crusading] army claimed they had never before seen such a numerous, well-equipped army with so many tents gathered together. According to a common consensus there were some 200,000 warriors. Day after day they burned down country villages, towns and castles and, eager to receive the [aforementioned papal] indulgence, they were even crueller than the heathens and they killed and burned those of both sexes, young as well as old. Fear and trembling seized the hearts of many people in the area of Žatec. Because of this some forsook the fortresses and fled to the cities. While there, some of them were subjected, without mercy, to burning like the rest.

In order to maintain their forces as well as their honor, they {the crusaders} sent off a contingent to King Sigismund and urged him, with reference to his oath at Constance, to come with the largest possible army in order to prosecute the heretics. If he would not come, the prince-electors [threatened] they would arrange to have another king of the Romans {i.e., replace Sigismund}. But before King Sigismund of Hungary was able to leave where he was at to join the army, the Lord Jesus heard the weeping and wailing and shouting of the women and the virgins and the widows, and the anger of God and a just vengeance came over all of the armies of the enemies. In some miraculous way, Almighty God put those inhuman armies to flight without so much as another attack. On October 2, in many places the tents of the army caught fire by the coincidence of God. Above the tents one could see a single yellow and brown pillar which went from one tent to the next and wherever it went a bolt of fire shot down into the tent. Abandoning their goods they [the crusaders] fled, some barely escaping with their lives. When the people of Žatec saw what was happening, they pursued the crusaders with about a thousand men and killed several hundred. They captured others alive and cast them into prison. Then they gave God praise with great thanksgiving because God had scattered their enemies and the persecutors of the truth had been put to flight.

Translated by Thomas A. Fudge from "Historia Hussitica," in *Fontes rerum bohemicarum*, ed. Jaroslav Goll, vol. 5 (Prague: Nákladem nadání Františka Palackého, 1893), pp. 511–13.

DOCUMENT 12
John Kaye's 1482 Translation of Guillaume Caoursin's Eyewitness Account of the 1480 Siege of Rhodes by the Ottoman Turks

The spelling and grammar of this fifteenth-century translation has been modernized. Note the garbled version of Islamic belief. Typically for Catholic Christians of this period, the writer believed that Muslims worshiped Muḥammad, not realizing that Muḥammad is in fact honored as a prophet. The writer describes the Turks' use of early cannons, called "bombards," that fired stone balls. The bombards are described as "casting," or "throwing," their ammunition more often than "firing" or "shooting." The traditional siege engines, which had been in use in warfare since the time of the old Roman Empire, had thrown stones, and the old terminology was still in use even though the artillery had changed. The writer also compares the Christian warriors to ancient Roman soldiers.

When the extract opens, the Turkish army is about to begin a major assault on the town of Rhodes. The town is being defended by its Greek and western European inhabitants, led by the brothers of the order of the

Hospital of St. John of Jerusalem, here called "knights of the Order of Rhodes."

Meanwhile, the Turks made themselves ready in their army to come and make an assault. A general announcement was made: that the great Turk [the sultan] would give them all the goods that were in Rhodes [town]; and that they should take all the young children in Rhodes and make them give up their [Christian] faith; and those who were aged between ten and twenty years should have their throats cut; and all those who were aged over that who were taken alive should be impaled with a long stake through their backsides and through the head. For this reason they should carry with them to the assault eight thousand stakes. The great Turk would be satisfied simply with a victory and with being supreme owner of Rhodes.

Soon after this announcement, all the Turks came toward Rhodes; but before they began their attack, in accordance with their false beliefs they called Muḥammad to their help, stripped themselves naked and washed themselves in running water, to represent the washing away of their sins. Afterward they each equipped themselves according to their status as warriors, and brought sacks with them, in which to put the goods of the town of Rhodes, and they tied ropes around their waists with which to tie up their prisoners, for they hoped in their God Muḥammad that they would without fail win a victory over Rhodes. The day before the great assault and battle, they cast and shot against the wall great stones from the greatest bombards that they had, and threw down the repairs and defenses that the Rhodians had made in the broken walls, so that they struck and slew the guards that were on the walls on the following night. For they never stopped throwing [stones from bombards] all through that day and the night and all the morning of the following day on which the great assault was made, so that nobody could stand safely on the walls or could prevent the walls being destroyed; for in a short time three hundred great stones were thrown.

After the Turks had finished shooting off their bombards, on the 28 July [1480] at about eight o'clock in the morning, they came together in a great multitude and number, and crossed over the ditch, which had been filled with the ruins from the broken walls of the city, and then they climbed nimbly on to the walls, more nimbly than the Rhodians could on their side, with ladders and steps. As soon as the Turks were on the walls they slew all the Christian men who were there in defense, and set up their standards and banners before the Rhodians were able to climb up the walls with ladders. But soon the Rhodians were there ready to hand, and from each side there went up a great and horrible shout: for all those from Rhodes cried to Jesus Christ; and the Turks cried "Muḥammad." And so the Rhodians, fighting manfully and heartily, resisted and withstood the great pressure from the Turks. There was the worshipful lord, the lord of Montelyon, captain of the men of war of Rhodes; and brother to the lord master [of the order of the Hospital: Pierre d'Aubusson].[17] And there were with him many knights of the Order of Rhodes and many other men of the city, some of whom were slain in that assault and battle, and many wounded.

There were on that side of the assault four great ladders in different places so that people could go up and down the walls, one of which was toward the Jews' Street. By that ladder and place the Turks came down into the city, but immediately the lord master commanded that it [the ladder] should be cut and pulled down. He himself went up on the walls at another place nearby with his company and there they fought against the enemies of Christ's faith, as manfully as ever the Romans did for their emperor, and slew many Turks, and finally beat them off. The lord master had five wounds, one of which was thought to endanger his life; but he was helped through the grace of God and help from leeches [doctors] and surgeons. He, because of his great manhood and noble heart toward God and toward his order, throughout all Rhodes was called the true father and defender of the city and of the faith of Jesus Christ. What great glory and praise he and his company with all the fighting men of Rhodes deserved that same day!

Source: Guillaume Caoursin, *The Siege of Rhodes (1482)*. Translated by John Kaye and Aesopus, *The Book of Subtyl Histories and Fables of Esope (1484)*, Facsimile Reproductions, introduction by Douglas Gray (Delmar, NY: Scholars' Facsimiles and Reprints, 1975). No folio numbers; actually folios 19r–20r.

NOTES

1. The Fatimid caliph and his ministers in Egypt did not know that the crusaders wished to capture Jerusalem for themselves. They hoped to use the crusaders as a military force to recover territory in Syria and Palestine that had

been lost to the Seljuk Turks. Jerusalem was Fatimid territory that had been captured by the Seljuks twenty years previously.

2. For modern analyses of the battle, see R. C. Smail, *Crusading Warfare, 1097–1193: Second Edition with a New Bibliographical Introduction by Christopher Marshall* (Cambridge and New York: Cambridge University Press, 1995), pp. 172–74; France, *Victory in the East*, pp. 282–96.

3. This was the lance-head that had been discovered in Antioch while the crusaders were besieged in the city. Contemporaries disagreed over whether it was really the lance-head that had pierced Christ's side when he was on the cross, as was claimed when it was found.

4. These were Byzantine saints who were not well known in the West before the crusades. See Christopher Walter, *The Warrior Saints in Byzantine Art and Tradition* (Aldershot, Hants., and Burlington, VT: Ashgate, 2003).

5. Translated by Peter Edbury in *The Conquest of Jerusalem and the Third Crusade: Sources in Translation* (Aldershot, Hants., and Brookfield, VT: Scolar, 1996), pp. 165–66.

6. Massé did not translate the next part of the text. There is a French translation in *Recueil des historiens des croisades, publié par les soins de l'Académie des inscriptions et belles-lettres. Historiens orientaux*, 5 vols. (Paris: Imprimerie nationale, 1872–1906; reprint, Farnborough: Gregg International, 1967), vol. 4, pp. 320–22.

7. Massé did not translate the next part of the text, which sets out the arrangement of the siege and a speech by Saladin in praise of the city and the Aqsa mosque. There is a French translation in *Recueil des historiens des croisades, Historiens orientaux*, vol. 4, pp. 322–26.

8. Peter of les Vaux-de-Cernay, *The History of the Albigensian Crusade*, pp. 292–93. The date is fixed by a reference later in the text to Conrad, cardinal bishop of Porto, being papal legate against the Albigensians. He held this post from late 1219 to 1223: Walter L. Wakefield, *Heresy, Crusade and Inquisition in Southern France, 1100–1250* (London: Allen and Unwin, 1974), p. 199.

9. Possibly the fortress of Lavaur; see Wakefield, *Heresy, Crusade and Inquisition*, p. 199.

10. Frederick did not crown himself king, but was staging a formal crown-wearing ceremony so that everyone could see that he was king. The patriarch was angry because according to the custom of the kingdom the patriarch himself should have placed the crown on Frederick's head as a symbol that Frederick's authority came from God.

11. King Philip II of France (d. 1223) had left money to the kingdom of Jerusalem in his will.

12. A wound could not be healed until the iron weapon that had caused it

had been removed. In other words, there were problems outstanding that meant peace could not yet be certain.

13. See also *The Chronicle of James I, King of Aragon, Surnamed the Conqueror (Written by Himself)*, trans. John Forster, introduction and notes by Pascual de Gayangos (London: Chapman and Hall, 1883; reprint, Farnborough: Gregg International, 1968), pp. 221–24; and *The Book of Deeds of James I of Aragon: A Translation of the Medieval Catalan 'Llibre dels Fets,'* trans. Damian Smith and Helena Buffery (Aldershot, Hants., and Burlington, VT: Ashgate, 2003), pp. 137–39.

14. These are all the names of Prussian tribes.

15. The word "Saracen" had become a synonym for "Muslim."

16. Note from Fudge, *The Crusade against Heretics in Bohemia*, p. 130: "in May 1421, Žižka conquered a small wooden fortress on the top of a hill near the town of Tiebusin near Litoměřice. The fortress belonged to the Knights of the Teutonic Order. He named the fortress 'Chalice' and made it his own."

17. This must be Antoine d'Aubusson, lord of Monteil-le-Vicomte.

GLOSSARY

Bull: An official document sent out by the pope or emperor, with the papal or imperial seal (*bulla*) attached to it.

Caliph: A Muslim leader who controlled both civil and religious affairs. The original caliphs were the successors of the Prophet Muḥammad. In the eleventh century, there were two caliphs in Islam: the Sunni caliph in Baghdad and the Shi'ite Fatimid caliph in Cairo, Egypt. The caliphate in Cairo ended in 1171. In 1258 the Mongols sacked Baghdad and murdered its caliph. Shortly afterward, the Mamluk Sultan Baibars installed a Sunni caliph in Cairo.

Cathars: A religious sect holding dualist beliefs, which means that they believed in two opposed gods: a good god of light and an evil god of darkness. The good god, they believed, created everything spiritual, while the evil god created everything physical. "Moderate Catharism" was quite similar to Christianity, with Satan as the evil god and the Holy Trinity as the good god. In its more extreme forms, Catharism was effectively a new religion.

Catholic: *See* Latin Christians.

Christian Orthodox: *See* Orthodox.

Cistercian Order: Catholic monastic order founded in 1098 at Cîteaux in central-eastern France, characterized by a "back to basics" approach to the monastic life. Its members set out to follow a simple Christian life separate from society.

Crusade indulgence: *See* Indulgence.

Crusader states: The lordships established by the crusaders in the eastern Mediterranean area. Most of the people who lived in them were not crusaders, but either local people or immigrants who had come out from Europe to settle there.

Emir: Originally meaning simply "commander," the title came to mean an independent Muslim ruler.

Empire, western: Theoretically a "reestablishment" of the Roman Empire in the west, which had disintegrated in the sixth century. By the eleventh century, this comprised what is now Germany, the Low Countries, the Alps, and northern Italy. The emperor was elected by certain German princes and lords, and crowned by the pope. Later called the Holy Roman Empire.

Franks: *See* Palestinian Franks.

Great Schism: Between 1378 and 1417 there was more than one pope in western Christendom. From 1378 to 1409 there were two, one in Avignon and one in Rome, and from 1409 to 1415 there was an additional pope in Pisa. These popes competed for religious supremacy, and the rulers of western Christendom supported whichever one suited them. The dispute led to the rise of the "conciliar movement," in which Church councils—at, for example, Constance and Basel—attempted to reform the Church.

Hanseatic League: A commercial league of merchant towns of north Germany, formed in the thirteenth century to protect their trading interests in the Baltic area and the North Sea. The league had bases in many towns, including Novgorod and London. In the later middle ages it had its own army and navy. In the sixteenth century it began to decline, as the main trading routes moved into the Atlantic and trade developed with the New World, but it survived in a much reduced form into the nineteenth century.

Heretic: A religious believer who stubbornly holds beliefs that differ from the beliefs laid down by the official religious body, and which are offensive to the authorities. In Medieval Europe, heretics were persecuted because they threatened the authority of the Church and monarch. Some were also a threat to the stability of society; for example, they refused to take oaths at a time when oaths of allegiance were an important binding force in society.

Holy Land: Christian term for the region of Palestine where Jesus Christ lived and worked.

Holy War: War for a religious cause, fought in the name of God or gods.

Indulgence: Used here in the sense of letting a person off the punishment due for their sin or wrongdoing. In the case of the crusade indulgence, those who went on crusades were let off doing the rest of the penance that was due for the sins that they had committed and confessed to a priest. Although the suffering that they would go through on the crusade itself might not actually be enough to compensate for their sin, the Catholic Church had, in theory, enough merits stored up from the good deeds of saints of the past to be able to make up any shortfall in merit after the crusade.

Latin Christians: Catholic (not Greek Orthodox) Christians, whose main religious writings are in Latin. Their religious leader is the pope, whose traditional seat is at Rome.

Latin kingdom of Jerusalem: The kingdom set up by the crusaders in Palestine in 1099 after their capture of the city of Jerusalem. Its capital was initially at Jerusalem, until Jerusalem was captured by Saladin in 1187. From 1191 its capital was at Acre.

Latin states: The territories ruled by the Palestinian Franks in the East: the kingdom of Jerusalem, the principality of Antioch, the counties of Edessa and Tripoli, and the kingdom of Cyprus.

Legate: Official representative, delegate, or ambassador.

Levant, the: The eastern Mediterranean area.

Mamluks: Originally the word meant "slave." The Mamluks who seized power in Egypt in 1250 were elite warriors, the slave bodyguards of the sultan. Between 1250 and 1257 they controlled the sultans of Egypt; in 1257 the mamluk Qutuz seized power in his own name. The Mamluks ruled Egypt and much of the Middle East until 1517.

Military religious order: A Latin Christian religious group with a rule of daily life approved by the Church authorities, whose members had vowed to help protect Christians and Christian territory. The members made the three monastic vows of poverty, chastity, and obedience, and wore a religious habit, but unlike monks, they could travel about in the course of their religious life. Some members of the order were warriors who formed an army to fight those who attacked Christians; others were support forces, such as servants, women (who gave prayer support to the warriors), and priests. The most famous military orders are the Order of the Temple, the Hospital of St. John of Jerusalem, and the Teutonic Order.

Mongols: Nomadic mounted warriors from northeastern Asia. They now live mainly in Mongolia.

Orthodox: Strictly speaking, "sound in doctrine"; in other words, a good Christian is orthodox. The Orthodox Church is a division of the Christian Church comprising several independent churches that all acknowledge the special spiritual authority of the patriarch of Constantinople. However, unlike the pope in the Latin or Catholic Church, the patriarch is not regarded as having spiritual supremacy. The Orthodox Church differs from the Catholic Church in various points of doctrine. The most obvious differences for outside observers are the importance of the veneration of icons in Orthodox religion; the fact that Orthodox parish priests may marry while Catholic priests may not; and the fact that the Orthodox do not accept the Catholic doctrine of purgatory.

Palestinian Franks: The western European Christians who settled in the Middle East after 1099. Most of the people on the First Crusade came from France or from the west of Germany, which were the lands that had historically been populated by the Franks, a Germanic people. Therefore, the crusaders and the settlers who followed them originally called themselves Franks, the Muslims called them Franks, and historians call them Palestinian Franks for convenience.

Parias: A form of tribute. A monetary sum paid regularly by the Muslim petty kings of al-Andalus to the Christian rulers of northern Spain.

Penance: Some action to compensate God for sin (wrongdoing or crime committed against God). Satisfactory penance wipes out the punishment due for the sin.

Pilgrimage: A journey, usually with hardships, undertaken to a holy place for the purpose of penance.

Schismatic: Someone who separates from the Church on the grounds of a difference of religious belief. In the Middle Ages, the Catholic Christians regarded the Orthodox Christians as schismatics. *See also* Great Schism.

Shi'ites: Islamic sect. Differ from the Sunnis in that they do not accept the Islamic teachings that are not included in the Koran, and they believe that Ali, husband of the prophet Muḥammad's daughter Fatima, was Muḥammad's true successor.

Sunnis: Orthodox branch of Islam, followed by the majority of Muslims. Differ from the Shi'ites in that they accept the *Sunna*, a collection of teachings based on Muḥammad's words not included in the Koran, and they accept that the first four caliphs were the true successors to Muḥammad.

Visigoths: "West Goths." A Germanic tribe that moved into the Black Sea area in the early centuries of the Roman Empire. In the fourth century, they were driven out by the Huns and entered the Roman

Empire as refugees. They fought and defeated the forces of the eastern Roman Empire in 378 at the battle of Adrianople, but were then taken into imperial service, where they acted as mercenary troops. They were employed by general Stilicho in the western Empire, but after Stilicho's fall, the Roman Senate refused to pay them, and in 410 they sacked Rome. They were later taken back into imperial employment and were used as military forces against other dangerous Gothic tribes, such as the Vandals and Alans. In 418 they were settled in Aquitaine, in southwest France, where they continued to supply military service to the emperor in return for land. In 456 they moved into the Iberian peninsula to attack another German tribe, the Sueves. They conquered the peninsula and set up their own government. The remaining imperial authorities in Italy approved, on the basis that the Visigoths could stop the Vandals invading Italy.

Vizier: A leading court official of a Muslim state; the equivalent of a prime minister in a western European state.

ANNOTATED
BIBLIOGRAPHY

Primary Sources

Crusades to the Holy Land, 1095–1291

Ambroise. *The Crusade of Richard Lionheart*. Translated by John L. La Monte and Merton Jerome Hubert. Reprint, New York: Octagon Books, 1976. *The History of the Holy War: Ambroise's Estoire de la guerre sainte*, ed. Marianne Ailes and Malcolm Barber with a translation by Marianne Ailes. Woodbridge, Suffolk, and Rochester, NY: Boydell Press, 2003. First-hand account of much of the Third Crusade, told by an Anglo-Norman historian-poet.

Arab Historians of the Crusades. Translated by Francesco Gabrieli, translated from the Italian by E. J. Costello. London: Routledge, 1969. Reprint, New York: Dorset Press, 1989. A selection of sources about the crusades and crusaders, translated from Arabic.

Christian Society and the Crusaders, 1198–1229: Sources in Translation, including "The Capture of Damietta" by Oliver of Paderborn. Translated by John J. Gavigan; edited by Edward Peters. Philadelphia: University of Pennsylvania Press, 1971. Oliver of Paderborn provides the best medieval account of the Fifth Crusade.

Chronicle of the Third Crusade: A Translation of the Itinerarium Peregrinorum et Gesta Regis Ricardi. Translated by Helen Nicholson. Aldershot, Hants., and Brookfield, VT: Ashgate, 1997. Partly based on Ambroise's history of the Third Crusade and partly on other firsthand evidence, this is the most complete medieval account of the Third Crusade.

The Conquest of Jerusalem and the Third Crusade: Sources in Translation. Translated by Peter W. Edbury. Aldershot, Hants., and Brookfield, VT: Scolar,

1996. A selection of sources about the fall of the kingdom of Jerusalem to Saladin in 1187 and the Third Crusade.

Crusader Syria in the Thirteenth Century: The Rothelin Continuation of the History of William of Tyre with Part of the Eracles or Acre Text. Translated by Janet Shirley. Aldershot, Hants., and Brookfield, VT: Ashgate, 1999. Contemporary thirteenth-century accounts of events in the Holy Land.

The Crusades: A Documentary Survey. Edited by James A. Brundage. Milwaukee: Marquette University Press, 1962. An authoritative collection of translated essential sources for the crusades.

Gesta Francorum et aliorum Hierosolimitanorum. Translated by Rosalind Hill. London: Nelson, 1962. The primary account of the First Crusade. Direct, lively, and readable.

Guibert of Nogent. *The Deeds of God through the Franks: Gesta Dei per Francos.* Translated by Robert Levine. Woodbridge, Suffolk, and Rochester, NY: Boydell, 1997. Based partly on the *Gesta Francorum*, this is a secondhand account in which the monk Guibert tried to deduce God's purpose for the crusaders.

A History of Deeds Done beyond the Sea, by William of Tyre. Translated by Emily A. Babcock and A. Krey. 2 vols. Reprint. New York: Octagon Books, 1976. The most important source for the history of the kingdom of Jerusalem in the period 1099–1184. Ends just before Saladin's conquest of the kingdom in 1187, but the future was already clear when Archbishop William stopped writing.

Ibn al-Fūrat. *Ayyubids, Mamlukes and Crusaders: Selections from the Tārīk al-Duwal wa'l-Mulūk of Ibn al-Fūrat.* Translated by U. and M. C. Lyons; introduction by Jonathan Riley-Smith. 2 vols. Cambridge: Heffer, 1971. Valuable account of the crusaders from the point of view of their opponents.

Ibn Shaddād, Bahā' al-Dīn Yūsuf ibn Rāfi'. *The Rare and Excellent History of Saladin.* Translated by D. S. Richards. Aldershot, Hants, and Brookfield, VT: Ashgate, 2001. Biography of Saladin by one of his closest friends.

'Imād al-Dīn al-Isfahānī. *Conquête de la Syrie et de la Palestine par Saladin (al-Fath al-qussî fî l-fath al-qudsî.* Translated by Henri Massé. Paris: Paul Geuthner 1972. French translation of this vital contemporary account of Saladin's campaigns.

Jerusalem Pilgrimage 1099–1185. Edited by John Wilkinson, J. Hill, and W. F. Ryan. 2nd series, vol. 167. London: Hakluyt Society, 1988. Medieval descriptions of the city of Jerusalem and its surrounds in the twelfth century, written by Christian pilgrims to the city.

Joinville and Villehardouin. *Chronicles of the Crusades*. Translated by M.R.B. Shaw. Harmondsworth: Penguin, 1963, pp. 161–353. Translation of the classic account by Jean de Joinville of King Louis IX's first crusade.

The Templars: Selected Sources. Translated by Malcolm Barber and Keith Bate. Manchester and New York: Manchester University Press, 2002. A collection of translated source material on the Templars, with commentary by Malcolm Barber—well known and respected for his studies of the Templars.

The Wars of Frederick II against the Ibelins in Syria and Cyprus, by Philip de Novare. Translated by John L. La Monte. New York: Columbia University Press, 1936. Philip of Novara wrote in a racy, acid-sharp style. His account is very hostile to Emperor Frederick II.

Crusades to Greece

Crusaders as Conquerors: The Chronicle of the Morea Translated from the Greek. Translated by Harold E. Lurier. New York and London: Columbia University Press, 1964. Exciting and detailed narrative account of the crusaders' conquest of southern Greece after the Fourth Crusade.

Joinville and Villehardouin. *Chronicles of the Crusades*. Translated by M.R.B Shaw. Harmondsworth: Penguin, 1963, pp. 27–160. Translation of the classic account by Geoffrey of Villehardouin of the Fourth Crusade and the capture of Constantinople in 1204.

Robert of Clari. *The Conquest of Constantinople*. Translated by Edgar Holmes McNeal. Toronto, Buffalo and London: University of Toronto Press, 1996. The Fourth Crusade from an ordinary knight's point of view.

Crusades in Spain and the Baltic

De expugnatione Lyxbonensi: The Conquest of Lisbon, Edited from the Unique Manuscript in Corpus Christi College, Cambridge. Translated by Charles Wendell David, with a foreword and bibliography by Jonathan Phillips. New York: Columbia University Press, 2001. Fascinating firsthand account of the siege of Lisbon in 1147.

James I, king of Aragon. *The Book of Deeds of James I of Aragon*. Translated by Damian Smith and Helena Buffery. Aldershot, Hants., and Burlington, VT: Ashgate, 2003. King James I of Aragon's autobiography, including his account of his conquest of the Balearic Islands and the kingdom of Valencia.

The Livonian Rhymed Chronicle. Translated by Jerry C. Smith and William L. Urban. 2nd ed. Chicago, IL: Lithuanian Research and Studies Center, 2001. Written by an anonymous author for the brothers of the Teutonic Order, this tells the story of the crusaders' invasion and conquest of Livonia, including the Teutonic Order's version of the battle on Lake Chud (Peipus) in 1242, famed as the centerpiece of Eisenstein's film *Alexander Nevsky.*

Crusades against Heretics

The Crusade against Heretics in Bohemia, 1418–1437: Sources and Documents for the Hussite Crusades. Translated by Thomas A. Fudge. Aldershot, Hants., and Burlington, VT: Ashgate, 2002. Very useful and wide-reaching collection of documents relating to the Hussite Crusades.

Peter of les Vaux-de-Cernay. *The History of the Albigensian Crusade: Peter of les Vaux-de-Cernay's Historia Albigensis.* Translated by W. A. and M. D. Sibly. Woodbridge, Suffolk, and Rochester, NY: Boydell, 1998. This and the following entry are the two most important pro-crusader accounts of the Albigensian Crusades.

William of Puylaurens. *The Chronicle of William of Puylaurens: The Albigensian Crusade and its Aftermath.* Translated by W. A. and M. D. Sibly. Woodbridge, Suffolk, and Rochester, NY: Boydell, 2003.

William of Tudela. *The Song of the Cathar Wars: A History of the Albigensian Crusade, by William of Tudela and an Anonymous Successor.* Translated by Janet Shirley. Aldershot, Hants., and Brookfield, VT: Scolar, 1996. The first part of this account supports the crusaders; the second part supports the people of the Languedoc.

Crusades after 1291

Documents on the Later Crusades, 1274–1580, edited and translated by Norman Housley. Basingstoke: Macmillan, 1996. Very useful collection of translated documents relating to the later crusades, including plans for new expeditions and accounts of crusades.

Secondary Works

Barber, Malcolm. *The Cathars: Dualist Heretics in Languedoc in the High Middle Ages*. Harlow: Longman, 2000. Detailed, authoritative, and readable account of Languedocian society, the Cathars, and the Albigensian Crusades. Includes a chronology of the campaigns.

Barber, Malcolm. *The New Knighthood: A History of the Order of the Temple*. Cambridge and New York: Cambridge University Press, 1994. The standard scholarly study of the Templars in English. Detailed and thorough.

Brundage, James A. *Medieval Canon Law and the Crusader*. Madison and London: University of Wisconsin Press, 1969. Essential reading for understanding how and why the legal status of crusading and crusaders developed as it did in the Middle Ages. Readable and thoroughly referenced.

Christiansen, Eric. *The Northern Crusades*. 2nd ed. London: Penguin, 1997. The standard one-volume work on the crusades to northeastern Europe in English. An analytical study, covering the period from the twelfth to the sixteenth centuries. Outstanding scholarship.

Constable, Giles. "The Second Crusade as Seen by Contemporaries." *Traditio* 9 (1953): 213–79. The standard modern account of the Second Crusade.

Folda, Jaroslav. *The Art of the Crusaders in the Holy Land, 1098–1187*. Cambridge and New York: Cambridge University Press, 1995. The authoritative scholarly work on the subject.

Forey, Alan. *The Military Orders: From the 12th to the Early 14th Centuries*. Basingstoke: Macmillan, 1992. Meticulous and detailed, the best scholarly account of all the military religious orders written in English.

France, John. *Victory in the East: A Military History of the First Crusade*. Cambridge and New York: Cambridge University Press, 1994. Readable and fascinating scholarly account of the First Crusade. Includes maps and battle plans.

Fudge, Thomas A. *The Magnificent Ride: The First Reformation in Hussite Bohemia*. Aldershot, Hants., and Brookfield, VT: Ashgate, 1998. Clear modern account of the Hussite movement, its beliefs and development. Well illustrated and with a good bibliography.

Gervers, Michael, ed. *The Second Crusade and the Cistercians*. New York: St. Martin's Press, 1992. A useful collection of articles on the early period of crusading.

Heymann, Frederick Gotthold. *John Žižka and the Hussite Revolution*. Princeton, NJ: Princeton University Press, 1955. Classic account of the life of John Žižka and his role in the Hussite crusades.

Hillenbrand, Carole. *The Crusades: Islamic Perspectives*. Edinburgh: Edinburgh University Press, 1999. Widely praised study of Muslim attitudes toward the crusades and the crusaders.

Housley, Norman. *The Crusaders*. Stroud: Tempus, 2002. A narrative history of the crusades from the First Crusade to the sixteenth century, arranged around four firsthand accounts of crusading. Using these sources, Housley considers why the crusaders went on crusade.

Housley, Norman. *The Later Crusades: From Lyons to Alcazar, 1274–1580*. Oxford and New York: Oxford University Press, 1992. A detailed and far-ranging book on the crusades that took place between the second Church council of Lyons in 1274—when Pope Gregory X tried and failed to raise a crusade to help the Holy Land—and the failed Portuguese expedition to Morocco in 1578.

Jordan, William Chester. *Louis IX and the Challenge of the Crusade: A Study in Rulership*. Princeton, NJ: Princeton University Press, 1979. An account of how Louis IX organized his crusades. As much a study of royal government as of war, this book gives a valuable insight into the complexities of planning a crusade campaign in the mid-thirteenth century. Scholarly but readable.

Kennedy, Hugh. *Crusader Castles*. Cambridge and New York: Cambridge University Press, 1994. The standard scholarly work on the subject. Well presented and readable.

Laiou, Angeliki E., and Roy Parviz Mottahedeh, eds. *The Crusades from the Perspective of Byzantium and the Muslim World*. Washington, DC: Dumbarton Oaks, 2001. An important collection of essays by leading scholars.

Madden, Thomas F. *A Concise History of the Crusades*. Lanham, MD: Rowman & Littlefield, 1999. Considers the crusades between 1095 and 1291. The focus is on the crusades to the East, but the Albigensian Crusades are also described.

Madden, Thomas F. *The Crusades: The Essential Readings*. Oxford and Malden, MA: Blackwell, 2002. Reprint of twelve authoritative articles on the crusades.

Mayer, Hans Eberhard. *The Crusades*. Translated by John Gillingham. 2nd ed. Oxford and New York: Oxford University Press, 1988. Standard and authoritative history of the crusades from 1095 to 1291, with detailed notes and a summary bibliography.

Nicholson, Helen. *The Knights Hospitaller*. Woodbridge, Suffolk, and Rochester, NY: Boydell, 2001. A general history of the order of the Hospital from its beginnings in the Holy Land in the eleventh century to the present day.

Nicholson, Helen. *The Knights Templar: A New History*. Stroud: Sutton, 2001. A well-illustrated history aimed at the general, nonspecialist reader.

O'Callaghan, Joseph F. *A History of Medieval Spain*. Ithaca and London: Cornell University Press, 1975. Classic history by a greatly respected scholar.

O'Callaghan, Joseph F. *Reconquest and Crusade in Medieval Spain*. Philadelphia: University of Pennsylvania Press, 2002. An important new study, based on both Muslim and Christian sources.

Phillips, Jonathan, and Martin Hoch, eds. *The Second Crusade: Scope and Consequences*. Manchester and New York: Manchester University Press, 2001. A collection of recent studies of the Second Crusade.

Powell, James M. *Anatomy of a Crusade, 1213–1221*. Philadelphia: University of Pennsylvania Press, 1986. The standard modern scholarly (and readable) account of the Fifth Crusade.

Pringle, Denys. *Secular Buildings in the Crusader Kingdom of Jerusalem: An Archaeological Gazetteer*. Cambridge and New York: Cambridge University Press, 1997. A comprehensive listing and description of secular buildings in the kingdom of Jerusalem. (Another 2-volume work by Pringle lists churches.) Includes analysis and many illustrations.

Queller, Donald E., and Thomas F. Madden. *The Fourth Crusade: The Conquest of Constantinople*, with an essay on primary sources by Alfred J. Andrea. 2nd ed. Philadelphia: University of Pennsylvania Press, 1997. Standard scholarly work on the Fourth Crusade, now updated and revised.

Richard, Jean. *The Crusades, c. 1071–c. 1291*. Translated by Jean Birrell. Cambridge and New York: Cambridge University Press, 1999. English translation of this history of the crusades by an internationally respected scholar.

Riley-Smith, Jonathan. *The First Crusade and the Idea of Crusading.* London: Athlone, 1986. Considers how the crusade ideal developed and why.

Riley-Smith, Jonathan. *The First Crusaders, 1095–1131.* Cambridge and New York: Cambridge University Press, 1997. An invaluable study examining who went on crusade between 1095 and 1131, their family connections and relations, why they went on crusade, how they prepared their expeditions, and what happened to them after they returned. Includes a list of all currently known crusaders in the period covered by the book.

Riley-Smith, Jonathan. *The Knights of St. John in Jerusalem and Cyprus c. 1050–1310.* Reprint, Basingstoke and New York: Palgrave Macmillan, 2003. Originally published in 1967, the standard scholarly work on the order of the Hospital in English for the period that the order was based in the Holy Land.

Riley-Smith, Jonathan. *What Were the Crusades?* 3rd ed. Basingstoke and New York: Palgrave Macmillan, 2002. Groundbreaking at its first edition and still essential reading for historians of the crusades. Not everyone will agree with Professor Riley-Smith's definition of crusading, but his discussion of the issues is fundamental.

Riley-Smith, Jonathan, ed. *The Atlas of the Crusades.* London: Times Books, 1991. Beautifully illustrated, with maps detailing crusade expeditions not only to the Holy Land but also throughout medieval Europe.

Riley-Smith, Jonathan, ed. *The Oxford Illustrated History of the Crusades.* Oxford and New York: Oxford University Press, 1995. A beautifully presented and well received survey of crusading activity from the late eleventh century to 1798, with concluding chapters that consider modern depictions of crusades and what survives of crusading in the modern world.

Schein, Sylvia. *Fideles crucis: The Papacy, the West, and the Recovery of the Holy Land, 1274–1314.* Oxford and New York: Oxford University Press, 1991. A study of European Christian reactions to the loss of the crusader states in 1291 and plans for the recovery of the holy places.

Setton, Kenneth M., ed. *A History of the Crusades.* 6 vols. 2nd ed. Madison, Wisconsin, and London: University of Wisconsin Press, 1969–89. Covers the crusades from the First Crusade to the fifteenth century. Individual volumes consider not only the military campaigns but also the art and architecture of the crusader states, and the impact of the crusades on Europe and on the Near East. Also available online at: http://libtext.library.wisc.edu/HistCrusades/.

Setton, Kenneth M. *The Papacy and the Levant, 1204–1571*. 4 vols. Philadelphia: American Philosophical Society, 1976–84. Authoritative, detailed, and carefully referenced account of the crusades to the eastern Mediterranean from the Fourth Crusade to the capture of Cyprus by the Ottoman Turks in 1571.

Siberry, Elizabeth. *Criticism of Crusading 1095–1274*. Oxford and New York: Oxford University Press, 1985. Detailed study, using a very wide variety of source material, of contemporary reactions to crusading.

Trotter, David A. *Medieval French Literature and the Crusades (1100–1300)*. Geneva: Droz, 1988. Not fully comprehensive, and his conclusions are rather negative, overlooking the fact that chronicle evidence carries the same problems of interpretation as fiction. Nevertheless, this is a good introduction to the subject.

Urban, William L. *The Baltic Crusade*. 2nd ed. Chicago, IL: Lithuanian Research and Studies Center, 1994. Readable account of the first hundred years of the crusades in the Baltic, including an account of the early years of the Teutonic Order.

Urban, William L. *The Livonian Crusade*. Blue Ridge Summit, PA: University Press of America, 1982. Traces the history of the crusade in Livonia from 1296 onward. The following two books carry the story forward in other areas of the crusading front.

Urban, William L. *The Prussian Crusade*. 2nd ed. Blue Ridge Summit, PA: University Press of America, 2000.

Urban, William L. *The Samogitian Crusade*. Chicago, IL: Lithuanian Research and Studies Center, 1989.

Urban, William L. *Tannenberg and After: Lithuania, Poland and the Teutonic Order in Search of Immortality*. Chicago, IL: Lithuanian Research and Studies Center, 2001. Continues the history of the Teutonic Order and its long-suffering neighbors beyond the defeat of the Teutonic Order in 1410, considering how the rivals tried to depict themselves to their contemporaries and posterity.

Urban, William. *The Teutonic Knights: A Military History*. London: Greenhill Books, 2003. A history of the Teutonic Order in English, written by a respected scholar.

Wakefield, Walter L. *Heresy, Crusade and Inquisition in Southern France 1100–1250*. London: Allen & Unwin, 1974. Classic scholarly account of the Albigensian Crusade.

Internet Resources

De re militari: the Society for Medieval Military History. Includes reprinted essays on various aspects of medieval warfare, bibliographies, translated primary sources, and many links. Much information on the crusades. www. deremilitari.org

Internet Medieval Sourcebook. Essays by crusading scholars, and a wide collection of translated primary sources. www.fordham.edu/halsall/sbook1k. html

Islam and Islamic History in Arabia and the Middle East: the Crusaders. The crusades to the East described from an Islamic viewpoint. www. islamicity.com/Mosque/ihame/Sec10.htm

The Jerusalem Mosaic: The Crusader and Ayyubid Period (1099–1250 c.e.). A history of Jerusalem in the crusader period, with information about sites, food, costume, people, and water supplies of the period. http://jeru.huji. ac.il/ef1.htm

Library of Iberian Resources online. Reprints of books about Spanish and Portuguese history, including many related to the crusades. http://libro.uca. edu/title.htm

ORB: online resource book. Contains essays by well-known western scholars. http://the-orb.net/encyclop/religion/crusades/crusade.html A separate section covers the history of the military religious orders, with essays and translated texts. http://the-orb.net/encyclop/religion/monastic/milindex. html

Vadum Iacob Research Project. Archaeological report into the excavation of the castle of Vadum Iacob, built by the Templars in the kingdom of Jerusalem and destroyed by Saladin in 1179. http://vadumiacob.huji.ac.il

INDEX

Abū 'Abd Allah Muḥammad XI, king of Granada, 33, 102–3

Acre ('Akko), xxxv, 13, 16, 48, 101–2, 120, 123, 137, 150–52

Adhémar of Monteil, bishop of Le Puy, 7, 134

Afonso I Henriques, ruler of Portugal, xxxii, 28

Afonso V, king of Portugal, 33

Aimery of Montréal, 60, 108–9

'Ain Jālūt, battle of (1260), xxxiv, 15, 101, 114

Albania, 81, 84, 91, 103, 121

Albert of Buxtehude, bishop of Riga, 44–45

Albigensian crusade, xlvii, 54, 58–65, 93, 108–9, 110–11, 113, 115, 145–48

Alcazar el-Kebir, xxxviii, 34

Aleppo (Haleb), 10, 13, 15, 17, 86, 122, 123, 131

Alexander II (pope), 26

Alexander VI (pope), 85

Alexander Nevsky, xxxiv, 43, 47

Alexandria, xxxvi, 80

Alexios Angelos (Byzantine emperor), 111

Alexios Comnenos (Byzantine emperor), 6, 7, 9, 104

Alfonso VI, king of Castile, xxxi, 21, 25–26, 28, 34–35

Alfonso X ("the wise"), king of Castile, 30, 31, 114

Alfonso XI, king of Castile, 30, 158–60

Algeciras, 30

Algiers, xxxviii, 33

alliances. See treaties

Almohads, xxxii, xxxiii, 28–29, 62, 113

Almoravids, xxxi, 28–29

Almourol castle, 27

Amaury (Amalric), king of Jerusalem, xxxii, 14, 122

Amedeo VI of Savoy, 80

Americas, 34, 72, 98

Anglo-French War (Hundred Years War), 51, 70, 73, 80, 81, 82

Anna Comnena, 104

Antioch (Antakya), xxxi, xliv, 6, 8, 15, 101, 104, 119–120, 129–36, 171

Aragon, kingdom of, xxxv, 25, 27, 29–30, 84, 102–3, 113–15. See *also* Ferdinand, king of Aragon; James I, king of Aragon; Peter II, king of Aragon

Armenia. *See* Cilician Armenia

Arnold Aimery, papal legate, 58, 60, 145, 147

Ascalon, xxxii, 137, 138

al-Ashraf Khalīl, sultan of Egypt, xxxv, 16

assessment of crusades, 9, 12, 16–18, 47–48, 52, 64–65, 72–74, 91–98

Asturias, kingdom of, 23

Audita tremendi, 140–44

Ayyūbids, xxxiii–xxxiv, 13, 78, 122–25. *See also* al-Kāmil, sultan of Egypt; Saladin, sultan of Egypt

Azores islands, 32

Baghdad, xxvi, xxxiv, 5, 122, 126, 131, 169

Baibars, sultan of Egypt, xxxiv–xxxv, 17, 97, 101–2, 169

Baldwin I of Boulogne, king of Jerusalem, xliv, 7, 8

Baldwin III, king of Jerusalem, xxxii

Baldwin IV, king of Jerusalem, xxxiii

Baldwin of Aulne, papal legate, 45

Balearic islands, 29, 114, 153–54

Baltic region, crusades to, xl, xlvii, xlviii, 12, 37–52, 92, 155–57

Barbastro, xxxi, xxxix, 4, 26

Basel, Church council of (1431–49), 71

Bayezid I, Ottoman sultan, xxxvi, 78, 81–83

Bayezid II, Ottoman sultan, 85–86

Beirut, 101, 137

Belgrade, xxxvii, 84, 86, 88, 117, 121, 126

Berengaria of Navarre, queen of England, xlii

Béziers, 60, 63, 147

Black Death, 81

Boabdil, king of Granada, 33, 102–3

Bohemia, 39, 41–42, 48, 67–74, 87, 93, 117–18, 160–63

Bohemond, xliv, 7, 8, 103–4, 132–33, 134

Bohemond VI, count of Tripoli, 15

Bosnia, 84, 112

Boucicaut, marshal of France, xxxvi, xlvi

bull, issued by pope to launch crusade, xlvi, 140–44, 169

Burgundy, 13, 26, 82, 84, 115

Burzenland, 110

Byzantine empire, xxvi, xxxix, xlv, xlviii, 6, 7, 9, 13, 17, 77, 80, 102–4, 111, 122, 130. *See also* Constantinople (Istanbul)

Cadiz, 29

Calatrava, Order of, 28

Calixtus III (pope), 33

Canary islands, 32–33

captives, 46, 59–60, 78, 81, 82, 125, 137, 141, 147–48, 157, 162–63, 164. *See also* slavery

Carcassonne, 60, 62, 63

Casimir III, king of Poland, 49, 50, 107

Castile, kingdom of, 25, 27, 29–35, 102–3, 114, 158–60

castles, 14–15, 16, 27, 29, 40, 42, 46, 50, 58, 60, 62, 64, 78, 82, 101–2, 108–9, 121, 123,

130, 131–32, 136, 137, 154, 161

Cathars, 53–65, 93, 108–9, 111, 145–48, 169

Celestine III (pope), 44

Ceuta, 32, 34

Charlemagne (emperor), 2, 95

Charles I of Anjou, king of Naples, xxxv, xliii

Charles IV (emperor), 67

Charles V (emperor), 86–87, 126

Charles VIII, king of France, 85

Charles ("the Hammer") Martel, 2

Childrens' Crusade, xxxiii, xlviii, xlix, 13–14

chivalry, xxvi, xlv–xlvi, 31, 39, 49, 57, 73–74, 92, 123, 159–60. *See also* motivations for crusading

Christ, Order of, 98

Christburg, treaty of (1249), 47

Christian, bishop of Prussia, 44–46

Christopher Colombus, 34, 98

Chud (Peipus), battle at Lake (1242), xxxiv, 47

"El Cid," 35

Cilician Armenia, xxxvi, 8, 12, 15, 80, 101, 102, 104, 130

Cistercians, 44, 45, 58, 59, 111, 145–47, 169

Clement V (pope), xxxv, 48

Clermont, Church council of (1095), xxxi, xxxix, 1, 6

colonization. *See* settlement and colonization

Conrad, duke of Cujavia-Masovia, 45, 46, 110

Conrad, marquis of Montferrat, 12

Conrad II, king of Jerusalem, 105, 106, 149

Conrad III, king of Germany, 12

Constance, Church council of (1414–18), 47, 51, 67, 68, 162

Constantinople (Istanbul), xxxiii, xxxv, xxxvii, 5, 6, 7, 12, 13, 17, 34, 80, 84, 111, 117, 120–21

conversion, 7, 22, 25, 32–34, 39, 40, 42–48, 50, 51, 58, 92, 93, 107, 112–14, 155–56

councils of the Church, xxxi, xxxv, xxxix, 1, 6, 47, 51, 62, 67, 68, 71, 111, 114

Crete, xxxviii, 87, 88

criticism of crusades, 12, 18

Crnomen, battle of (1371), 81

Crusade cycle, 95

crusaders' views of Muslims, 1–2, 78, 93–95, 96–97, 105, 163–65

crusades, definition of, xxxix–xlii, xlvi–xlix

cultural exchange, 93–95. *See also* science, study of; toleration

Cyprus, xxxvi, xxxviii, xxxix, 12, 16, 80, 83, 87, 105–6, 149, 152, 171

Damascus (Dimashq), xxxii, 10, 12, 13, 15, 17, 106, 122, 123, 131, 148, 150

Damietta, xxxiv, 124

Daniil of Galich-Volyn', 41, 48

Defenestration of Prague: first, 68; second, 72

Denis, king of Portugal, 98

Denmark, 39, 42, 51

diplomacy, 8, 13, 18, 25, 30, 50, 70, 71, 74, 86, 87, 125, 131, 149. *See also* treaties

Djerba, island, 127

Dobrin, Order of, 45–46
Dominican friars, 58, 152
Dyrrachium (Durrës), 103–4

Economic factors, xliv, 95–96
Edessa (Urfa), xxxii, xliv, 8, 10, 142, 171
Edward I, king of England, xxxv, 18, 102
Egypt, xxxii–xxxv, xxxvii, 14, 80, 86, 101, 105–6, 122–25, 129, 131, 149, 151–52
Eleanor, duchess of Aquitaine, xlii
Elizabeth I, queen of England, 86
England, kingdom of, xxxv, xxxviii, 12–13, 18, 31, 38, 51, 60, 67, 70, 73, 80, 81, 82, 86, 96, 102, 119–20, 137, 158
Eric VI, king of Denmark, 42
Estonia, 37, 40, 42, 52, 92–93

Fatimids, xxvi, 5, 6, 8, 122, 129, 169
Ferdinand, king of Aragon, xxxvii, 33–34, 93, 102–3
Field of Blood, battle of (1119), xxxi
Fifth Crusade, xxxiii, 14, 105, 110, 112, 145
Finland, 38, 42–43, 93
First Crusade, xxv, xxxi, xlii, 1, 6–9, 16, 17, 26, 129–36
Flanders, xxxii, 7, 134–35, 136, 159
Fourth Crusade, xxxiii, 13, 17, 60, 110–11
France, kingdom of, xxxiv–xxxvi, xli, xlii, xxxiii, xlv–xlvi, xlvii, 1, 2, 4, 7, 12–13, 14, 18, 26, 38, 51, 54, 57–65, 70, 73, 80, 81, 82, 85, 86–87, 91, 94–97,

105, 108–9, 111, 120, 124–25, 126, 129, 134–35, 145–48, 150
Francis I, king of France, 86, 87, 126
Franciscan friars, 57, 111, 117, 152
Frederick I Barbarossa (emperor), 12
Frederick II of Hohenstaufen (emperor), xxxiii, 14, 46, 47, 105–6, 109–110, 148–52
Frederick III (emperor), 115
Frederick of Hohenzollern, elector of Brandenburg, 70
Friars, 57, 58, 111, 117, 152

Galich, 41, 48, 50
Gallipoli, 80
Gdańsk (Danzig), 48–49
Gediminas, prince of Lithuania, 49, 50, 106–8
Genoa, xxxix, 8, 15, 80, 81, 84, 96
Geoffrey de Charny, knight, xlv–xlvi
Geoffrey Chaucer, 31
George Branković, of Serbia, 84
George Castriota Scanderbeg, 121
George of Poděbrady, king of Bohemia, 71, 117
German Crusade, xxxiii
Germany, xxxii–xxxiii, 7, 12, 14, 37–47, 49, 51–52, 57, 67, 69–70, 72–73, 86–88, 91, 92, 105, 109, 112–13, 145, 147, 156–57, 161–62
Gibraltar, 30
Giraude, lady of Lavaur, 60, 108–9
Godfrey de Bouillon, first Latin ruler of Jerusalem, 7, 135
Golden Bull of Rimini, 110
Gottfried of Lekno, abbot, 44

Granada, kingdom of, xxxvii, xlv, 29–34, 49, 92, 93, 102–3, 114, 159–60

"great schism," 81

Greece. *See* Byzantine empire; Morea

Gregory VII (pope), 4–5

Gregory VIII (pope), 123, 140–44

Gregory IX (pope), 45, 46, 105, 109–110, 148

Gregory X (pope), 114

Gregory XI (pope), xxxvi, 81

Grunwald (Tannenberg), battle of (1410), xxxvi, 51, 113, 117

Guibert of Nogent, xlii

Guy of Lusignan, king of Jerusalem, 123, 137, 140–41

al-Hakim Bi-amr Allah, caliph, 5

Hanseatic League, 107, 170

Hartwig II, archbishop of Bremen, 43–44

Hattin, battle of (1187), 123, 136–38, 140–41

Henry, count of Champagne, 13

Henry IV (emperor), 4, 6

Henry the Lion, duke of Saxony, xxxii, xlviii

Henry the Navigator, 32

heresy, 48, 53–57, 65, 67–68, 71–74, 108–9, 111, 127, 145–48, 171

Hermann von Salza, grand master of Teutonic Order, 46, 109–110

Hetoum, king of Cilician Armenia, 15

Holy Land, crusades to, xxv–xxvi, xxxi–xxxv, xxxix–xlix, 1, 5–19, 28, 48, 49, 64, 91–92, 93, 105, 114, 129–36, 140–44, 148–52, 158–59

Holy Sepulchre, 5, 106, 135, 150

Honorius III (pope), 63, 105, 145

Hospital of St. John of Jerusalem, Order of, xxxii, xxxv–xxxviii, xlviii, 16, 27, 80, 81, 83, 86–88, 102, 126–27, 139, 141, 150, 153–54, 163–65

Hugh III, duke of Burgundy, 13

Hugh III, king of Cyprus and Jerusalem, 101

Hugh of Vermandois, 134–35

Hundred Years War, 51, 70, 73, 80, 81, 82

Hungary, kingdom of, 81, 82, 84–88, 91, 110, 112, 115, 117, 121, 126–27, 162. *See also* Sigismund

Hussite crusades, xxxvi, xli, xlvii, 69–74, 93, 115, 117–19, 160–63

Hussite heresy, 53, 65, 67–68, 71–74, 93

Ibelin family, 101, 137, 149

Iberian peninsula, crusades to, xxxix, xl–xli, xlvii, 4, 12, 21–36, 38, 92, 93, 95, 98, 102–3, 113–15, 153–54, 159–60

India, 34, 127

Indulgence, crusade, xxvii, xliii–xliv, xlvii, 26, 32, 33, 38, 44, 59, 85, 86, 144, 156, 162, 171

Innocent III (pope), xliii, 13, 38, 42, 44, 58–59, 62, 105, 110–12, 113, 145

Innocent IV (pope), 106

Innocent VI (pope), 80

Iran, 77, 85, 126, 127

Iraq, xxvi, 85, 127, 130, 131. *See also* Baghdad; Mosul

Isabel I, queen of Jerusalem, 13

Isabel II, queen of Jerusalem, 105, 149

Isabella, queen of Castile, xxxvii, 33–34, 93, 102–3

Islamic views: of Christianity, 10, 28, 138–40; of crusades, xxvi, 8, 9, 16–17, 97. *See also* jihād

Italy, crusades in, xliii, xlv, xlvii, 17–18, 59

Ivan III, grand prince of Moscow, 51

Ivan IV "the Terrible," grand prince of Moscow, 51

Jadwiga, queen of Poland, xxxvi, 51, 108, 112–13

Jaffa (Joppa, now Tel Aviv Yafo), 8, 101, 149, 150, 152

Jagiełło (Władysław), king of Poland and duke of Lithuania, xxxvi, 51, 69, 108, 112–13, 117

James I, king of Aragon, xxxiii–xxxiv, 28, 29, 113–15, 153–54

James II, king of Aragon, 30

James Douglas, 158–60

Jatwingia, 40, 47

Jean Froissart, 31

Jem, Ottoman pretender, 85

Jerba, island, 127

Jerusalem: city of, xxxi–xxxiv, xxxix–xli, 1, 5, 8–10, 14, 34, 98, 104, 106, 119, 123, 131, 138–40, 142, 148–50, 159; kingdom of, xxvi, xxxi, 9–17, 101, 119–20, 122–23, 136–38, 141, 148–52

Jerusalem, Order of St. John of. *See* Hospital of St. John of Jerusalem, Order of

Jews, xxxiv, xxxvi, 7, 22, 30, 34, 78, 93

jihād, xxv, 10, 17, 31, 121, 122, 127

Joan of Arc, 70, 73

Jogailo. *See* Jagiełło (Władysław), king of Poland and duke of Lithuania

Johan Sverkersson, king of Sweden, 42

John XXII (pope), 49, 50, 107

John Albert, king of Poland, 85

John of Capistrano, 117

John Hunyadi, xxxvii, 84, 85, 115–17, 121

John Hus, 67, 68

John Wycliffe, 67, 70

John Zápolya, king of Hungary, 87

John Žižmka, 69–70, 117–19, 160–61

justification for Christian warfare, xxv, xxvii, xli, 3–5, 21, 23, 26, 31–32, 39, 53

al-Kāmil, sultan of Egypt, xxxiii, 14, 106, 125, 148–52

Karelia, 43

Kerbogha of Mosul, 8, 129, 134–35

Königsberg (Kaliningrad), 42

Korybut of Lithuania, king-elect of Bohemia, 69, 70, 118

Kosovo, battle of (1448), 115

Kosovo Polje, battle of (1389), xxxvi, 81

Kraków, 48, 112

Kulm (Chełmno), 46, 110

Kurland, 43, 51

Kutná Hora, 69, 118

Ladislas the Jagiełłonian
(Władysław III), 84, 115
Ladislas Postumus (László V), 71,
115, 117
La Forbie, battle of (1244), 14
Las Navas de Tolosa, battle of
(1212), xxxiii, 29, 62, 113
Lateran, fourth Church council at
the (1215), 62, 111
Latin empire of Constantinople, 13,
111
Latvia, 37, 40, 44, 52, 92, 93. *See
also* Livonia
Lavaur, 58, 60, 108–9, 147
Lazar, prince of Serbia, 81
Lepanto, battle of (1571), xxxviii,
88
Lipany, battle of (1434), xxxvi, 71
Lisbon, xxxii, 28
Lithuania, xxxvi, 37, 39–40, 47–
52, 69, 86, 92, 93, 106–8, 112–
13
Livonia, xxxiv, 40, 42–48, 50, 51,
110. *See also* Latvia
Louis I of Anjou, king of Hungary,
81, 82, 112
Louis II, king of Hungary, 87
Louis IV of Bavaria (emperor), 49,
107
Louis VII, king of France, xlii, 12,
58
Louis VIII, king of France, 62–63
Louis IX, king of France, xxxiv,
xxxv, 14, 18, 63–64, 94, 96,
124–25
Lyons, second Church council of
(1274), xxxv, 114

Maccabees, 144, 147
Madeira, 32

al-Mahdiyyah, xxxi, xxxvi, xxxix,
4, 82
Malta, xxxvii, xlviii, 87, 127
Malta, Order of. *See* Hospital of St.
John of Jerusalem, Order of
Mamluks, xxxiv, xxxvii, 9, 13, 15,
16, 80, 85, 86, 101–2, 114,
124–25, 126, 169, 172
Manṣūra, battle of (1250), xxxiv,
125
Manzikert, battle of (1071), 6
Margaret, queen of France, 125
Margaret of Beverley, 119–20
Marienburg (Malbork), xxxv, 39,
51
Marj Dabiq, battle of (1516), 86
Marqab castle, 16
Martin V (pope), 70
Martin Luther, xxxvii, xliii–iv, 87,
98
martyrdom, 78, 131, 156–57
Mary, queen of Hungary, 68, 82,
112
Matthias Corvinus, king of Hun-
gary, 85, 117, 121
Mehmed I, Ottoman sultan, 83
Mehmed II, Ottoman sultan,
xxxvii, 78, 84–85, 116–17, 120–
21, 164
Melilla, xxxvii, 34
Michael VIII Palaeologos (Byzan-
tine emperor), xxxv, 13
Milan, 86
military religious orders, 27–28, 39–
40, 45, 172. *See also* Calatrava,
Order of; Christ, Order of;
Dobrin, Order of; Hospital of
St. John of Jerusalem, Order of;
Santa Maria, Order of; Santi-
ago, Order of; Swordbrothers,

Order of; Temple, Order of the;
Teutonic Order (Teutonic
knights)
Mindaugas of Lithuania, 47–48
mission. *See* conversion
Móhacs, battle of (1526), 87
Mongols, xxvi, xxxiv, 15, 18, 50,
77, 101, 102, 107, 114
Montgisard, battle of (1177), xxxiii
Montségur, 64
Morea, xxxviii, 81, 121
Morocco, xxxviii, 28, 29, 30, 32
Moscow, 51, 93
Mosul, xxv, xxxii, 8, 10, 122, 125,
129, 134
motivations for crusading, xliv–xlvi,
1–3, 9, 31–32, 104, 156. *See
also* chivalry
Muḥammad, prophet of Islam, 2,
163–65
Muḥammad IV, king of Granada,
159–60
Murad I, Ottoman sultan, 80, 81
Murad II, Ottoman sultan, 84, 115,
120
Murcia, 29, 114
Muret, battle of (1213), xxxiii, 62,
113

Naples, xxxv, 33, 86
Napoleon, xxxviii, xlviii
al-Nāsīr, Almohad caliph, 29, 113
al-Nāṣir Dā'ūd, sultan of Damascus,
148, 150–52
naval leagues, xxxvi, xxxviii, xlvii,
xlviii, 80, 87
naval war, xxxi, xxxii, xxxvi,
xxxix, xlvii–xlviii, 29, 30, 83–
88, 115, 121, 123, 126–27
Navarre, kingdom of, xxxiv, xlii

Negroponte (Euboea), 85, 121
Nicaea, 7, 130
Nicopolis, battle of (1396), xxxvi,
82–83
Novgorod the Great, 41–43, 47, 49,
93, 170
Nūr al-Dīn, sultan of Damascus,
xxv, xxxii, 10, 12, 17, 97, 122

Oran, xxxviii, 33, 34
Orebites, 69–71, 73, 118–19
organization of crusades, xlvi–xlviii.
See also papal role in crusading;
strategy of crusades
Orlando, epic hero, 95
Ösel island, 42, 43
Otranto, xxxvii, 78, 85, 121
Otto IV of Brunswick (emperor),
105, 111, 145
Ottoman Turks, xxvi, xxxvi–
xxxviii, xlvii, 16, 34, 51–52,
73, 77–100, 115–17, 120–21,
126–27, 163–65

papal role in crusading, xxxix, xliii,
xlvi–xlviii, 1–6, 26, 33, 38,
44, 47, 50, 70, 73, 81, 84, 96.
*See also names of individual
popes*
parias, 24–25
Paris, peace of (1229), 63–64
Paschal II (pope), 26
"peace of God," 4
Peipus (Chud), battle at Lake
(1242), xxxiv, 47
Peloponnese, xxxviii, 81, 121
personnel in crusade armies, xlii–
xliii, xlvii, 7, 117, 131–33, 134–
35, 147, 156–57, 161–62
Peter I, king of Cyprus, xxxvi, 80

Peter II, king of Aragon, xxxiii, 62, 108, 113

Peter of Castelnau, papal legate, 58–59, 111

Peter Thomas, papal legate, 80

Philip II, king of Spain, 126–27

Philip II Augustus, king of France xlvii, 12–13, 59, 62, 63, 96, 105, 111, 120, 150

Philip of Alsace, count of Flanders, xxxii, 136

Philip the Good, duke of Burgundy, 84

Philippe de Mezières, 82

Piacenza, Church council at (1095), 6

Pierre d'Aubusson, grand master of Hospital of St. John, 121, 165

pilgrimage, xxxix, xli–xlii, xlvii, 3, 38, 39, 92, 119–20, 123, 149–52, 156, 173

piracy, 30, 39, 42, 43, 85, 87, 126

Pisa, xxxix, 15, 96

Poland, kingdom of, xxxvi, 39–41, 44–51, 69, 85, 86, 112–13, 115, 117

Portugal, country and kingdom of, xxxii, xxxviii, 25, 27–29, 32–34, 98, 127

Prague: city of, 67–69, 71–75, 117–18, 161; Four Articles of, 65, 67, 69, 72

preaching crusades, xlvi–xlvii, xlviii, 7, 31, 38, 80, 117, 145, 147, 156

Přemysl II, king of Poland, 48

Přemysl Ottokar II, king of Bohemia, 42, 48

Prokop Holý, 70, 71

Prokůpek, 70, 71

propaganda, 23, 25–26, 34–35, 45, 47, 48, 50, 70–71, 84, 127

Protestant Reformation, xliv, 34, 51, 72, 87–88, 98

Prussia, xxxiii, xxxv, xlv, 37–42, 44–51, 92, 110, 112–13, 155–57

Pskov, 47, 49

Qalawun, sultan of Egypt, 16

Qansuh Ghawri, sultan of Egypt, 86

al-Qaşr-al-Kabīr, xxxviii, 34

Quia maior (1213), xliii, 112

Qutuz, sultan of Egypt, 15, 101, 125, 172

Raymond, count of St. Gilles, 7, 132–33, 134

Raymond III, count of Tripoli, 122, 136–37

Raymond V, count of Toulouse, 58

Raymond VI, count of Toulouse (St. Gilles), 58–63, 111, 148

Raymond VII, count of Toulouse, 62–64

Raymond Roger Trencavel, 60, 62

reconquista, 21, 23, 25–26, 29–30, 32–35, 93

Reval (Tallinn), 42

Reynald of Châtillon, 122

Rhodes, xxxv, xxxvii, 80, 85, 86, 121, 126, 163–65

Rhodes, Order of. *See* Hospital of St. John of Jerusalem, Order of

Ricaut Bonomel, Templar, xliii

Richard I, the Lionheart, king of England, xlii, xlvii, 12–13, 14, 96, 120

Riga, 44, 48, 49

Robert, count of Flanders, 7, 134

Robert I, the Bruce, king of Scotland, 158–59
Robert Curthose, duke of Normandy, 7, 134–35
Roger Trencavel II, 58
Roman Empire, 3–4, 21–22, 23, 32, 55, 84, 163, 170
Romania. *See* Byzantine Empire
Rus', 39, 41, 46–47, 49
Russia, 51–52, 85, 91, 92–93
Ruthenia. *See* Galich

Sagrajas, battle of (1086), xxxi, 28
St. George, 8, 135
St. James of Compostella, 34
St. John of Jerusalem, Order of. *See* Hospital of St. John of Jerusalem, Order of
St. Margaret of Antioch, 119
St. Mary the Virgin, 30, 46, 49, 120, 161
Saladin, sultan of Egypt, xxvi, xxxii–xxxiii, 10, 12–13, 15–17, 91, 97, 119–20, 122–23, 136–38, 138–40
Salado, battle at (1340), 30
al-Ṣāliḥ Ayyūb, sultan of Egypt, xxxiv, 101, 123–25
al-Ṣāliḥ Ismāʿīl, ruler of Damascus, xxxiv
Sancho I, king of Portugal, 28
Santa Maria, Order of, 30
Santiago, Order of, 28
Saule, battle of (1236), 45
science, study of, 26, 31, 93
Scotland, kingdom of, 158–59
Second Crusade, xxxii, xlii, 10, 12, 17, 28
Selim I, Ottoman sultan, xxxvii, 86, 126

Seljuk Turks, xxvi, xxxi, xxxix, 5–9, 12, 77, 102, 104, 130–33, 135–36
Serbia, 81, 84, 121
settlement and colonization, xliv, 10, 23, 25, 32, 35, 39, 42, 92, 110
Seville, 28, 29
Shajar al-Durr, sultana of Egypt, 123–25
Shepherds' Crusades, xxxiv–xxxvi, xlviii
Shiʿites, 5, 6, 122, 127, 169, 173
Sicilian Vespers, revolt (1282), xxxv
Sicily, kingdom of, xxxv, xlvii, 14, 17–18, 104, 105
Sigismund, king of Hungary (and western emperor), 68–71, 73, 82–84, 112, 115, 117–18, 162
Sigurd, king of Norway, xxxi
Simon de Montfort the elder, 60, 62–63, 108, 113, 148
slavery, 30, 77–78, 87, 119
Smyrna (Izmir), xxxvi, 80, 81
Sofia, 81, 115
Song of Roland, 95
Sophia, queen of Bohemia, 68, 117
Spanish Armada (1588), xxxviii
Speyer, diet of (1526), 87
Spring of the Cresson, battle at (1187), 123, 136–37
Stephen, count of Blois, 7, 129–33
strategy of crusades, 12, 14, 18, 46, 47, 69–71, 114, 115, 154
Süleyman "the magnificent," Ottoman sultan, xxxvii, 86–88, 126–27
Sunni Muslims, xxvi, 5, 6, 122, 169, 173

Sweden, 39, 42–43, 49, 51
Swordbrothers, Order of, xxxiv, 45, 110
Syria, xxvi, xxxix, 6, 8, 10, 15, 86, 92, 97, 130–31, 149

Taborites, 68–71, 73, 74, 118, 161
Tamerlane (Timur the Lame), xxxvi, 82
Tancred, Bohemond's nephew, xliv, 7, 104, 134, 136
Tangier, 33
Tannenberg (Grunwald), battle of (1410), xxxvi, 51, 113, 117
taxation for crusades, xxvii, 33, 57, 77–78, 95–96, 114
Temple, Order of the, xxxii, xxxv, xliii, 27, 45, 98, 102, 106, 113, 136–38, 139, 141, 148, 150–52
Teutonic Order (Teutonic knights), xxxiii–xxxvi, 37, 39, 42, 45–52, 86, 88, 102, 107–8, 109–110, 112–13, 117, 155–57
Thessaloníki, 81, 84
Thierry (Terricus) grand commander of the Temple, 136–38
Third Crusade, xxxiii, xlii, xlvii, 10, 12–13, 14, 15, 17, 28, 46, 119–20, 123
Thorn (Toruń): city, 46; second treaty of (1466), 51
Tiberias, 123, 137
Timur the Lame (Tamerlane), xxxvi, 82
Toledo, xxxi, 22, 25–26, 28, 34, 93
toleration, 22, 25, 30–31, 35, 92, 114, 120
Torquato Tasso, 95
Toulouse, 62, 63, 147–48
trade, xlii, 14, 15, 17, 29, 32–33, 39–44, 47, 48, 80, 84, 94, 96, 122
treaties, 13, 14, 15, 24, 29–30, 47–51, 63–64, 71, 80, 81, 85, 86, 101–4, 106, 107, 121, 122, 126. *See also* diplomacy
Trebizond (Trabzon), 84, 121
Trencavel family, 58, 60, 62
tribute, 24–25, 29, 33, 47
Tripoli (North Africa), xxxvii, 126
Tripoli (Tarābalus in Lebanon), 15, 102, 120, 122
truces. *See* treaties
Tunis, xxxv, xxxviii
Tunisia, 82
Tūrān Shāh, Mamluk sultan, 101, 124–25
Turks, xxxvi, 80, 85, 120, 121, 123. *See also* Ottoman Turks; Seljuk Turks
Tyre (Sūr), xxxii, 101–2, 119, 123, 137–38

Ukraine, 41
Urban II (pope), xxxi, xxxix, 1, 3, 5–6
Urban III (pope), 136
Usamā Ibn Munqidh, 94
Uzun Hasan, 85

Václav. *See* Waclaw, king of Poland; Wenceslas IV, king of Bohemia
Valdemar II, king of Denmark, 42
Valencia, kingdom of, xxxiv, 29, 30, 114, 153–54, 160
Vandals, 33
Varna, battle of (1444), xxxvii, 84, 115
Venice, xxxii, xxxvii, xxxviii,

xlviii, 15, 48, 80, 81, 83–86, 96, 115, 121

Vienna, siege of: (1529), xxxvii, 87–88, 91, 126; (1683), xxxviii, 87

Visigoths, 21–23, 25–26, 32, 33, 173–74

Volyn', 41, 48, 50

Waclaw, king of Poland, 42

Waldensian heretics, 57, 111

Wallachia, 84

warfare, 8–9, 15, 18, 31, 40, 44, 46, 49–50, 59–60, 63, 73, 78, 82, 115, 118, 130–40, 147–48, 155–57, 161–65

Wenceslas IV, king of Bohemia, 68, 117

Wends, 42

Witold, grand duke of Lithuania, 69, 113

Władysław III, king of Poland (Ladislas the Jagiełłonian), 84, 115

Władysław IV Łokietek, duke of Greater Poland, king of Poland, 48–50, 107

Władysław Jagiełło, king of Poland. *See* Jagiełło (Władysław), king of Poland and duke of Lithuania

Women, role in crusading, xlii, 63, 112, 119–20, 125

Žatek, 69, 160–63

Zengi of Mosul, xxv, xxxii, 10, 12

Zenta, battle of (1697), 88

About the Author

HELEN NICHOLSON is Senior Lecturer in History at the University of Cardiff, Wales, UK. She is the author of *The Knights Hospitaller* (2001), *The Knights Templar: A New History* (2001), *Love, War, and the Grail: Templars, Hospitallers,* and *Teutonic Knights in Medieval Epic and Romance, 1150–1500* (2001), and a number of books and articles on the Military Orders and on the Crusades in the twelfth, thirteenth, and fourteenth centuries. In 1997 she published a translation of an early thirteenth-century account of the Third Crusade: *Chronicle of the Third Crusade: A Translation of the "Itinerarium Peregrinorum et gesta regis Ricardi,"* and she edited the proceedings of the second international Clerkenwell conference on the Military Orders: *The Military Orders, vol. 2: Welfare and Warfare* (1998). She is currently researching into the activities and reputation of the Knights Hospitaller in the British Isles in the fourteenth century.